THIS TRUCKIN' LIFE

The Reminiscences of a Truck Driver

Laurie Driver

AuthorHouse™ UK Ltd.
500 Avebury Boulevard
Central Milton Keynes, MK9 2BE
www.authorhouse.co.uk
Phone: 08001974150

First published by AuthorHouse 7/19/2010

ISBN: 978-1-4490-9044-9 (sc)

This book is printed on acid-free paper.

FOREWORD

THIS book is an anecdotal volume, all the incidents within these pages are true. I only hope that the incidents portrayed retain their humour, or pathos, when transposed to the written page. Because of passage of time there may be the occasional chronological error. I have researched through various channels and stretched my memory, but certain dates and times have eluded me and I have included the anecdotes where they seem to sit most readily. There is, in some cases, the use of a little poetic licence, to hopefully enhance the tale. I hope I will be excused these lapses and additions and hope they don't detract from any pleasure given from the overall exercise.

Because I had to have a base to work on, the following pages are somewhat autobiographical. Names have been changed to protect the innocent............and the guilty.

Most of the early parts of the book take place in and around Manchester, which is where the incidents occurred, and which is my home town. Later incidents take place further afield as I matured into a long distance tramper.

The majority of us that work for a living go to their place of employment with one motive, to earn money. If one achieves job satisfaction and a love for the type of occupation embarked upon, then so much the better. Few modes of employment can be classed as vocational and these include Ministers of Faith, the teaching and medical professions, firemen and policemen etc.

Even people in these vocational positions can and are motivated by the pecuniary advantage that these posts offer.

The LGV or HGV driving licence is known or classed as a vocational licence, whether this elevates the job of a professional driver to a vocational position is a moot point.

Most other forms of work are seen as a necessary evil and a means to an end. These ends being the opportunity of making enough cash to, hopefully, live in relative comfort. A great many jobs are mundane and soul destroying and few of the working class, hoi polloi make enough money to retire early or live in luxury. This, despite the long and excessive hours worked and shift differentials and weekend working, is our lot as we chase the ever elusive fortune.

Because most of us have never had wealth, we chase it by doing the football pools and the lottery, going to Bingo and buying Premium Bonds. The odds, in these forms of gambling, are stacked so heavily against the punter that very few people realise their objectives.

I have worked in the transport industry for most of my working life, and because of the nature of the job, have worked for numerous haulage companies, both large and small. The transient nature of employment within the transport industry stems from the break up of the system which had been nationalised after the 2nd world war.

When independents started surfacing again there was a shortage of drivers and a good driver could always find work and would change jobs for the promise of a tanner (6d or 2½p in new money), or less, an hour or more than he was already earning, in the pursuance of a higher paid occupation in his quest to raise himself and his family above the state of poverty and penury.

There is a lot of somewhat saucy or risqué language and plain spoken, no nonsense expletives are used frequently because this is the normal language within the trucking fraternity. This is borne from the fact, that until recently, it was a male dominated industry. The distaff side seem to have come into the game since the advent of synchromesh gearboxes, and the sleeper cab, and the demise of roping and sheeting, and the hand-bailing of twenty ton loads, and also the fact that we had to change our own wheels if tyres were punctured, whether loaded or empty or in fine weather or foul. Those drivers that worked for small independents would also be responsible for oil and filter changes. Now I am not saying that the gentler sex couldn't do the job in those days, but why on Earth should they want to? A wet sheet could weigh well over 1cwt; and would, often, have to be lifted manually from the ground onto the bed of the wagon, and up on to the load, water would run down ones neck mixed with the grime and grease of well used sheets, I mean, it could smudge a girls make-up, and who wanted a girlfriend or wife with the well calloused hands of an experienced roper and sheeter and wheel changer, well, I suppose you never know, do you? The whole scenario of hand-balling and roping and sheeting was hard physical labour, and could be very dirty, and I think in those more gentlemanly days, would have offended the sensibilities of the average female, upon saying that, there was always the exception to dis-prove the rule of which later. The folding of sheets, once pulled off the load, in wet, windy, cold weather was sometimes enough to bring despair to the most macho of men.

Drivers' hours have always been long and anti-social with some employees working all the hours God sends and a few extra that the Devil throws in, in order to make ends meet, as drivers pay, for the responsibility involved, has always been notoriously low. I believe it was because of the long hours and poor pay that some of the more unscrupulous drivers turned to thievery, thus getting all drivers tarred with the same brush and begetting the saying 'it fell off the back of a lorry,' for any goods of a suspect nature; drivers, it seems, are bigger sinners than the Borgia's. Of course there were always the unscrupulous gaffers who would turn a blind eye and offer inducements of bonuses and night out money to *run bent* to increase their own profits.

Transport cafes and transport digs were the male's domain. The sleeping quarters ranged from good to downright bloody awful, from single rooms to rooms with 2 beds to dormitories with up to 50 beds or more where other drivers would be getting up to start work at all hours through the night. There would be farting, snoring, masturbating, and God knows what going on. There were communal showers and mainly very poor washing facilities; try shaving in luke-warm water at three or four in the morning. Again, I think, the average gentlewoman would have been somewhat offended. I still cannot think what would make a modern female want to sleep in the back of a cab, in a strange town, on a lorry park, with either no amenities or with just the basics, unless the female psyche is becoming more like the male. Transport, especially truck driving and the trials and tribulations of a driver within the industry and his tactics to keep body, soul and family together over a 40+ years career are what we endeavour to deal with, within these pages. The world of haulage is a strange phenomenon, once you are in; you're hooked. It is hard to get out. It is addictive, like heroin, or cocaine. One has to be of a certain breed to be a truck driver..........it is not a job, it is a way of life.

CHAPTER ONE
RAILWAYS TO ALL GROUPS LICENSE

THE YOUTH EMPLOYMENT OFFICE

The early 1960's were my mid teen age years and it was during this time that my life in transport started. It was in 1962 to be exact, when I was a callow, naïve youth of sixteen years of age, and freshly redundant from my first job after leaving school. That first job was with J. T. Hedley and Son, Gold Blockers and Embossers, where I had been sent by The Youth Employment Office. I was taken on, as an apprentice gold blocker and embosser to learn the trade of printing in gold and silver leaf and various other coloured foils. The printing trade was my chosen profession. There was, as it turned out, not enough work to sustain the workforce, and approximately 9 months after leaving school with a handful of GCE's., I was thrust onto the open job market, leaving the brewing up, cleaning up and errand running to the next most junior boy.

My first port of call, after my redundancy from Hedley's, was the Youth Employment Office, to sign on and seek further employment. It was only 9 months since I last called upon the YEO when, after sitting my GCE 'O' Levels I left school and placed myself on the employment market with the intentions of earning enough money to enable me to discontinue the practise of depending on spends from my parents and to be somewhat self sufficient.

The Youth Employment Office, or the Teenage Dole Office, as it was known, was, in 1962, situated at the Liverpool Road end of Deansgate in Manchester. I took my place, at about 0930, with the other out of work youths and was eventually summoned, at about noon, by a bald, shiny headed, painfully thin Youth Employment Officer and Advisor, who was doing his best to exude authority, but failing miserably. This puny, emaciated, somewhat insignificant looking individual, whose off the peg, pin stripe suit looked at least 2 sizes too big and hung loosely from his Spartan frame, invited me into an austere cubicle cum interview room where a table and two hard seated, straight backed utility chairs were situated. He pointed to one of the chairs and gestured for me to sit. He took a seat on the opposite side of the table. In his claw like, skeletal hands he held my life history, encased in a cardboard file, which he placed on the table between his skinny forearms. Needless to say the file was as slim as he was thin; it was not at all substantial.

This sartorially challenged, haggard looking, narrow backed beanpole then lifted his half lens spectacles, which were hanging by a cord around his scrawny neck, balanced them, somewhat precariously on the end of his hawk like beak and peered, with little interest, over the top of what I took to be National Health glasses, firstly at the contents of the file then rather studiously at me. He looked like a moth-eaten, Dickensian lawyer. He then began to speak in a monotone drawl, as he did so his very prominent Adam's apple bobbed up and down, like a cork in rough water. He repeatedly lifted his left arm and glanced at his watch. His tone and manner of speech conveyed to me his lack of interest in myself, my welfare, or the job he was paid to do. It seemed that I was responsible for keeping him from his lunch. To him I was just another spotty faced, out of work, lazy juvenile punk wasting his time. The conversation that ensued went something like this:

'Right Mr. Laurie Driver what can we, here at the Youth Employment Office, do for you?'

'I need a job and I thought that you sir, having my recent history before you, may have understood that that's why I'm here at the Youth Employment Office, seeking work.'

'A job doing what, young man.'

'I rather thought that you, as a youth employment advisor, might be able to advise me, sir, as all I have previously done is before you in my records.'

'Ah, and what have you been doing so far in your working life?'

'I presumed that you might have known from the documentation in front of you, that I have been working as an apprentice Gold Blocker and Embosser in the printing industry, and I would like to continue in that trade, sir.'

'Well you don't seem to have a lot of experience.'

'I only left school 9 months ago.'

'Ah yes, so it says, here in your records that I have before me. Well we have no vacancies in the printing trade for apprentices, but I think I have just the position for you, it s a job that offers lots of scope and opportunities for a bright young thing like yourself, and you could go right to the top, and in years to come earn vast amounts. Do you know the whereabouts of Deansgate Railway yard, just across the road?'

'No sir, but I rather think that if it is just across the road, I shouldn't have too much difficulty locating it.' I said, with a hint of sarcasm, which went completely over his glossy, bald, raptorish, be-spectacled head.

'Very good then, young Driver,' he said as he handed me a written youth employment card, which he had been writing as he interviewed me 'here's an introduction card, you're to see an Inspector Etchells or an Inspector Carroll. By the way the position is for a trailer boy/van lad. Off you go young man and good luck.'

'Good bye sir and thank you.' I said, thinking to myself, what an idiot and useless excuse for a civil servant. If I had bumped into this cadaverous, hollow cheeked, excuse for a civil servant in the street 2 minutes later, I doubt he would have recognised me; he was not interested in me or my future prospects just as long as he could get through the day trouble free.

AN INTRODUCTION TO THE RAILWAYS

I ambled across the road, with a feeling of foreboding and trepidation, to Deansgate Railway Depot, where I might start earning again and possibly go right to the top and command vast amounts from the money tree. The entrance was actually at the junction of Watson Street and Lower Bridgewater Street, just off Deansgate. It was a ground level yard situated beneath an upper yard which was held up by massive iron stanchions every 30 feet, or so, all around a central, raised loading dock, approximately 100 yards long by 25 yards wide. On each of the loading docks lengths were numerous loading bays where goods vehicles reversed on, to either load or unload. The upper yard was, as I remember, used as a marshalling yard for Central Railway Station. These were still the days of the steam train, although the diesel/electric locomotive engine was coming into prominence. The first of these to be introduced on a commercial basis was the Deltic, Class 55 built in 1961 of which there had been prototypes and tests since 1955 and discussions and tests had been conducted on various diesel/electrics since 1945.

Both upper and lower yards of Deansgate Depot had rail lines running into the massive Great Northern Railway warehouse at the end of Watson Street and behind Peter Street, sadly the whole upper and lower tiers of Deansgate Railway Yard are now car parks, and Central Station is now the G-Mex Exhibition Hall. The GNR warehouse is used for other commercial enterprises.

As I peered through the entrance between the massive, open wooden gates of the yard, situated opposite the Watson Street railway arches and almost beneath the Bridgewater Street railway bridge, in the mid-afternoon of a sunny day, everything appeared dismal and in shadow. There were varying hues of grey and brown but the overall shade was black. The actual surrounding wall was of black brick as if contrived to add to the Stygian gloom. I felt like Livingstone about to enter the Dark Continent.

The yard itself was cobbled with granite setts and the only true colours I could see, at that time, was the green of a few blades of grass and weeds and the yellow of a few dandelions sprouting up between the cobblestones nearest the gate, which just caught the rays of the afternoon sun. The overall impression was one of dankness, dampness, and darkness, although once the yard was fully accessed, it opened up and was not as depressing as at first I had thought, with its block end, red rusty, rail lines, overgrown with weeds and brambles. It was obvious that no locos or carriages had moved along this section of track for a long time. Next to the track were old, disused stables which had not accommodated any equine workers for a number of years. Different types of goods vehicles and trailers were parked up along the loading dock and along the perimeter roadway. Whilst pondering whether to venture forth or not, numerous railway liveried vehicles were entering and exiting the yard, like so many bumble bees to-ing and fro-ing between the pollen donors and the hive. I finally plucked up enough courage and strode through the open portal, on my exploratory voyage to the world of British Rail.

As I entered into the yard I noticed a dim light emanating from the uncleaned windows of a small, slate roofed, badly pointed brick structure. I traipsed around it until I found the entrance, upon the door was screwed an unpolished and tarnished, brass sign with the legend INSPECTOR'S OFFICE. I hesitated for a moment then knocked rather tentatively, and a deep pleasant voice bade me enter. I opened the door and made my entrance, into the single roomed structure, to be confronted by a rather tall, middle aged gentleman with thinning, grey, wavy hair, stood with his back to a small pot-bellied stove, upon which sat a kettle, gently simmering away.

This man of some stature had on his large frame a Railway great coat beneath which was a railway blazer and a waistcoat adorned with a silver chain which held a railway issue pocket watch. The waistcoat covered and disguised the Inspector's slight paunch. He wore well tailored, well pressed Inspector's uniform trousers and his shoes were polished to a patent leather finish. His railway shirt was neatly ironed and his railway tie was finished with a neat Windsor knot. His hands were behind his back underneath his coat as to raise it to the heat, much in the manner of a Victorian gentleman in a tailed coat. This was Inspector Ernest Etchells, the Number 1 Inspector, who had ultimate control for the immediate vicinity that was Deansgate Depot. The opposing shift was under the supervision of Number 2 Inspector, Mr Harold Carroll, who was Inspector Etchells second in command. The Inspectors shifts overlapped to accommodate any de-briefing and problems. The two Inspectors covered the hours between 0700 and 1900, the hours of darkness being supervised by a foreman.

'Good afternoon, young man, my name is Inspector Etchells,' this gentleman said, 'How may I help you?' he then asked.

'Good afternoon sir, I've come about the job for a trailer boy, my name is Driver and I have an introduction card from the Youth Employment Office.' I replied.

'Very well,' he said 'hand me the card and allow me to tell you something about the position in question. Please be seated.' He gestured towards an empty chair.

'Thank you.' I said as I took the seat he had offered.

This single roomed office contained 2 chairs, a desk with a typewriter upon it, a small filing cabinet and a coat stand. There was the aforementioned stove and kettle, plus a small sink with just a cold water tap affixed to it and a logistics board screwed to one of the walls. This it seemed was all an Inspector needed.

The Inspector read the card and addressed me thus 'it says on this card that you have a number of GCE's, which is unusual for the post of trailer boy, and it says your last position was as an apprentice to a printing company and to be truthful, I don't think you will find this position as challenging as your last, young man. You will be using your brawn somewhat more than your brain.' He then continued so, 'The job on offer, young chap, if you decide to take it on, will be to help a driver in the preparation of his vehicle and load, and also in the delivery of envelopes, parcels, packages, crates, chests, cartons, boxes, perishable goods and livestock in cages and containers, including live fish, dogs, cats, birds, certain wild breeds and other more domesticated creatures on a dedicated round, and for collection of same for despatch to places further afield. If you're good at your job, well behaved, polite and a good and punctual timekeeper, when you reach the age of 18, we may send you to our driving school, and hopefully, young Laurie Driver, you will become a young lorry driver, ha, ha, ha.' He laughed at his own little joke. When his mirth had subsided he carried on, 'if not you will stay as a driver's mate until a portering vacancy becomes available and you will then take on that said position. You may apply for the driving school no more than 3 times and other vacancies will be posted on the notice board on a monthly basis. Feel free, after satisfactorily completing a 3 months probationary period, to apply for any vacancy that you think you may be capable of fulfilling, clerical or manual. May I suggest, with your education, you try to avail yourself of a clerical post later, as the pay is a little better and the work a little cleaner. You will be taken on initially for the 3 months probationary period I have mentioned and paid £3.00, per 42 hour week with annual increments, and will be liable for shift work at 18 years of age, for which you will be paid a differential...........'

'But the man at the Youth Employment said I could go right to the top,' I interrupted.

'That son, is the top. So what do you say? I've others to see you know.'

'I'll give it a try, sir,' I said in a tone that betrayed my lack of conviction.

'Right you are, we'll fix you up for a medical with our company doctor and get you a starting date in anticipation of your passing. Expect notification for your medical within the next 7 days and thank you for your interest, and for now, good-bye young fellow, we'll meet again soon, I'm sure.'

'Good-bye Inspector Etchells,' I said 'and thank you.'

Thereby was conducted my interview. There was no interviewing panel or inquisition. No references were pursued to my knowledge. I could have had a criminal record as long as my arm. I could have been a kleptomaniac larcenist of a violent and lethal disposition, but that didn't seem to matter, I was to be a trailer boy on British Rail, LM region, so ultimately a railwayman with the perks of free rail travel, uniform, pension, et al, pending the passing of the medical.

I had been wished good luck by a totally uninterested Youth Employment Officer, for a job I considered a trained chimpanzee, or perhaps even an untrained chimpanzee could so. So much for the General Certificate of Education I had studied so hard and long for. Still, I thought, it'll do as a stepping stone for a couple of weeks until something better comes along. How wrong I was.

Nowadays one would have to undergo checks for a criminal record and obtain at least 2 references to secure a position on the railways, but in the 60's it was a much more straightforward proposition, especially for the lowly capacity of driver's mate.

I got a date the following week, for my medical, which I passed as I was, then, a fit young man. By the end of the week I received a letter, telling me to report to Deansgate Depot the following Monday morning at 08.00hrs with my P45. Deansgate Rail Depot only delivered and collected goods that were small enough to travel on passenger services as opposed to the goods depots like Liverpool Road and Ardwick East that carried goods for heavy industry, e.g., bulk steel, bulk timber, paper pulp and containers etc. Monday morning came around and I was up bright and early to get myself ready. My mum had bought me a brown workman's haversack and a white, enamelled brew can, with all the makings for tea and coffee. You weren't a railway man without a haversack, brew can and the makings. She had also made me a sandwich for my dinner, which I found out wasn't really necessary, as all railway depots had their own subsidised canteens, though some employees still preferred to bring sandwiches, especially van lads and trailer boys that could not afford to pay for these cheap meals on such a meagre income.

I arrived at the depot early, along with 2 other new starters, each carrying a brown haversack, over his shoulder and clutching a white enamel brew can. We looked as alike as 3 peas in a pod. We were put through what was then the B.R., induction course, which consisted of a lecture on safe working practises, a thumbnail sketch of the railways history, holiday entitlement, pay and working conditions and measurement for our uniforms. We were told about our entitlement to subsidised and free rails travel to which we would be given rights after a qualifying period. We were then introduced to our drivers to be. The driver that I was to work with was a guy called Jake. That was my first day on the railways.

The free and subsidised travel was little used by the van lads. Most of the continental railways had reciprocative agreements with British Rail which allowed their foreign counterparts to enjoy rail travel throughout the length and breadth of the UK. The more mature drivers and their families travelled all over the continent on their concessionary passes. The lowly van lad used his for days out to Blackpool.

The next morning I and the other new recruits reported for duty at 0800hrs, looking as much alike as the previous day. We were given clock cards, shown where to clock on, and directed to the mess room to find our drivers. I could hear the buzz and hum of numerous discordant voices from outside and I opened the door, with a certain wariness. The sight that greeted me was reminiscent of the western saloons I had seen in old John Wayne films, but minus the firearms, dancing girls and the liquor, the liquor being replaced with tea and coffee. There was a thick blue-grey pall of stale tobacco smoke hanging in the air. The mess room was a large brick building which was actually made up of 2 rooms with a wall containing an archway separating them. Each section had its own entrance from outside. An unshaded, nicotine stained light bulb hung, by its wire, from a ceiling rose in each of the rooms to shed a meagre luminescence throughout the mess. Very little natural light was able to make its way through the begrimed windows of the mess and so the lamps were left switched on at all times. The section that we had entered had a number of tables which were taken up by various card schools. Different games, including Poker, 3 Card Blind Brag, Don, etc., were being played, the less skilful games being played by lads of my own age or slightly older, the big money games and the more skilful by the drivers and porters. I had no idea of the legality of it all but there were piles of cash on the tables, notes and coinage, more money than I had ever seen at such a tender age. There were people arguing, shouting, shoving and pushing. It was like a cross between a bear garden and Donnybrook Fair.

Through this imbroglio and hotch potch of characters Jake saw me enter, and called me over, he pointed to the hot water geyser and told me to get myself a brew, whilst he finished his game of cards, and then we would load up and set about our deliveries. The other new starters were matched up with their drivers, and they had the same look of incredulity, upon their faces, as I believe I must have had.

I weaved my way through the Bedlamic chaos, followed by the other new boys, towards the hot water heater which was in the corner of the room to the right of the door as one entered. It was positioned to the side of and above a large brownstone Belfast sink. There was the mirror image of this set-up on the other side of the partition wall in the other half of the mess room. Whilst making my way to the geyser I heard little asides, and comments from the older drivers' mates and the younger drivers, about the new kids and what would be done to them. Luckily these juvenile threats were just that, made to make us initiates feel ill at ease, but no real threat to our well being.

I finally made it to the geyser and prepared myself a brew and tried to make myself as inconspicuous as I could. One of the older drivers, who I later found out was called Harold, had filled his brew can prior to me and he was swinging it backwards and forwards in ever increasing arcs until he was swinging it full circle to *'mash the brew.'*

During one of these revolutions, at a somewhat inopportune moment, the brew can separated company with its handle and it and its contents flew across the room and hit one of the card playing drivers on the back of the head, spilling a good deal of the contents down his back. There was a shout of 'Good Jesus, Mary and Joseph!' The card player, an Irish guy named Mick, jumped up, steam rising from the back and shoulders of his greatcoat like the morning mist on a lowlands swamp. He ascertained from whence the offending object had come, made his way across the room to the driver stood gawping, in complete bewilderment, at his hand which still clutched the handle of the brew can. Mick took up a pugilistic stance and a bout of fisticuffs ensued, although it was soon broken up, and apologies and handshakes were exchanged. The Irish card player had on, at the time, his full uniform and as such had more skins than an onion, so apart from the bump on the back of his bonce he was relatively unscathed. As I watched the scene unfolding before my eyes I felt a tap on my shoulder. I turned round with a terrified look on my countenance to be confronted by Jake who, by the wide grin on his face, had obviously seen a great deal of humour at my introduction to the railwayman's pre-duty social activities.

Fights and brawls were fairly commonplace and were usually over card games and usually between trailer boys and van lads. These altercations usually took the form of a duel with fists, whereby the 2 combatants would go around the rear of the mess room, by the coal pile, and have a stand up set to, loosely based on the Marquis of Queensbury rules. The bout would finish after a knock down or when one had had enough. Very rarely were there any serious injuries, other than the occasional bloody nose, black eye or cut or swollen lip, sustained during these scuffles and scrambles.

One rough and tumble, which could have had serious consequences, occurred between an 18 year old Negro porter, called Geddes Yates and a strapping 16 year old, white lad known as Clarkie. This was over the contents of the kitty of a game of blind brag. Tables were overturned, chairs were thrown, punches and kicks were exchanged. There was scratching and gouging and Clarkie was well in front on points when Yates pulled out a bone handled sheaf knife, with a blade of approximately 6 inches in length. This was probably in lieu of any firearms. Yates made a couple of feints followed by a couple of lunges before a couple of the older drivers stepped in and wrestled Yates to the floor. The knife skidded across the stone floor and was picked up and secreted away by one Eddie Hunston. By this time Inspector Etchells had been summoned, by one of the porters who had dashed to his office. The Inspector arrived within a couple of minutes, questions were asked but the Cosa Nostra Law of Omerta prevailed. Warnings were issued to the two combatants. Inspector Etchells dealt with the issue within the confines of the depot issuing the two lads with severe disciplinary notices and the threat of the sack if there were any further transgressions. The adversaries shook hands and promised to get along in the future. I cannot remember what happened to the money that was in the kitty.

The following Monday when old Tom, who at 70 years of age, had been kept on after retirement, to come in at 0500 hrs to set the two pot-bellied stoves for the early shift and do a bit of cleaning, was raking the ashes out of one of the stoves, which the night shift had a tendency to let go out, when the well charred, bent but unmistakeable blade of the sheaf knife came to light. But by then the incident was regarded as being in the past and so life went on and the misshapen, blackened blade was thrown in the rubbish bin.

Jake ushered me out of the mess room, brew in hand, and told me to follow him to the loading bay. I did as I was told and followed like a timid child behind a strict parent. He had already backed his vehicle on to the bay in preparation for loading. Jake's trailer was of the box type with a rear roller shutter and tail board. He proceeded to show me the correct loading procedure; basically it was a job you picked up as you went along, loading as close as possible, in drop order. He also showed me how to become competent in the use of the steel toe-capped tyre pressure gauge, which, basically meant giving each tyre a hefty kick to ascertain whether there were any punctures or under inflated tyres. Not the most accurate or reliable method, but tried and tested. There was also the oil and water to be checked on a daily basis, along with the fuel.

A couple of the trailers were flat beds whilst the rest were box types, approximately 20ft long. The units or prime movers were 3 wheel Scammell Scarabs, commonly called the mechanical horse, after the horses and carts they were brought in to replace, they were known as urban artics and the coupling device was Scammell's own automatic coupling as opposed to the fifth wheel coupling of larger, heavier vehicles. The rest of the fleet were rigid 4 wheelers consisting of 1951, 6 cylinder Bedford 'M' or 'O' types with either petrol or diesel engines, 4D Ford Thames powered by a 3.6 litre 4D four cylinder diesel, or Ford's petrol engine, 3 ton Austin K series and Morris CV11/40 with a 3.5 litre petrol engine, and an old Thorneycroft, and a couple of Dennis. All were bonneted trucks except the Dennis. The Dennis' were the F8 model with a 4.25 Rolls Royce petrol engine or the Perkins diesel engine. Later, Commer and Karrier Bantams and a streamlined Scamell known as the Townsman were introduced as prime movers. The Karrier Bantam was powered by a 2.260

litre Perkins diesel engine. The Townsman was also diesel powered, using the Leyland OE160, it also had an air assisted trailer release button. Also introduced were TK Bedford's with Bedford's own 330D engine in an attempt to standardise on diesel powered vehicles.

When I started at the railways, the vehicle colours were a yellowy cream and maroon, known as the blood and custard livery. This colour scheme could be seen in railway stations and railway waiting rooms the length and breadth of the country. The livery for the later trucks changed to yellow when National Carriers Limited took over the railways road transport in the late sixties.

At the time I was introduced to Jake, I was also introduced to the trailer boy I was to replace. He was and still is, known as Knocker, a corruption of his true name, Norman Hocker. Knocker had just reached 18 years of age, and so was about to go on shift work but he had applied for the driving school and been accepted so he would only do a couple of weeks as a mate on shifts before he went to the school. Knocker and I became good friends and that friendship still exists today as does my friendship with Jake. At the time I met Jake I thought he was getting on a bit, but in truth he was only 12 years my senior, but to a 16 year old anyone over 20 was so far advanced in age as to be ancient.

There was a lot of older drivers coming up to retirement age, these older men had been on delivery rounds with horses and carts in the past and when the horseless carriage was introduced, it was said, they moved onto them without ever taking a driving test for a motorised vehicle, other than the railways own domestic test. They were awarded their licenses by grandfather rights and most of them drove as if they still had Dobbin drawing a wain. There was John 'Jolly' Carter, Percy 'Longprong' Longton, Teddy 'Horseman' Taylor, Billy 'Tug' Wilson, John 'Chalky' White and

Dave 'RSM' Lee, and a few others whose names now elude me. 'RSM' was so called because of his military bearing and as far as I know, was the only one of the older drivers to have served in the war, the others falling back on the protected industry status of railwaymen. It seemed that every worker on the railway's was awarded a nickname. Some of the younger drivers had been through National Service, and had passed their driving tests in the forces, though they still had to be tested on each vehicle and have that vehicle registered on their British Railway domestic licenses which were licenses issued to each driver to ensure that they were conversant with each vehicle driven. Jake had done his National Service but his job on the Railways was kept open. His posting was to Germany and after his National Service he returned to Deansgate Depot to resume his career.

After a couple of days on the job I was issued with my uniform which consisted of 2 pairs of trousers, 3 shirts, 2 ties, 1 jacket, 2 long sleeved waistcoats, 1 hat and 1 Railway greatcoat. The Railway greatcoats were of such a length that they hung down to ones feet and so one appeared to be floating on air and moving along like a wraith. Most of the staff that were issued with this overlong accoutrement had them shortened by their wives or girlfriends or even by professional seamstresses. Safety shoes had to be purchased at a discounted price.

Health and Safety has certainly changed, and for the better. Nowadays Hi-Viz vests and safety footwear plus other personal protective equipment (PPE) are supplied at no cost to the employee. If anyone was caught working out of uniform they would be reported to the powers that be and the disciplinary procedure would be invoked, 3 disciplinary notices would result in dismissal, needless to say most people wore the uniform, or as much or as little of it that they could get away with.

I worked with Jake, as a trailer boy, for 18 months during which period we won the annual award for best kept and cleanest truck in the depot, we spent hours on bull-shit and elbow grease, touching up the paintwork, blacking the tyres, cleaning the glasswork etc. We won such a good prize that after all these years I can't, for the life of me, remember what it was.

Jake was a man of integrity and he taught me respect and a sense of values within the workplace. He treated me as an equal and instilled me with confidence; he also taught me the basics of driving the Scammell, in a quiet corner of the yard, to prepare me for the day I went to the driving school. This wasn't easy for someone who had never sat behind the wheel of a vehicle before, let alone a commercial articulated truck. The vehicle had a constant mesh gearbox with a gate shift, situated to the right of the driver; one had to virtually clamber over the gear shift to get into the driving seat. Well, on my first attempt at driving and shifting gear I rattled the cogs in that gearbox, making all kinds of grinding and crunching noises. Jake said he thought I was trying to play God Save The Queen or even Beethoven's Moonlight Sonata through the gearbox, but as we all know, practice makes perfect and I persevered until I was somewhere near competent.

Our delivery round was around the Gaythorn, Hulme and Bridgewater areas. We did the deliveries in the morning and collections in the afternoon, but the first port of call was Aston's Café on Cambridge Street for breakfast with other drivers and van lads, where the drivers, as a matter of tradition, paid for their lads. Steve Aston who owned the establishment was a member of the Aston footballing family which included Johnny Aston and young John who played for Manchester United. Some of the more famous companies on Jake's round were The Dunlop Rubber Company, Odham's Press, The Hotspur Press, The Daily Herald building, The Dot Motorcycle Company and Selas Gas which, I believe, later became part of British Gas, but there was also a lot more lesser known, local companies and a great deal of domestic mail order deliveries. Coming up to Christmas the mail order deliveries increased tenfold and we received tenfold the amount of gratuities from both domestic and commercial customers. At that time I had a mate who worked on refuse collection colloquially known as 'on the bins.' One night over the Christmas period we were discussing the tips we'd made. I asked 'how did you make out with tips on your job?

He replied 'okay, but I went to this house, knocked on the door, when the door opened I said to the householder 'compliments of the season, I'm the man who empties your bin' and he said 'same to you, I'm the man who fills it.' And slammed the door, so one way or another he'll be shown the error of his ways over the coming year.'

Through the year, Jake let me keep any tips that we made. The only time he took any of the gratuities was at the Christmas period when some firms would give a bottle of whisky or even a fiver for the service we had supplied. At this time the tips, be they monetary or in kind were split 50-50, or as close as possible. Jake would keep the alcoholic spirits and give me extra cash in lieu. I had never been so well off in my life. I could afford to buy Christmas presents and still have cash left to spend on myself. This was my first inkling of how good a little extra cash could make one feel. It had the ability to turn an insignificant trailer boy into a person with bargaining power and a will to obtain more. My pockets were full and I revelled in it.

A FEW CHARACTERS

It was while working with Jake, at Deansgate that an old schoolmate and friend of mine became unemployed and was looking for a temporary position until he went into the army. His name was 'Dusty' Rhodes and he approached me to ascertain whether there were any jobs going at Deansgate. I, in turn, approached Ernie Etchells and told him of Dusty's dilemma. Inspector Etchells asked me to tell my friend to pop down for an interview the following day. Dusty went for the interview, got a date for his medical and started a week or so later as a van lad at Deansgate.

Dusty and I had gone to primary school together where we had both done well in the 11+ examinations and were granted places in the Grammar Stream at the local Secondary Modern School. The Grammar or Alpha Stream as it was also known was for those students who had not secured a scholarship to Grammar School or those that were borderline pass cases in the 11+.

Of the students that were in the same class as Dusty and I were a number that went on to take 'A' level GCE's and go on to University to get degrees. One such was 'Porky' Pawson who became a chartered Accountant and went to work in the Caribbean and then New York, making a lot of money on the way. There was also Philip 'Pip' Lloyd who became a teacher and later emigrated to Australia where he secured a Headmastership. Others from our class went on to get degrees and took on high flying jobs as trainee scientists, doctors, vets and the like.

Dusty and I were not destined for such lofty achievements. Dusty was a jester and saw life as one big joke and treated it accordingly. A couple of examples of his wit and humour were seen whilst we were both still in the Grammar Stream.

When we were attending a lesson on woodwork theory, the teacher, a Mr Coakley, was explaining to the class the make up of trees in general. He had explained how the bark was the outer protective covering and was telling us about the sap, which is virtually the life blood of a tree, and the sapwood which grows between the bark and the heartwood. He went on to talk of the annual rings, by which you can date a tree trunk, and star shakes and cup shakes caused by storms. He then told us of the medullary rays that radiate from the medulla or the pith, which is the central part of plants and various other living tissue, and I suppose equates to bone marrow in humans. Upon finishing the lecture, the teacher asked 'Can anybody present tell me what the pith is?'

In a flash, Rhodes' hand shot into the air, and he blurted out, with no hesitation 'YETH THIR, I KNOW WHAT THE PITH ITH.' With this outburst the class started, as one, to laugh and Coakley could not coax us to stop.

On another occasion in a Physics lesson we were learning about the firmament and the planets etc. The teacher singled out Dusty and asked 'Rhodes, will you be so kind as to tell myself and the class the name of the Dog Star?'

Now Dusty knew full well that Sirius was the Dog Star but his sense of humour caused him to answer 'Me, tell you, sir? I thought you would have known, it's Pluto, isn't it, sir?' Once again the class burst into laughter at Dusty's apparent stupidity.

Dusty was dropped from the Grammar Stream in the 3rd year because of his low marks and his disruptive influence on other pupils. He left school at 15 years of age with no qualifications, and took a number of menial, mediocre jobs. His father was a draughtsman at A.V. Roe plane makers, at Greengate, Chadderton, now British Aerospace and he secured his son a place as an apprentice draughtsman. Dusty hated it and after a year or so and against his father's wishes, he handed in his notice and took himself off to the Army Recruitment Office where he enrolled as a boy soldier with the Royal Engineers. It was in the short period between leaving AVRO's and being accepted by the army that Dusty filled in his time working as a trailer boy.

The Railways at that time, the early sixties, employed a lot of African and Afro-Caribbean people who had come to Britain for a better life in the 1940's and 1950's. Quite a lot of them ended up doing the more tedious, menial and mundane jobs such as portering on the Railways or working on the buses, or such jobs as his white brethren would not do. One such was a tall, well built African called George Achi O Tutu. Who was as strong as an ox, black as the Ace of Spades and suffered a religious fervour, bordering on fanaticism and when he wasn't praying, well, praying was easier than working, would regale anyone that would listen with excerpts from the good book in his best deep baritone. Unfortunately his quotes were more often mis-quotes, such as the story of how Samson slew the Philistines with the *arse bone of a giraffe*, and the story of Shadrach, Meshach and *To bed we go*, and the *wisecracking* of Solomon, and how Jesus performed the *mackerel* of bringing *Lazy Arse* back from the dead, and many more.

There was a black guy called Raymonde D'Aguilera who came from one of the French African Colonies, although black he had distinctly white features and may have been of mixed race. Then there was George Pembo who was a close friend of Jake's who had come to Britain as a child from the Caribbean, with his parents and siblings in the 40's. George played in a Caribbean steel band. Another black guy from the West Indies was Clive Thorney who *'walked the walk and talked the talk'* and considered himself to be the answer to any maiden's prayer. He had endeavoured to straighten his hair and affected a white man's hairstyle with a side parting, his hands were well manicured and he appeared never to get dirty.

He was definitely workshy and when he went into hospital for a hernia operation another driver was heard to say 'He must have got that hernia breaking wind, because that's the only time he ever strains himself.'

At least 20% of the driver/van lad workforce at Deansgate, and most probably at all the other rail yards and stations, were second generation blacks or of mixed race born over here. Most rail yards were cosmopolitan melting pots and as well as the Afros' and Jamaics' there was the usual smattering of Irish, Scottish and Welsh and the occasional Chinee' and at Deansgate there was even an Hawaiian named Kim who came to work on a 650cc Triumph motor cycle and his party piece was to offer the local office girls 'A ride for a ride'. Whether or not this offer was ever taken up I know not, but I never saw any nubile office girls fighting to clamber onto his pillion or anything else for that matter.

There was a driver at Deansgate called Albert de Toper and his round covered parts of Hulme that Jake's did not and also part of Moss Side and Old Trafford. On his round were two breweries and Pomona Dock where the Guinness boats docked from Ireland. Albert liked a tipple, well, he was an out and out sot really, and whether he had anything to deliver to the breweries and Guinness or not he would call in for his 'allowance'.

Because he was well established on the round and everybody knew him, he was made quite welcome at Guinness and the breweries with the result that his nose and cheeks took on a rather florid complexion with outbreaks of pustules. When I say florid, it was anything from pink through purple to puce and was once described by another driver as 'redder than a baboon's arse.'

Albert lived in Old Trafford and one morning as he was making his way to work at approximately 05.00hrs, he was coming on early for pre-rostered overtime, he passed a particular house and saw smoke coming from under the door. He peered through a gap in the curtains and saw flames. Albert did no more, but shoulder charged the door until it gave way. He entered the premises and was responsible for rescuing the family that resided there, with no injuries to the family or himself. The noise made by Albert's efforts to force the door woke the neighbours who telephoned the emergency services, who arrived within minutes. The upshot of this reminiscence is that Albert got a commendation for his bravery and public spiritedness, but he also got an award, from the public purse, for the 'atrocious burns' he received to his face.

Amongst the drivers was one cantankerous and much disliked fellow, Bill Bailey, who nobody wanted to work with. He had been Knocker's driver for Knocker's first year on the Railways and Knocker had nothing but scorn for Bailey. He took all the tips from his van lads and would not allow them in the cab of the vehicle. He made his lads ride on the rear of the truck in all kinds of weather. He never bought his van lad a meal, as did all the other drivers. Consequently he was always the last roundsman driver to leave the depot at the end of the day as none of the lads or drivers would clock him out, which, unbeknown to the inspectors or management, was common practice at the time.

Knocker passed his driving test, after a month's intensive course of the Railways' Driving School, which was situated in Hollinwood, a borough of Oldham. He came back to Deansgate, at 18 years of age, as a fully fledged Railway Road Vehicle Driver, and his earnings shot up to a basic wage of £9-10s (£9.50p) per 42 hour week, plus overtime and shift differential. A king's ransom to a young man in those days.

Time passed and I reached 18 years of age. The first Monday after my birthday I left Jake and the delivery round and was put on shifts, and I was allowed to work overtime. It was a shock to the system having to rise at 0430hrs. Until then, I had foolishly believed that there was only one 4.30 in the day and that was in the afternoon. At that time I had to rely on public transport to get me to and from work. Not being used to working 12 hours I frequently fell asleep on the bus home and missed my stop causing me to arrive home later than expected.

My first driver on shifts was Knocker and we were to start at 05.30hrs. I met him walking through Albert Square at 05.15hrs. He was in front of me but I knew it was him from the back by the black, finger tip, drape jacket, and the drainpipe trousers, finished off by wedged heeled, crepe soled, brothel creeper shoes. From a distance he looked like a walking blackboard and easel. He, like me, was one of the last of the Teddy boys. I affected similar garb, but not for work.

That morning after Knocker had changed into his uniform he was allocated a diesel powered Dennis to drive. The vehicle was low on fuel so the first job was to fill her up. The Railways had their own bunkering stations; central Manchester's being on Baring Street next to Mayfield Station. Knocker pulled up to the pumps and proceeded to put in the fuel, unfortunately he inadvertently put in petrol instead of diesel. We then proceeded to Piccadilly, and as we reached the security box by the livestock office there was one almighty BOOM! The engine cover, in the cab, blew off, the cab filled up with black, oily smoke. The vehicle came to a halt, Knocker and me blindly clambered out of the black, pungent atmosphere of the cab into the acrid, smog-like atmosphere that surrounded the vehicle's exterior. We were both retching and coughing and our eyes were watering profusely. Our faces were smeared with the sooty, greasy deposits from the engine much to the amusement of everybody within the immediate vicinity. We must have looked like the poor relations of The Black and White Minstrel Show. The vehicle had to be towed away to the workshops which were situated in the Railway arches beneath Mayfield Station, on North Western Street, for remedial work, whilst Knocker and myself were taken back to Deansgate to clean ourselves up.

There was another guy, Walter Wall, who started on the Railway before me. He was a cousin of mine and actually started as a driver. Having past his test prior to starting on the Railway.

Walter was 2 years my senior and he went straight on to shift work but had to pass tests on each of the Railway vehicles he drove, these passes were noted on the B.R. Domestic License which was issued to every driver to ensure that one was capable of driving and conversant with each type of vehicle.

Walter was notorious for his inability to get up early and he was overjoyed when I reached 18 years of age and went on turns as they called shift work on the Railway. This move to shifts benefited both of us as we both lived in the Blackley area, about a mile apart, and I had to pass Walt's house on the way to work. At the time Walt was the owner of a big black, Humber Hawk limousine, which, to me, looked like a de-commissioned hearse, in which I would get a lift to work on the occasions that we were on the same shift. As I stated earlier, Walter was pretty damn useless at getting up early. He had a bad back. He couldn't get it off the bed, and so he depended on me to knock him up. This I did by a combination of banging on the front door and throwing small stones at the bedroom window. Walt did try mind, he set two old wind-up alarm clocks, the type with a pair of bells and a striker on the top. He placed these on top of an empty biscuit tin, with the lid sitting loosely askew on top, both alarms would go off simultaneously, rattling the loose lid, causing the clocks to fall into the empty tin to continue the cacophony in a somewhat more resonant and reverberant mode. There was enough noise to waken the dead, but not to waken Walter, though he did receive numerous complaints from his neighbours. His wife had taken to using the spare bedroom through the working week, to avoid the noise of the amplified alarm clocks. He eventually went on nights to escape the early starts.

BELLE VUE

One of the jobs allocated to shift drivers was to pick up livestock from Manchester Piccadilly Station, e.g; crates of new-born chicks for the reptile house at Belle Vue Zoological Gardens which was situated in Gorton on the A57 Hyde Road. Those reptiles loved those tender, juicy, new born chicks. Occasionally live specimens of some wild beasts were delivered by the Railway's, although these were of the less dangerous type.

Belle Vue was opened in 1836 by one John Jennison, (1793-1869). The Jennison family owned the zoo until 1925. It was the 3rd oldest zoological gardens in the world. Belle Vue finally closed its doors to the public in early 1982.

Now in the 40's, 50's and 60's Belle Vue was Manchester's own Disneyland before Disneyland had even opened, which was, incidentally, in 1955. It was a famous zoological gardens and funfair with all kinds of exotic animals. It had its own boating lake and it had white knuckle rides including a wooden roller-coaster known as the Bobs, water flumes, The Wild Mouse, carousels, a haunted house etc. It hosted speedway racing and had its own team, the Belle Vue Aces. It boasted Kings Hall where international boxing and wrestling took place, where such wrestlers as Billy Two Rivers, Jack and Dominic Pye and Jackie Pallo fought, as did the famous boxers of the day, such as Jackie Brown and Brian London. Belle Vue also hosted band and dance nights, an annual Christmas circus, brass band shows and fireworks displays.

The first woman reporter to report a boxing match, did so from Belle Vue's King's Hall. The match took place in 1932 between Jackie Brown and Jim Maharg. The lady reporter was a Dora Taylor and she reported for the Manchester Evening News. Sadly Belle Vue is no more, and in its place is a multi-plex cinema, bowling alley and fast food outlets, although the Speedway is still there, as is Belle Vue Greyhound Racing Track.

On Saturdays, for overtime, Knocker would volunteer to do

the livestock job, and so the van would be loaded with the new born chicks and whatever other items of livestock and perishable goods were needed at Belle Vue, plus a secondary cargo of trailer boys and van lads. The rear shutter of the van was pulled down. Knocker would then drive to the rear goods and trade entrance of Belle Vue and yell 'LIVESTOCK!' to the security guard, who would then lift the barrier and let the van in. Once in, and out of sight of the security man, Knocker stopped and opened the rear shutter and a half a dozen or more lads jumped out and scurried off into the park, like so many escapees from a paddy wagon, having saved the entrance fee to one of Manchester's major attractions. Knocker and his legitimate van lad made the delivery, parked the van and joined the rest of the lads for an hour or so of unbridled enjoyment before everyone piled into the back of the van and returned to the depot, and for this we were paid the princely rate of time and a quarter.

SALFORD YOUTHS

DURING the mid 60's, an influx of youths from the City of Salford started work at Deansgate. They were all from the Ordsall area and all knew each other. I think it may be pertinent here to use only their Christian names. There was George, Charlie, Eddie, Pete and John. They had all recently left Ordsall Secondary Modern School and had been sent by the Salford Youth Employment Office to Deansgate to fill the positions for van lads. All five started on the same day. All five of them always had upon their persons plenty of cigarettes and, for van lads, plenty of cash. The reason for this abundance of cigs and dosh came to light when Charlie told his driver, a lad not much more than two years older than Charlie, how this situation came about.

In those days most cigarettes cost less than half a crown (12½p) for a pack of ten. The cigarette machines outside retail outlets for the out of hours smokers took a half crown coin and issued the requisite change. Charlie explained how he and the others sellotaped a piece of cotton to a half crown coin, deposited the said coin into a cigarette machine. When the coin dropped into the machine and hit the trip mechanism, the coin was pulled back a smidgin' and taped into place on the front of the machine via the piece of cotton. Then each column of cigarettes would be emptied by opening and shutting the drawers, as each pack of cigs was removed the requisite change fell down the change chute. When the machine was empty, the cotton was untaped from the machine, the half crown fell into the machine to be rejected because the machine was empty. Thus all the cigarettes and all the change were taken and the half crown, used to perpetrate the crime was recovered to be used at the next machine.

Various drivers and the Salford van lads emptied machines all over Manchester, Salford and Trafford. There was even an article in the Manchester Evening News of the day, stating that thieves had found an ingenious method of emptying cigarette machines and that the police were at a loss as to how it was happening. Railway vans were to be seen outside newsagents and off licenses at the quiet and unsociable hours of the day and night and if any passers by would have taken the trouble to investigate, they would have seen drivers frantically pulling the drawers in and out and depositing cigarettes into a bag as the van lad tried to catch all the change being ejected from the machine, occasionally scrabbling around the floor for elusive coins. Luckily no one suspected anything and nobody caught on and the scam only came to an end when the price of cigarettes went up and the single half crown coin could not be used.

DOGS, CATS AND OTHER BEASTS

The Railway always had its fair share of characters, and Piccadilly livestock and perishable office was no exception. In those days people would send dogs and cats amongst more exotic animals by rail, in tea chests, cardboard boxes or custom made crates. There was a porter at Piccadilly named Justin Case, who was a dedicated animal lover and would feed and water any transient beast passing through the station. He even bought a dog leash and collar so that he could exercise any poor dogs mid way through their journey, a very noble gesture which relieved the animal of a lot of stress during its journey without its owner.

One day a racing greyhound arrived in a large wooden box, with a hinged, mesh door at one end. The animal looked obviously distressed, so Justin, after having gained the mutt's trust, opened the box, placed, around its neck, the collar and lead. He then persuaded the pooch out of the box and tied it to a pallet, and gave it a little food and water. After the racing canine had finished its repast Justin untied it, grasped the lead and proceeded to take this quick and agile quadruped on its constitutional down the nearest platform, which was a goods and mail platform as opposed to a passenger platform. As he strolled along the platform one of Piccadilly station's feral, flea-bitten, feline rat catchers appeared, it saw the greyhound, the fur on is back rose, it's backbone arched, it hissed and spat, but discretion being the better part of valour, it turned tail and shot off down the platform, down the 4ft and along the railway track away from the station. The greyhound, being a dog of pursuit, leapt forward dragging the leash from its walker's hand and sped after the cat with the porter in hot pursuit, shouting at the top of his voice 'STOP THAT DOG, IT'S A PARCEL!' The hound disappeared down the 4ft and raced down the permanent way after the cat, never to be seen again. Needless to say Justin never seemed to have the same affection for animals after that incident, and to add insult to injury he was paraded in front of the management and the disciplinary procedure was invoked. All this for his kindness and devotion to our four legged friends.

Not much later and once again at Piccadilly Station there was another animal escapee escapade, concerning a pig that sought its freedom and ran amok down a passenger platform during the rush hour. The driver that had been sent to pick up the porker for delivery was a giant of a man named Roger Cronshaw, known as 'The Bear' or sometimes 'Brother Grumble' because of his deep, stentorian voice. How the porcine creature escaped was never ascertained, although the van lad, a somewhat inquisitive individual, was the number 1 suspect, but escape it did. The said beast, which must have weighted in at about 20 stones, charged down one of the main platforms scattering, like ninepins, bowler hated business men who tried to fend it off with their briefcases and rolled up umbrellas. Women and girls screamed and dived unceremoniously into the open doors of the slam door rolling stock, which was in common usage at the time, showing great expanses of thigh, stocking tops and suspender belts as they did so, other passengers jumped onto the pull along parcel trucks that littered the platforms, or hid behind the metal stanchions which supported the station. Some became frozen to the spot, whilst schoolchildren giggled uncontrollably at the events unfolding before them. Big Rog and his van lad aided by half a dozen or so porters were trying to corner this bacon on the trotter, which was grunting and snorting at all and sundry, and by sheer luck drove it to the doors of the guards van of a local train. The doors opened outwards and were in the open position. The guards van was self contained and had no through doors to passenger coaches, so once the hog was inside and the doors closed, it was captured.

The problem which then arose was how to get the swine back into its crate and into the back of the trailer for delivery. The solution was to put the crate onto the rear of the trailer along with the van lad and half a dozen porters, back the trailer up towards the guards van doors, the doors of the guards van were then opened, and then the trailer was hurriedly reversed the last few feet before the snorting beast gained access back to the platform. The gap between the open doors was less than the width of the trailer and a couple of stout scaffolding planks, which had been commandeered from a building team that were doing some ongoing maintenance work to the station, were laid from the back end of the trailer and the crate to the floor of the guards van. These planks were reinforced by use of a portable wheelchair ramp, of which each platform had one. The porters and the van lad then went into the guards van and after much urging, cajoling, and man-handling accompanied by much shouting, swearing and porcine squealing the huge boar was finally enticed up the gently sloping ramp and returned to its crate. The crate, whose floor had a generous covering of hay, was immediately, firmly secured, and the poor, rather distressed animal sent to its destination.

The train in which the pig was captured was, because of the event, late leaving the station, but the occurrence gave a good half an hour of free entertainment and amusement for a number of passengers and is a better excuse for late running trains than leaves on the line or the wrong type of snow.

All railway yards and stations had at least one cat and sometimes up to half a dozen of these velvet pawed, razor clawed felines, they were of the feral type, who seemed to know, as cats do, on which side their bread is buttered. Their main undertaking, of course, was the pursuit and destruction of the rat and mouse population which proliferated in dark, dingy railway yards and stations.

At Deansgate yard one Friday evening, before finishing time on the late shift, and prior to the night shift starting, myself and a few other van lads were waiting to clock ourselves and our respective drivers off, this was a drivers perk, gained by the drivers for buying breakfast and dinner and generally looking after the lads. The yard was almost deserted, I and a couple of other drivers mates found the depot cat, a big, one-eared, ginger She cat, atop of the coal pile at the rear of the mess room building. It was lying motionless, with numerous lacerations about its face and body, and clumps of fur missing. It had obviously lost its fight with rats or a dog or even an urban fox and was in a comatose state.

One of the lads present prodded it with a stick, it mewled quietly but still didn't move. Everyone around agreed that the cat was close to death, so one of the lads, known as Mitch, volunteered to put it out of its misery. The method used wasn't exactly clinical, there was no lethal injection or humane killer available, and so he picked up the coal shovel, whirled it round his head a couple of times and, with a flourish, brought it down, CLANG! on the unconscious moggie's noggin. This done he shovelled the old grimalkin up and took it into the mess room, with its head and front paws lolling over the edge of the shovel. He opened all the windows and doors, and put the poor one eared, mini tigress, which was still lying spread out on the shovel into the gas oven and turned on the gas and came outside. The rest of us watched from the mess room door. The cat was left in the oven, to breathe in the toxic fumes, for approximately a quarter of an hour, when Mitch went back in and turned off the gas and closed the windows. He took the supposedly dead pussycat back to where it was found and threw it behind the coal pile, hoping that whatever carnivorous beasties were about would dispose of the body. Whilst all this was going on the two pot bellied stoves in the mess room were merrily burning away and I assume that they devoured the gas before any build up took place, otherwise we may have been charged with causing an explosion and arson, or nowadays, accused of terrorism.

On the following Monday morning, I arrived at the depot at 05.25, for a 05.30 start. I clocked on and made my way to the mess room. I opened the door and there to my complete and utter surprise, sat in front of the pot-bellied stove, grooming itself, keeping Old Tom company, was the big, ginger Puss, looking still dishevelled but slightly better than it had on the preceding Friday. Now I've heard of cats having nine lives, I thought, but this is ridiculous. The same cat was still keeping down the rodent population at Deansgate when I left. I now realise that when Mitch performed his act of mercy, the shovel must have hit the coal prior to or simultaneously to the cat's head, thus resulting in the said Moggy receiving only a glancing blow and sending it into a deeper comatose state. The secondary act of mercy, i.e. the gassing to supposedly make sure that the cat was truly dead did not work, I assume, because of the cat's low breathing and the open windows in the messroom.

Another cat incident that happened around the same time, took place at Victoria Station perishable and livestock office and concerned a prize winning Persian cat which came into the office to be put on to a connecting train. There was a Rosette on the rigid cardboard box and an embossed card proclaiming the breed, class and the fact that it had won 1st prize, best in show. One of the young inquisitive van lads from Victoria decided that he must see this prize winning majestic beauty, so he peered through a slight gap in the top of the box, he couldn't see anything so he slowly opened the box a little wider, still not enough, he opened the box fully and the beautiful Persian cat, with a blue riband around its neck, immediately leapt out of the box through the door and disappeared from view. The van lad immediately grabbed hold of one of the stations flea bitten, feral felines, and with a fair amount of hissing, spitting and scratching, from the semi-wild marmalade, mangy, mouser, managed to tie a piece of string in a bow around its neck, stuff it into the box, seal it up and send it on its way. I never heard anymore about this incident, but I imagine the owner was more than a little upset upon opening the box that was delivered to him and finding an animal that resembled his prize winner only insomuch as it belonged to the family *Felidae*. I suspect a claim ensued. It was said that a litter of kittens, born some time later, to the railways feral cat population, had about them, a distinct Persian look.

A NIGHTTIMES INCIDENT

I remember an incident that occurred whilst I was a driver's mate on nights, which came around every 3rd week, on a rotational shift basis. The fact that I was on nights means I had turned 18 years of age and I place this incident early in 1964. The night shift was from 22.00hrs to 06.00hrs with the opportunity to work 12 hours if required and the hours for this were 18.00hrs until 06.00hrs. I was working with a driver called Phil Landerer on the night in question. We had completed the first part of our night's duties and had returned to Deansgate at slightly later than 12 midnight and made our way to the mess room. Phil said he was going to 'get his head down for a couple of hours,' and duly prostrated himself along the length of one of the dining tables in front of the pot bellied stove. I pulled up a couple of chairs in front of the pot belled stove in the other section of the mess room. I couldn't sleep and so tried, with difficulty, to read a newspaper by the feeble light. At 0230 I went into the other room to waken Phil. As I entered I saw, by the flickering light of the pot bellied stove and the dim light from the other half of the mess room, the shadowy silhouette of a rat that appeared larger than the railway cat, which was, at this time, sleeping on a chair in the other half of the messroom. The buck toothed, coarse haired, rodent was sat on Phil's chest sniffing his face, its whiskers tickling his nose. The bristling hairs touching his hooter caused him to waken. He opened his eyes to see the rat's face in all its close up, nose twitching, horrible, bestiality. He let out a high pitched, loud scream. The rat raised itself on its haunches and, using Phil's chest as a launching pad, bounded over his face, off the table onto the floor and disappeared under the door. At the same instant Phil leapt from the table gibbering, somewhat belatedly, 'Gerritoff, gerritoff!' and brushing his chest and face with this hands. Most unfortunately, judging by the deposit the rat had left on Phil's chest, the beast must have been as startled as he was. It had literally shit and peed itself and the rat faeces and urine were now smeared over Phil's face. After I had stopped laughing and Phil had calmed down and cleaned this movement of the rat's bowels and urinary tract off his hands, face and clothes as best he could and because we were blissfully unaware of such things as Weil's disease we returned to the lorry and set off on our last job of the night.

Weil's disease is an infectious and often fatal disease that is transmitted via rats' urine. Sufferers may experience flu like symptoms, jaundice and liver failure. The death rate from the disease is approximately 25 per cent

Our last job was to load up at the Victoria - Exchange Station platform, which incidentally was the longest railway passenger platform in Britain if not in Europe, with a load of newspapers for a distributor in Rochdale. We were on our return leg of the journey back into Manchester, proceeding in a southerly direction down the A664, Rochdale Road. As we were passing through the Collyhurst district of Manchester at about 04.30hrs we both noticed a fellow crossing the road a little in front of us. It was pitch black. The street lighting was not very bright and the man was dressed in dark clothing. Because of these factors what we didn't notice was the pole he carried over his shoulder. Phil said 'he doesn't seem to have seen us, let's give him a fright.' He gunned the engine and accelerated towards this chap intending to miss him by a yard or so. The bodywork of our vehicle, a

1953 'O' series, petrol powered, 3 ton Bedford hit the pole with a resounding crack. Phil looked at me in astonishment and asked 'What the bloody hell was that?' I didn't reply, instead I leaned out of the cab window and looked to the rear to see the darkly clad pedestrian doing an involuntary pirouette in the middle of the road, before he fell down. Phil saw him in his mirrors, slowed down, saw the man pick himself and his pole up and start shouting and waving his fist at us. He was, obviously, not badly hurt but was most certainly badly annoyed.

Phil dropped a cog and accelerated away. We related the incident back at the yard and we were told that the guy that we set twirling like a spinning top, strange though it may seem, was the last of a long line of knockers-up from the Collyhurst area, and the pole was his knocking up implement. He was, obviously out and about at that early hour in pursuance of his livelihood without a thought of being mown down by a speeding railway, road vehicle.

THE DRIVING SCHOOL

Having turned 18 years of age in 1964, I applied for my provisional Driver's license and put in an application for the driving school, and after about 2 months my application was processed and I was accepted along with 2 other lads from Deansgate and 3 from Victoria, and so began a 4 weeks intensive driving course at the Hollinwood Driving School. The hours were 08.00hrs until 17.00hrs Monday to Friday. The tuition was based on a 1 to 1 basis, i.e., one instructor per individual driver. The first day was classroom based, learning the Highway Code, maintenance etc. The second day we were allocated our vehicles and shown the basics of servicing and maintenance, daily checks and general familiarisation with our learning vehicle and other types of vehicles at the school. I was allocated a Scammell Scarab, mechanical horse with a flat bed trailer, as were the other two Deansgate lads, John Olafson, a lad from the Cheetham area of Manchester, of Swedish descent and a half caste African lad called Stuart Onigbanjo from the Moss Side area whose father was African and whose mother was English. One of the Victoria lads was also allocated a Scammel whilst the other 2 were allocated rigid 4 wheelers. Each week one day was set aside for the theoretical aspect of driving and one day for maintenance, the rest of the time was solely driving.

On the third day we started the actual driving tuition, we never left the yard, indeed, we never left the yard for the first week. Those of us that were allocated Scammells were being shown, *en bloc,* by one of the instructors, the correct procedure for coupling and uncoupling the tractor and trailer. Now the interior of the Scammell Scarab was totally basic and utilitarian. The gear shift was as described earlier. The steering wheel had metal spokes which, I am sure, were capable of severing a finger if one hit a brick or other obstacle that might cause the single front wheel to turn suddenly, as the Scammell Scarab was a 3 wheeled unit capable of turning on its own axis. There was an in-cab, manual trailer brake for controlling the trailer in the event of a skid or Jack Knife situation, a trailer release handle and as in every railway road vehicle there was, within easy access a Pyrene, hand pump, fire extinguisher. Behind the driver's seat was the radiator. There was no protective cover, just a bloody hot brass top and filler pipe which extended through the bodywork to the exterior of the vehicle. This radiator projected out from the back of the seat, about 6 inches towards the centre of the rear body panel. The Scammell Scarab 3 ton version was produced until 1965, and was powered by a 1.6 litre Perkins diesel engine.

We were taught to reverse under the vehicle using our mirrors then ensure it was properly coupled by selecting a low forward gear and attempting to pull forward whilst the external trailer brake was still applied. When my turn came to perform the manoeuvre I started to reverse using my mirrors, as I got closer to the trailer I cheated by surreptitiously half turning to look through the rear window, as I did so, my forearm came into contact with the radiator. There was a loud yelp followed by a shout of 'FUCKING HELL!' and I ended up with a blister about the size of a Half Crown just below my elbow, much to the amusement of the onlookers.

After completing the coupling process, I then had to do the manoeuvre in reverse, thus dropping and disconnecting the trailer. I put the vehicle in gear, pulled the trailer release and started to edge forward. Temptation got the better of me, however, and I again attempted to peer through the rear window to ascertain how things were progressing. As I did so my elbow once again came into contact with the radiator in exactly the same already injured spot. I screamed the usual well known profanities, my foot slipped off the clutch, the nose of the Scammell rose in the air and the vehicle leapt forward so fast that the jockey wheels on the trailer didn't have time to descend, and the trailer dropped straight on its knees. Panic was immediate and the bystanders and onlookers fled into hiding behind stationary trucks and trailers at a pace a little faster than the norm, expecting to be flattened by a trailer or killed by a young maniac in an out of control Scammell Scarab. The vehicle, after divesting itself of the trailer, actually stalled and stopped. The instructor was first out of hiding, he approached the cab, reached in and applied the handbrake, and turned off the ignition, he then dragged me bodily from the vehicle saying 'You stupid, useless young tosser.' Nowadays that might be seen as somewhat politically incorrect, but at the time I'm sure everybody around shared his sentiments. At that moment in time I thought my driving career had come to an end before it had started, but after a severe verbal lambasting, and a lecture on what not to do, I was allowed to continue my training, much to my relief.

I can't remember the name of my one to one instructor but he was a dead ringer for the late actor Sid James, so everyone called him Sid. I'm not saying his countenance was craggy but after a few days I had the feeling I was looking at a relief map of the Pennines. So rugged was his face that it was said that Sid used a 4 wheel drive electric razor to shave. Sid was a show off and his party piece was to watch his pupil of the day make a complete cock up of their first attempt at reversing an artic. He would then take the pupils place behind the wheel telling the said learner, 'Now I'll show you how a proper driver reverses.' He would then position himself and proceed to reverse around a corner, keeping the rear trailer wheels approximately six inches from the kerb and finish with the vehicle in perfect alignment. He would then pull forward to his original starting position and say 'Now I'll show you how the best driver reverses.' He would then select reverse, set the vehicle in motion, as the unit and trailer started their backwards journey Sid would climb out of the cab and at walking pace would steer the vehicle around the corner from outside until the whole rig was in perfect alignment, six inches from the kerb when he would climb back inside, cut the engine and apply the hand brake. He was an excellent driver, a bloody good teacher, but an out and out big headed bastard.

Sid always carried with him a 12" wooden ruler, the type used by schoolchildren of the day and I soon found out what it was for. If, whilst driving along, the learner, who at the time happened to be me, rested or left his foot on the clutch pedal the ruler was brought down, rather viciously, on the thigh of the said leaner. This soon cured me or any other of Sid's trainees of riding the clutch.

The 4 weeks training flew by and all of a sudden test day was upon us. Everyone was nervous and asking each other last minute questions on the Highway Code. There were two examiners from the Ministry of Transport Licensing Authority for six tests, I was third to go. We had to do all relevant vehicle checks beforehand and then the dreaded road test. Each test consisted of approximately two hours of driving on all types of road, then the Highway Code and then the crunch, pass or failure.

On my test I went all round Hollinwood, Failsworth, Moston, Blackley, Middleton, Royton, Shaw and into Oldham town centre. In Oldham we went down narrow, cobbled, side streets near Oldham Market on market day. There were cars and vans parked anywhere and anyhow they could. At one particularly narrow point between two vehicles my examiner got out of the vehicle and beckoned me through via hand signals. I edged forward, my brow perspiring with apprehension. My mirrors passed between the stationary vehicles, we had been taught that if the mirrors, being the widest part of the vehicle, pass through a gap then the rest of the vehicle will follow, so I proceeded through with about 1½″ on either side to spare. It went through my head at the time that if the examiner trusted me enough, to get out of the cab and watch me as I drove through the gap then I reckoned I had passed. We did the reversing at a spot where the houses had been demolished and just the roadways remained, this was near the Clough Hotel off Victoria Avenue East in Blackley. We then returned to the driving school and after a few questions on the Highway Code I was congratulated by the examiner and handed my pass certificate. So at 18 years of age in 1964 I became a British Rail Road Vehicle driver, my first step to a lifetime of haulage. On the day all but one Victoria lad passed, though he did pass at his second attempt.

Back at our home depot we handed in our provisional licenses, and pass certificates which the company then sent off to the Licensing Authority, and we were issued with blank

Railway Domestic Licenses upon which was immediately stamped SCARAB, SCAMMELL, 3 TON. It was then just a case of awaiting the return of our full licenses and we were up and running or rather up and driving.

THIEVERY AND SKULDUGGERY

One of the jobs given to newly passed drivers entailed trailer change overs at a local mail order company in Ardwick which had about six bays solely for the use of railway vehicles, one of which was always left empty. There might have been up to 4 drivers working all day on this job. The drivers would take a trailer full of mail order returns from Deansgate to the mail order company, exchange it for a trailer loaded with new goods and return to Deansgate where the trailer would be off-loaded and the parcels sorted for various destinations further afield. It seemed that almost as many goods were returned as new goods were sent out. The drivers would do 4 trailers each way with an extra one for overtime. After about 3 months on this particular job, Johnny Olafson started coming to work in a second hand, almost new Mark 10 Jaguar. This vehicle was 3 litres or more, it didn't have a cigarette lighter it had a cigar lighter, it had a cocktail bar and cocktail table in the rear, and real leather upholstery. At the time, the average railway road vehicle driver ran an old banger, if he had his own transport at all. Ernie Etchells, the depot inspector, only had an old 100E Ford Anglia and there was Olafson, a newly passed out driver, swanning around in a top of the range Jaguar Limousine.

It transpired that a rich aunt in Sweden had died and left him a large legacy, or so we were led to believe, until the police spotted a railway vehicle being unloaded at a lock up garage in Cheetham Hill, late at night. The garage was used for storage by a Jewish market trader and the driver of the railway vehicle was............Johnny Olafson.

Apparently Olafson would finish his 12 hour shift at 18.00 hrs or 22.00hrs depending which shift he was on, he would go home and have his tea or whatever, come back a couple hours later with an accomplice, when there were very few people about, jump into a Scammell, back it under a trailer of returned mail order goods, drive, nonchalantly through the gates and deliver the misappropriated load to he market trader, and return to the depot, park up the vehicle and he and his accomplice would walk out of the yard. Nobody knew how much Johnny and his accomplice, and of course the market trader, made out of this little scam or how long it had been going on and indeed how long it might have continued but for the eagle-eyed bobbies, but all three ended up with custodial sentences.

The mail order company, as do a lot of retail and catalogue outlets, write off a percentage of their profits as damaged or stolen goods and I believe Olafson's misdeeds, although they may have impacted on the Manchester office of the mail order company, had little effect on the national operation. Olafson and his accomplice were small time crooks not big time racketeers.

Another incidence of thievery on the Railways was performed by a clerk on regular nights. Whether or not the idea was gleaned from Olafson's shenanigans, or whether it had been going on for years prior, I don't know, but once again it was the mail order returns that were being purloined. There were no inspectors on nights and just the one clerk and a couple of porters and a foreman who spent most of the night in the mess room.

The clerk knew what time the drivers left and what time they'd be back and so knew when the yard would be empty and for approximately how long. He allowed the porters to go to the mess room for a couple of hour's kip. Armed with the knowledge that he was alone, he would phone an accomplice who had his own van. The nefarious driver would turn up, the vehicle would be loaded with the requisite goods and the van and driver would depart. Somehow, maybe because of a tip off or because of reported losses by the mail order company, the British Transport Police had become suspicious and were watching and gathering evidence. One night they pounced and the unsuspecting clerk, as do most thieves, got caught. He was charged and convicted and received a custodial sentence. He probably made a few hundred pounds. The shady van driver was never caught and he probably made thousands. This may have been due to the code of honour amongst thieves.

SOMETIMES THINGS GO WRONG

The week after I had passed my test, in 1964, I worked 06.00 - 18.00, Monday to Friday and 06.00 until 12 noon on Saturday. The following week I received my pay slip and wage packet. After the tax man and the National Insurance had taken their lump, and a little amount towards my pension, I was left with the grand sum of £15-15s, or 15 guineas (£15-75p). I gave my mum a set amount for my keep, went out and bought a new pair of Wrangler jeans and matching jacket and still had enough left to take my girlfriend out. I realised the value of the work ethic and the power of the pound, which gave me a certain independence and a desire for much more.

Drivers that had recently passed their tests were more likely to be involved in minor prangs or incidents due to their lack of experience and road sense, coupled with that unknown quantity, the mad, impetuosity of youth. One such incident happened involving Stuart, the mixed race African lad, it could have had more serious consequences but for the fact that Piccadilly Station was almost empty due to the fact that it was prior to 06.00hrs.

Stuart and I had started at 05.30hrs at Deansgate; his unit was already coupled to his trailer, courtesy of the night driver, and mine wasn't. Stuart did his vehicle checks, made out his log sheet, and he and his trailer boy headed for Piccadilly while I was still sorting my vehicle out.

Being that time of the morning and there being little traffic about he drove up Piccadilly approach at about 40 mph., forgetting about the speed ramps at the approach to the security box, he hit the ramps at the same 40 mph., and literally became airborne. He landed with a bone shaking thud to see his trailer overtake him and carry on for about 20 yards down the platform and come to rest against a massive pile of mail bags at a rather precarious angle. The mountain of mail bags, which were awaiting loading on to the Royal Mail train, prevented the trailer toppling on to its side. Fortunately there was no great damage except for a couple of gouges in the tarmac, caused by the steel wheels of the undercarriage of the trailer after it had inadvertently separated company from the unit. There were no witnesses except for the security man and a couple of postal workers and a couple of porters, plus the railway cat, who didn't seem interested at all. So with the help of all present including me, as I had, by then, arrived at the station, we cleared some of the mail bags to make some room, righted the trailer, by brute force and ignorance and re-coupled it with the unit and the job continued with Stuart driving rather less recklessly and at a more sedate pace.

The little Scammell urban artic with a box trailer had a tendency to turn over if badly loaded and driven too fast around corners. This happened to a driver named Vinny Powell who, when heading for Piccadilly from Deansgate, was in the process of turning left off Peter Street into Mount Street in an attempt to beat the lights. He ended up with his trailer leaning, at 45 degrees, against a lamp post at this road junction. I was following Vinny and saw the whole incident. I pulled up and went to help. As I reached the stricken vehicle, Vinny's van lad had gotten out of the unit and was stood by the truck, pretending to strum a banjo and giving a very good rendition of George Formby singing *'I'm leaning on a lamp post at the corner of the street, in case a certain little lady comes by.'* Much to the amusement of passers by, Vinny was still sat behind the wheel looking somewhat miserable. The Railway recovery vehicle was called, the Council was notified and apparently all claims were settled.

Around this time in the mid 60's, my sister married a guy who was a driver at Mother's Pride bakery in Old Trafford. One of the Railways biggest customers at that time was Knightsbridge Cakes, another bakery just around the corner from Mother's Pride. The Railway drivers on the way to Knightsbridge Cakes would call at Val's Café on Skerton Road, directly opposite the Mother's Pride bakery. One day I was sat at the window in Val's munching and enjoying the delights of a well crisped and greasy bacon butty when I saw my new brother in law pull out of the bakery garage into Skerton Road. There were 5 or 6 Railway vehicles parked on one side and various other vehicles parked on the other side, which left room for only one vehicle to proceed along a two way street. I saw my brother in law stop so I went to the door and looked up the street. There was a big American car driven by a rather large black gentleman, stopped, facing the Mother's Pride van. Both drivers were gesticulating to each other to reverse out of the way, this then turned to shouting at each other but of course, in their bloody mindedness, neither of them wanted to lose face. The black guy pulled out a newspaper and spread it across the steering wheel and started to read, glancing up every few seconds to weigh up the situation. My sister's new husband, in retort, got out a magazine. After a couple of minutes, and in exasperation, he jumped out of his cab and went to remonstrate with the driver of the car. The next thing I saw was him walk back to his vehicle, jump into it and reverse to let the black guy through.

It wasn't until I saw the new in-law at the weekend that I noticed the swelling under his eye.

'What happened to your eye?' I said.

'What happened?' he repeated 'I had an argument with a black guy on Skerton Road. That's what happened.' He replied.

'I know, I was in Val's Café at the time, but that doesn't explain the bruisin'.'

'Well when I went over to him I said are you backin' up or what? An' he said 'Fuck off honky! You back up.' So I stuck my head through the window and said 'Don't tell me to fuck off.'

'So what did he do?'

'He hit me.'

'So what did you do?'

'I backed up. Didn't I?' Discretion, once again, plays its part.

After a couple of months driving on the Railways, the new drivers were put through domestic tests on other types of vehicles to broaden their ability and flexibility. I was taken out in a 3 ton Dennis with my cousin Walter as my training driver. The Dennis, like most vehicles of the day, had no electric signalling devices and all signals were given by hand. The Dennis also had a 5 speed constant mesh gearbox, which meant double de-clutching and getting the revs right before the next gear could be smoothly selected. I was driving along towards Mayfield Station with Walter sat in the passenger seat giving instructions. As we approached a corner Walter instructed thus, 'Clutch pedal down! Neutral! Clutch out! Rev! Signal! Clutch down! Third gear!' and I suddenly found myself with one hand on the gear lever and the other out of the side window frantically signalling. Walter grabbed the steering wheel and shouted at me 'Bloody 'ell Laurie, who's drivin' this bloody truck, you or me.'

After I had acquired a few more vehicles on my domestic license, these being the Dennis, Fordson and Bedford rigid 3 tonners, I was sent to Knightsbridge Bakery to pick up a load for Mayfield Station for an ongoing train. Mayfield Station, I believe, was the main passenger station before London Road was opened, but at the time was used solely for goods. The station approach was a fairly steep roadway about 350 yards long up to the platform and was paved with red brick and on the day in question it was raining which turned the red brick roadway into a red brick skid-pan, as I was about to find out.

The approach road was approximately 20ft wide and walled on both sides with a narrow footway on the left hand side as you entered. The vehicle I was driving was a petrol powered Dennis which was about 18ft long and loaded out to 3 tons with Iced Genoa and fruit cake for various destinations.

On this wet day and with me still being wet behind the ears as far as my driving experience was concerned, I turned off Fairfield Street into the station approach road which had a left hand turn just after the entrance had been cleared. I dropped a gear, gunned the engine, took the corner too fast and because of the weight and speed of the vehicle, lost control, and went into a skid. The vehicle spun round a full 360 degrees and then a further 180 degrees, whilst still sliding forwards, finally coming to a halt, leaving me facing back the way I had come. My van lad's face had turned a whiter shade of pale as I had fought to control the sliding vehicle. We were both shaking with fright and I think we came very close to the need for a change of underwear. It would have been virtually impossible to do a 3 point turn due to the lack of room, yet we had spun round 1½ times and not even touched either wall, or sustained any damage other than to my injured pride. I had to then drive down the approach, around the block and re-enter the approach. Needless to say the second attempt was executed with a lot more wariness and caution than the first.

MY FIRST INDUSTRIAL ACCIDENT

In my first year as a driver I was asked to cover Jake's job when he took his annual leave. By this time, 1966, van lads and trailer boys were no longer employed on delivery rounds, though they were still employed on shift work and were now known as driver's mates. The majority of the drivers had decided to sell the lads down the river for a few extra shillings in their pay packets, something Jake and one or two others voted against. So I covered Jake's round without a mate. On the second day I was delivering some large but light boxes to a clothing firm on Marlborough Street, just off Hulme Street, near Oxford Road. I drove in to the cobbled yard, spun the Scammell Scarab around and reversed down the yard to the unloading point. I parked the vehicle and went to the rear where I climbed up into the back of the trailer and loaded myself up with the boxes for delivery. I thought I had put the trailer tail board up on chains, unfortunately this was not the case and I walked straight off the end of the trailer into thin air. Being unable to float or levitate, I instantly fell to the ground landing awkwardly with one foot between 2 cobblestones, twisting the ankle violently, and scattering parcels all over the place. Once the onlookers had stopped laughing, and realised the tumble was probably not so funny various people ran to my assistance.

I was aided in standing and a chair was brought for me to use to take the weight off my injured ankle, my boot was removed and the ankle visibly started to expand. Deansgate depot was phoned and Ernie Etchells was notified about the incident. Accident books were duly filled in and all the correct procedures were followed. Knocker was brought to the yard to take over my deliveries and collections. Arrangements were made to take me to Manchester Royal Infirmary, where I thought I would have the ankle strapped up, given some pain killers, and sent home. Oh no! Firstly my sock was surgically removed to reveal a much swollen and misshapen joint that had turned a bluish-purpley colour with added redness where there were a couple of small lacerations.

I was then ferried to the X-ray Department, by means of a wheel chair, where a few transparencies were taken. I was then ushered into a consultant/specialist radiologist's office with my hospital snaps. Upon viewing them, clipped to a light box, this expert in the interpretation of Mr Roentgen's photographic results took a sharp intake of breath, looked at me and said, 'We're going to have to operate on this ankle, young fella me lad.'

'Why, Doc? What 'ave I done to meself?' I asked.

'You have broken your ankle, severed the tendons and surgery is required to put things right.' He told me. 'And you will be in plaster for at least a couple of and up to 3 months or more.'

I was put on a push along hospital trolley bed and wheeled down to the operating theatre where I was given a pre-med which, despite the pain I was in, set me off into fits of the giggles which only subsided when the full anaesthetic was administered. I woke up much later on a surgical ward with my leg in plaster up to the knee and now in no mood for giggling due to the considerable pain I was suffering. I was confined to the hospital bed for over a week and in plaster and on crutches for 3½ months. When I was finally able to get out of bed I found it almost impossible to stand after being on my back for such a period without the use of my legs. They literally turned to jelly when I imposed by body weight upon them. Luckily 2 nurses were at hand to make sure that I didn't inflict any more damage to myself.

During the time I was confined to bed I unwillingly had to use urine bottles and bed pans to perform my toilet needs, so unwillingly that I had not taken advantage of the dreaded bed pan for 2 days. I never, as long as I live, want to go through the embarrassment of having to use a bed pan again. The first time I used this stainless steel, portable latrine, the nurse was summoned. A nice, helpful lady, but built like a brick outhouse. The curtains were drawn around the bed, my PJ's were pulled down and I was hoisted onto the silver potty by the burly, latter day Florence Nightingale, who then left me to do my business. I sat on the stainless steel rim of the pan and bore down. There then followed one almighty explosion as all the trapped wind made good its escape. At the same moment I started to pee. Unfortunately, I hadn't noticed that my odd trick was hanging over the edge of the pan and I urinated all over the sheets and blankets. When I had finished and attempted to wipe myself, I again called for the hefty female medical attendant who had to complete the wiping and cleansing of my derriere, much to my embarrassment. The place stank and believe me it does not make one feel any better to be told by the nurse, 'Never mind, sonny, accidents will happen and don't you worry I've seen it all before, you know.'

My soggy mattress and bed linen were changed and a rubber under sheet was fitted to my bed as a precaution and, it seems, to cause me further embarrassment.

Once I had proved that I could perambulate, with the aid of a pair of crutches, I was discharged as an in-patient and had to make my next appointment through the out-patients department. My first appointment was only a week later for a change of Plaster of Paris, which was badly discoloured due to the seepage of blood after the operation and also to check on the stitches and to clean up the post operative site. After another fortnight the stitches were removed which necessitated another change of plaster.

I was in plaster and on crutches for 3½ months and off work for 4½ months. I returned to work and back to shifts after the 4½ months rest, recuperation and physiotherapy. My ankle, although healed has since been weak and I am constantly falling over and twisting it.

I reported the accident to the relevant authorities and it was recorded as an industrial accident so I got a little extra sick pay and after a few months a compensatory lump sum. In these more litigious days I may have tried to sue one or other of the parties but in those less litigious days and being somewhat naïve, I accepted the accident for what it was and banked the lump sum which, when added to my sick pay, equated to my loss of earnings. All in all I was quite happy with the outcome although the lump sum had whetted my appetite and lust to savour more of the tasty root of all evil, which possessed a pleasant and addictive flavour.

Whilst working on the late shifts as a mate and as a driver, I and others would frequent a pub near Victoria Goods Yard. The pub was called The Crown and it was here that, prior to the broken ankle accident, I had met the girl who, a couple of years later, would become my wife. The building that was once the Crown is still there but is now a retail outlet of some kind. Knocker and his girlfriend and I and my new girlfriend went out regularly as a foursome and used The Crown on a regular basis. We got married within a year of each other, Knocker being the first to give up his freedom, and as one of the others drivers said, 'What's he gone and done that for? She's not even bloody pregnant.'

Now that I was on a drivers rate and working 12 hour shifts, earning copious amounts of the green folding stuff, my girlfriend and I decided we would marry, so we got engaged and so about a year after Knocker and 2 weeks before my 21st birthday in January 1967 we tied the knot, and luckily through life's ups and downs, that knot is still secure.

THE PRECIOUS ALL GROUPS LICENSE

Upon reaching my 21st birthday I was granted my all groups licence, which allowed me to drive what would nowadays be class one LGV vehicles. During the years 1964 - 1967, there was a road improvement scheme being undertaken in Manchester. This finalised in 1967 with the opening of the A57(M), Mancunian Way, linking the A6 Downing Street, Ardwick to the A56 Chester Road at Hulme. During this time, some drivers were loaned out from their home depots to Ardwick East goods yard to carry over length loads to the Mancunian Way site. Being just 21, I volunteered my services, and was accepted and although the round trip was less than two miles, I learned the operation of trombone trailers. These are trailers that can be lengthened by stretching the chassis by means of a pin that can be removed, the trailer is then stretched by pulling forwards whilst the trailer brake is applied and when the required length is obtained the pin is relocated in the appropriate hole. The longer the trailer was stretched, the less pay load it would take. I also learned the use of sylvesters and chains as load restraints. The trailers we used were 30ft's stretched to 40ft, with a 10ft overhang at the rear and because of the short journey involved, dispensation was given to do the runs without a police escort, thus I was involved in the last year of the construction of the Mancunian Way. I also used these types of trailers and load restraints whilst loaned out to British Rail's Bolton Depot at Halliwell for a short period carrying steel. The motto for loading steel was 'STEEL ON STEEL, UNREAL - STEEL ON WOOD, VERY GOOD,' and it was at the Bolton depot where I honed my roping and sheeting skills. Roping and sheeting when properly executed is a work of art and sadly a dying skill with the advent of box vans, tautliners and containers. There are very few drivers still *au fait* with the knowledge of roping and sheeting that are able to fold and unfold sheets, and throw them out and tie them down correctly, using the sheet ties, let alone able to rope up and tie dollies. There are only a handful of firms still in the general haulage sector that run flat bed semi-trailers. One such is Swain's Haulage from Rochester, Kent whose work is mainly rope and sheet loads on flat bed trailers. There are a few others but most use a selection of trailers and maybe keep one flat bed for unusual loads.

CHAPTER 2
LIVERIES, NAMES, LOGOS AND SLOGANS

I MENTIONED earlier the Blood and Custard livery of Railway vehicles. Liveries of commercial vehicles have always been used as an advertising medium, this practice carried on into the motorised world, although nowadays most liveries are sprayed, but now and then one meets the haulier who is willing to pay, at a premium, for a good coach painting job.

Holland's Pies of Baxenden, near Accrington, was one such company. At one time all their Bedford TK's were coach painted by an expert craftsman from Preston. Wallace Thorburn, a meat haulier from Liverpool saw what a beautiful job was effected on the Holland's vehicles, so he had his first 14 litre Scania 141, V8 painted by the same artist, for this is what he surely was or still is. Wally wanted something simple but outstanding so he opted for a pure, black paint job with a minimum of custom lines ending in a flourish at the corners. The end result was outstanding, the depth of colour and the finish could only be described as perfect in its sublimity. That was in the 70's and Wallace has built his fleet to about 15 motors all finished to the same spec. His vehicles are a pleasure to behold in their simplicity.

H. J. Van Bentum's of the Nederland's has a very striking livery of blue and silver and with the Scania T cab Van Bentum's vehicles really stand out. There are few others who reach this standard, but not many.

Other liveries, as an advertising medium, are *'straight in your face'* i.e; the name of the company in 3 foot high letters down the length of a 44 ft trailer. It works, but it's hardly an exercise in subtlety.

Subtlety, I think works best, in 1984 in a Truck Stop on old Route 66 in California, I came across a Kenworth conventional hooked up to a 53ft semi-trailer. The whole rig was in jet black. The only writing to be seen was the owner driver's name address and phone number, painted discreetly on the fuel tank, but on either side of the trailer, in the bottom rear corners were hand painted, in full colour, Mickey Mouse motifs, approximately 2ft high. I don't think I need to tell you for which international company this driver was hauling 'Subtlety.'

Some of the *'in your face'* liveries work because of the quality of the paint job. One that springs to mind is Eddie 'Steady Eddie' Stobart, with his red, green. White and yellow colour scheme, although Stobart's livery has recently undergone a makeover, becoming multi tone green and white, which is still impressive. Stobart's trucks whether wagon and drags or artics are almost always immaculately turned out as are his drivers, though I believe the requirement to wear a necktie has been dropped. All his trucks carry the names of ladies, for which I believe there is a long queue. The most notable of these being the *'Sally B,'* named after Radio 2's Sally Boazman, aka Sally Traffic, who keeps all us truckers informed of the traffic situation and the weather along with Lynn Bowles.

The naming of trucks is nothing new and I think the first to do it in a big way was Stobart's county cousin, Robson of Carlisle, known as Robson's Border Transport. Robson ran a big fleet of mainly Atki Borderers and each truck was named in the same manner i.e; Border Reiver, Border Chieftain and Border Warrior etc., although Robson also ran some S39 cabbed Fodens with the

150 Gardiner engine, one such was the Border Banshee. Sadly Robsons' was bought out by UCI.

Another haulier to christen his vehicles is J. Barrett. Barrett is a small fleet owner from Oldham, which, as we know, is situated at the foothills of the Pennines on the Lancashire side. Thus all Barrett's motors are named Pennine Queen, Pennine Trooper etc. Barrett's breakdown truck is named Pennine Hercules for obvious reasons. Yet another haulier to christen his fleet is a company from castle Eden, County Durham, whose vehicles all carry a name with the prefix Eden, as in Eden Kestrel etc.

Names and logos play a great part in the recognition of a company, and some of them are quite humorous whether intentional or not.

Near the town of Northampton lies the little village of Old, where lived a haulier called Knight, hence Knights of Old, with the logo 'Service with Honour.' Incidentally the year 2003 marked a hundred years in the transport industry for Knights.

Then there's Mont Blanc Transport from Heywood, Greater Manchester who say 'We Will Move Mountains For You.'

There is a removal company, seen often on the highways and byways of Britain, called Bishop's Removals whose livery consists of a partial chessboard on which stands the Bishop with the logo 'Bishops Move,' and also written alongside this partial chessboard is the legend 'Better Across The Board.' Then there's the piano mover and carrier from Blackpool who is 'Big Enough to Cope, Small Enough to Care.' Vic Graham (Potato Merchant), has signwritten on the rear of his vehicles 'In case of fire........... chip pan in cab.'

I happened, one night, to be parked on Penrith Truck Stop. Parked next to my plain yellow British Telecom rig was a 14 litre Scania 142 V8, painted in a striking pale blue with dark blue custom lines on each panel. In the step well of the passenger side was scripted the proclamation '3 Steps to Heaven,' and in the step well of the driver's side, written in the same flowing style was the dictum 'If This Cab is Rocking - Don't Bother Knocking.'

On the same lorry park, on the same night, was a steel haulier with a coil carrier trailer, the type that most steel carriers use nowadays, and which looks like a larger version of the 19th century pioneer's, Prairie Schooner, covered wagons which were also known as the Conestoga wagon after the town of Conestoga in Pennsylvania, where they were first built for the purpose of transporting the pioneers westward. Their canvass covers were known as tilts, a term still used today for soft sided vehicles. The vehicle parked up on this night at Penrith was owned by a company called King, and down the side of his tilt was the proclamation that, 'Quality is King - King is Quality.'

There are a lot of companies that incorporate the words drive or driving into their slogans, there are too many to mention all, but as a couple of examples, there is R.T. Keedwell who is 'Driving Your Business Forward,' and in the same vein, RDS Transport's 'Helping to Drive Industry Forward.'

Another method used to catch the eye is alliteration as in Continental Cargo carriers, Lloyds of Ludlow, or Todd's Tippers, or the long established Sutton's of St Helens, or Baybutts of Burscough and Jack Richards of Fakenham, Norfolk who has Richards Reliable Road Services, across his trailer back doors followed by the slogan 'You're Following One of the Best, signed Jack.

I appreciate that if ones surname has the same initial as the town from which one is based it does not take a great deal of imagination, but even so 'Preston's of Potto' trips off the tongue much more readily than 'Taylor's of Martley,' but I am more interested in the witty or humorous, such as the rhyming names or slogans like 'Boole's Tools' of Stockport or another in the same vein on the truck of a company that makes nuts, bolts and screws which reads 'Heads and Threads.' Then there's the removal firm of Nelson's from Durham with the little verse 'Moving a Thing? Give us a Ring.' I also spotted, on the A1, a Luton van with the ditty 'Want a Van? – I'm Your Man,' and along the same lines, an artic with the slogan '…..Something to Haul, Give us a Call,' and the HIAB vehicle with the promise 'We'll Lift it and Shift it.' There is also the brick and block paving carrier who logo is Stock's Blocks, similarly, I saw a van that was used in the delivery of plants and suchlike for a garden centre or florists which and on its sides the name of the establishment, which was, 'Roots and Shoots,' and lastly there's C&M Haulage of Fitzwilliam near Wakefield, Yorks, with their little rhyme 'You Call, We Haul.'

The pun is also used and one that springs to mind is on the front of an FH12 Volvo Globetrotter, from Newcastle Upon Tyne, which reads 'TORQUE OF THE TOON!' Another pun, seen often, is on Dean Auld's rigs this one reads 'Hauled by Auld.' Then there is Chadwick's of Sandbach who deliver for Bargain Booze, and their pun reads 'Making Life Richer, For the Pourer.' On the rear panel of a Cummins powered ERF spotted in Trafford Park was signwritten 'Heaven is here on ERF.'

A lot of Scottish hauliers have a band of tartan across the front of or around the front and sides of their tractor units or cabs. Whether or not these tartan bands represent the clan tartan of the haulier I don't know, but it would be nice to think that this is the case. McWilliams of Huntly, Aberdeenshire, who specialises in bulk tipper work, is one such company with a narrow band of tartan around his motors as is Scotlee of Irvine and Hayton Coulthard of Twynholm, Kirkcudbright. Then there is Pollock's of Edinburgh and the family timber hauliers J and A Hedley from Ellon between Aberdeen and Peterhead. These are just a few of the Scottish companies that adorn their vehicles thus but there are very many more.

The Scottish are a patriotic lot and a lot of their trucks have the cross of St Andrew with the word *'Ecosse'* below it, painted on one or more of the body panels, and others have a full colour painting or a silhouette of a kilted Highland piper, complete with a Glengarry Bonnet or the ceremonial Bearskin. One such is McGonagall's of Arbroath who has the almost life size full colour depiction of the piper on the side panels of a Renault Magnum. Yet others have the slogans 'Scotland the Brave' or 'Scotland Forever,' or a mixture of 2 or 3 of these constituent parts. Another Scottish vehicle that I have seen on a number of occasions has a large thistle painted on the doors with the words 'Scottish and Proud of it.'

Specialist hauliers also, deserve a mention, such as Gilbert Brown from Ambleside in the Lake District who specialises in hauling boats, usually lake, canal or river cabin cruisers, on trailers specially constructed for this purpose. On the rear of a unit I saw was the phrase, 'Just Cruising thru' and on another 'Just Sailin' By.' Then there is the Scouse haulier Thomas Kelly (Liverpool), who has the little witticism 'Not the Biggest in the Pond, but the Best in the Pool.' I saw a small wagon and drag with tilt bodywork belonging to a haulier called R.A. Mann who must have been a fan of the wartime radio series ITMA, for on the back of his tilt trailer was the legend 'It's That Mann Again.'

I've seen scripted across the back panels of various tractor units phrases alluding to the power of the said vehicles and the owner or driver such as '580 Horses and 1 Stallion' similarly, '450 Horses and 1 Donkey or Mule or Ass.' There's one that has used the name of a well known TV comedy program as its basis which reads 'Only One Fool and 420 Horses.'

Then there's the totally unique and unusual such as Robert Wiseman's trucks. Mr Wiseman is in the milk processing and delivery business and has depots in Edinburgh, Glasgow, Aberdeen, London and Manchester and his trailer livery is a really eye catching, abstract design in black and white to resemble a cow's hide.

On the under-run bar on the back of one LGV I saw was the offer 'Free air-bag test starts here, come closer for more information.'

The true stars of the liveried truck are the air brush jobs; some are so good that they actually look as if photographs have been applied to the truck panels. There's one truck from Italy that has scenes from the film The Untouchables. The painted likenesses of Kevin Costner, Sean Connery etc., are so lifelike it's uncanny. Closer to home is Joe Sharp of Rochdale whose Scania Toplines were turned over to Haydon Autospray of Bath and a true artist with the airbrush Matt Pennycott. One of the trucks is the Norwegian Dream, the other the Atlantic Dream, both done in shades of pink, blue and white. Then there's E.W. Gardner of Avonmouth, who owns two tastefully air brushed 164 V8, 580 Topline Scanias. One is the Viking Bitch featuring semi naked Viking ladies, the other, Naughty Boys, features the infamous Kray Twins, Mad Frankie Frazer and Lenny McLean. Once again the airbrushing was done by Matt. Julian Arnold, generally known as Arnie who runs TLC European, owns two Daf XF95's one a 480 and the other a 530hp. The 530 has eye catching scenes from Thunderbirds airbrushed onto most of the body panels and is christened the Lady Penelope. The 480 continues the cartoon and puppet theme and is airbrushed with scenes from Captain Scarlet and is named the Lady destiny. The airbrush artist in this case is Paul Yeomans.

Bristol based Matt Pennycott is probably the most renowned of the airbrush artists in the transport world and another fleet he has done remarkable work for is Roy Gill's in the Peak District. The fleet, mainly Dafs, has one dedicated to Princess Di called the Queen of Hearts, one called Soap Daft, featuring all the well known faces from the popular soap operas, and another called

Comedy Classics featuring the likes of Tony Hancock, Norman Wisdom, Clive Dunn and many, many more. The likenesses are once again like photographic images. Most of these trucks and lots more can be seen at any of the Truckfests held annually at various venues up and down the country.

Then of course there are the messages scrawled in the grime on the rear of some vehicles such as the proclamation on the back of a very dirty white van which read 'Also available in white,' and on the back end of a 4 wheeler that was filthy and in a poor state of repair was written 'Cleaning and maintenance carried out by Stevie Wonder.' Then there was the Mail Order Parcels delivery van with the statement 'More Drops than Santa Claus,' scratched in the dirt.

CHAPTER 3
LEARNING THE GAME

LOTS OF JOBS IN A SHORT SPACE OF TIME

TWO years prior to my 21st birthday there was a massive shift away from wagon and drag to articulation following the 1964 Construction and Use regulations which permitted articulated vehicles to operate at up to 32 tons gross vehicle weight. This was the first major change since the 1955 Construction and Use Regulations which permitted a 24 ton gross weight on 4 axle artics and 20 tons gross on rigid 6 wheelers. These new regulations meant that a driver's earning potential had risen substantially allowing him to further line his pockets and elevate his position within the labour market.

With this in mind, when in my 22nd year, I left the Railways, whose pay scale I now considered paltry, and went working for an Irish tipper firm based on Store Street at the back of and below Piccadilly Station for the promise of untold wealth and substantial bonuses, which seemed to answer my prayers to Mammon and to sate my hunger for more dough or bread, metaphorically speaking. I was taken on even though I had no experience of tipper work. I was shown how to engage the tipping gear, via the PTO (power take off), and sent on my way. I was directed to load hard-core at a demolition site for a new build, tipping site. When I arrived at the new build site with my load, there was a queue to tip. The queue slowly moved forwards until it was my turn. I was called to the tipping area which was on the edge of a steep embankment. I reversed to the edge, engaged the tipping gear, and fed power to the hydraulics. The body began to rise. Unfortunately, I had forgotten to release the tailgate and as the load started its backwards journey towards its exit, which was firmly closed, the transference of weight took the truck over the edge of the embankment and it slid, on its rear axle, 20ft to the bottom of the crater. As the vehicle slowly slid down the embankment the realisation of what had happened slowly slid into my mind. When the truck had finished its descent and had come to a halt, with the cab facing skywards and the front axle in the air, like a begging dog, there appeared, peering through the side window of the cab, a very pale frightened and bewildered countenance belonging to yours truly. The only thing that stopped the vehicle from doing a complete back flip was the elevated bodywork which became jammed on the already tipped rubble. A bulldozer was brought to the scene, a chain was attached to the stricken vehicle. As the 'dozer' took the strain and started to pull, the tail gate was released and the front end of the vehicle, because the load acted as a counterbalance, came slowly down to earth, the front wheels making contact with a gentle, satisfying, dull thud. As the vehicle started its humiliating ascent back up the embankment, its load was evenly shed. Luckily the tipper and I were relatively unscathed, and as tippers experience a very hard life anyway, I lowered the tipping gear, secured the tail gate, apologised for any inconvenience and went back for a second load. I carried on using the same vehicle with its few extra battle scars which, because of my embarrassment, I did not report.

Because of my lack of experience of tippers and site work I was snapping half shafts like carrots and continually getting bogged down and having to ask the machine drivers to push or tow me out of whatever bog I was stuck in. After a couple of weeks the Irish owners decided that I was a thick, useless Englishman and that I was surplus to requirements and sacked me before I had earned any decent wages or substantial bonuses, or maybe sent them into bankruptcy. So with my all groups licence in my pocket I walked round to the Employment Office on Aytoun Street, in the centre of Manchester, where I found a vacancy for an artic driver for Bridgewater Transport off Egerton Street, by the side of the Bridgewater canal. They were mainly a long distance outfit working off the docks, but as a new starter I was employed to drive an Atkinson Borderer, powered by a 180 Gardner, doing two runs a day down to Stafford, loaded with approximately 20 tons of steel to use in reinforced concrete, on a 33ft flat bed semi trailer. The experience I had acquired working on the Mancunian Way project served me well here, though the job was only short lived. Into my second week and before I had done any real distance work, my brother in law phoned me. He had left Mother's Pride Bakery and started at Barratt's Meat Haulage and he was phoning to let me know a vacancy had arisen and he had recommended me and that Dennis Barratt wanted to see me for an interview. Dennis was the younger of two brothers, the elder being Arthur, who were both butchers by trade but who had diversified into haulage as a sideline, but the haulage side grew and took over. Not wanting to let a family member down, I went to see Dennis Barratt. I was offered the job and took it, mainly, because the money, which was the main motivation for working was better for driving a 4 wheeler for Barratt's than for driving artics for Bridgewater, although the vehicles weren't that good. There was a couple of Thames Traders with the 3.6ltre 4D diesel to power them and some series D Ford Customs which had the same power unit. There were also a couple of 6 leggers used for bulk loads.

When I started for Barratt's, reefers (refrigerated vehicles), were rare so Barratt's had insulated vehicles and when we loaded frozen produce we had to put blocks of 'Cardice' which is frozen Co2, known as dry ice, in every leg of the load, to keep it frozen. Co2 does not melt but reverts to a gaseous state which then disperses.

Besides edible meat, we carried meat and offal unfit for human consumption. This included beef lungs, cow's udders, and a product with a name something like Ashpet which, we were told, consisted of ground up cock's combs, lower legs, feet and claws and bones which went into pet foods. Waste not, want not, I suppose. But then when you see what's happened, nowadays, to our cattle herds through BSE, I think a little more consideration should be given to what we feed animals of any kind, whether they be reared for human consumption or whether they are pets.

As well as working from the meat market, Barratt's had a contract with Buxted Poultry, at Davyhulme, latterly part of the Ross frozen foods empire, delivering frozen chickens and turkeys to supermarket chains. Somebody, no doubt a quick thinking, smart arse driver, realised or found out that the average house brick weighted 7lbs, and was roughly the same size as a 7lb fowl, so if boxes of 7lb chickens or turkeys were amongst a delivery, the end of the box would be prized open, one of the carcasses removed and replaced by a house brick and the box resealed. Ill gotten gains were often swapped for various other comestibles from bakery delivery men or, fruit and veg men or other such providers of provender, or sold in cafes and corner shops or taken home and so the driver always had plenty of spending money, the larder at home was always well stocked and the supermarket manager had enough bricks to build himself a 4 bedroom detached house. It seems that most drivers no matter what commodity they haul had a fiddle of one kind or another to supplement their normal earnings and their diet.

Another contract that the Barratt's had was for the delivery of all Mars products i.e.; Mars Bars, Spangles, Opal Fruits etc., from the Bay Tree Mill of Middleton, Manchester. These were delivered to various retail outlets including corner shops and off licenses from North Wales and Staffordshire to Northumbria and Cumbria. This was before the days of bar codes and sell by dates, and there was very little check on returned goods, so a driver would pick up returns at one shop and, if the packaging was intact, mix them in with the next delivery and so dispose of them. After 30 or 40 drops, over a couple of days, a driver would have built up a handy little stockpile of new products which were sold on to local market traders to enhance the driver's lifestyle. Any damaged goods were returned to Bay Tree Mill, from where they were either disposed of via the local refuse collection, sent back to Mars at Slough or went for pig swill to the local farms.

The Barratt Brothers also had a contract with a company called SPD (Speedy, Prompt Delivery) which was a general groceries job which like the other contracts consisted of multi drops to both small and large retail outlets. The same fiddles applied to this contract.

When we were sent out with up to 40 drops on any of these contracts, to North Yorkshire and South Yorkshire, for example, it was impossible to do them all in a day, so if a driver's last drop of the day was at Barnsley, he would book off in his log book there and run the vehicle home, run back to next day and continue his deliveries. Of course, this was illegal and was known as running bent, but the driver gleaned up to 3 nights out allowance, which was a bonus for the underpaid employee. When parked at home with a load of goodies in the back of the vehicle, a padlock would be used and as extra security the Unfit for Human Consumption plate would be put in place on the back doors.

There were two drivers employed on regular long distance work usually pulling out a Gland Supplies at Potato Wharf next door to the old Water Street Abattoir. Gland Supplies supplied animal glands such as the pituitary, pancreas and other glands to medical and pharmaceutical companies, what was left was separated, frozen and loaded on to Barratt's 6 wheelers for delivery to Spillers pet foods at Barr Head in Scotland or Pedigree pet foods at St Helens or any of the other pet food factories. Jack Barratt, a cousin of the Barratt brothers was one of these distance men. The other was a guy who went under the name of Andy Mann. If the need arose any driver could be called on to do distance work.

At that time, even though I was married, I was still a little irresponsible and I ducked a couple of Mondays. Arthur Barratt said to my brother in law, 'You're kids ducked it again. I'm gonna have to buy him a Monday morning clock.'

One day I had a big argument with Dennis Barratt, it was over these occasional absences, and it ended up with him yelling at me 'You're sacked; now get the hell off my property.' To which I responded 'Stick your job up your arse ya fat bastard,' and walked off site. At 6.0.clock the following morning the phone woke me up. It was Dennis Barratt shouting 'Where the bloody hell are you? You was supposed to be on the meat market at half five.' Thus I was reinstated. This happened with Dennis and various drivers but grudges were never held.

Thirty years later, and I hadn't seen the Barratts in that thirty years. I was on holiday in Cyprus, my wife and I were sat in the hotel reception area when this big chap walks in with his wife. He was seventy odd years old and a bit overweight. I said to my wife 'I'm sure that's Dennis Barratt.'

She said 'Well go over and ask him.'

To which I replied 'Well I'm not sure.'

The following day the same couple were on a trip out from the hotel on the same coach as my wife and I. When we stopped for lunch we found ourselves sitting next to the couple and we started conversing. I said to the man 'Where are you from?'

He replied 'I'm from South Manchester.'

I said 'I'm from North Manchester, Blackley to be exact. What did you do before you retired?'

He said 'I'm a butcher by trade, but I went into haulage.'

'You're Dennis Barratt aren't you? I used to work for you.'

'You know,' he said 'I saw you in the hotel and I said to the wife, I'm sure that's Driver that used to work for me, and she said go over and ask him and I said I'm not that sure.'

So we had a few drinks and reminisced about the good old days. He told me Arthur had passed away and I phoned my brother in law from where we were and Dennis had a good chat with him. It was akin to a reunion of long lost brothers.

I soon tired of the meat haulage and multi drops and so I put in my notice and left Barratt's. My brother in law left not long after and went working directly for Buxted Poultry, where he eventually became the transport manager.

A couple of years later I met Andy Mann who told me that Barratt's had bought a 40ft reefer and an ERF unit to use on Gland's Supplies but he had put his son through the class 1 test instead of putting Andy or his cousin Jack on it, much to their chagrin. This apparently backfired on the Barratt's when the novice son pulled out of Gland's Supplies with a fully freighted trailer without first checking the coupling and all other points of safety. As he was negotiating the turn off Water Street into Regent Road (A57), Salford the trailer became detached from the unit and dropped on its knees mid way across the lights. This was in the rush hour at one of Manchester's busiest through routes and intersections.

Young Barratt, without any assistance, had successfully blocked up the junction for half the day causing all sorts of problems for commuters and travellers generally. The police arrived on the scene. Two heavy fork lift trucks were brought from the Meat Market and Gland's Supplies and after a number of hours the unit and trailer were re-connected. Whether young Barratt was prosecuted for his stupidity, I don't know.

I finished at Barratt's because I heard that plenty of money could be earned as a private hire taxi driver. I applied to the Manchester Watch Committee for my private hire license and took a job with Badger's cabs of Canal Street, Ancoats. My hours were supposed to be from 1400hrs until 0200hrs, although to make the massive earnings that had been promised, I ended up working 15 to 18 hours a day, which I considered over and above the length of a reasonable working day. Driving cabs is a mundane occupation but driving trucks is a much more skilful and satisfying pursuit and so, after a few months I returned to my vocational position.

Because I had been told that the earnings were high I took up a position for a short spell for MAT Transport, I think it was 2 days. MAT operated out of the Manchester International Freight Terminal (MIFT), in Trafford Park and I was allocated an Atki Borderer, with a Gardner 180 power unit, to work on local container work. I got the sack because I forgot about the rising barrier on the floor at the entrance to the terminal and when the security man lifted the standard barrier I drove forward. I came to an abrupt halt to the sound of the crunching and cracking of the vehicles bodywork as it came into contact with the rising floor barrier ripping the front bumper and light cluster off the Atki and splitting the fibre glass body panels. My embarrassment, when I went to report the damage, must have shone through the office door window. I must have been glowing like a beacon over this delicate situation. My earnings for this adventure were nil and I was too embarrassed to pursue a claim for the 2 days worked.

It was then 1969 and after being dismissed from MAT I applied for a job at a Motor Factors company in Rochdale. This position, if I count MAT, was the second job of 1969. The company was called Paul Backhouse & Co., and, I completely and conveniently forgot to tell the transport manager that I had been sacked from my previous post. I was employed to drive a 7½ tonne, 4 wheeler, Tautliner delivering and collecting stock to and from other Paul Backhouse depots of which there were 3, these being at Crewe, Warrington and Preston, Rochdale being the main supply depot. I would start at 0800 and load up with motor spares packed in wheeled cages. I'd leave the depot at 0830 and head for Crewe where I would deliver what was needed and pick up any returns, then on to Warrington and finally to Preston from whence I would return to Rochdale. The wages were less than my living standards deemed necessary and the repetitiveness of the tasks I had to perform made it a totally boring undertaking. I lasted a month or so, but at least I was earning a little something until a better situation came along which happened to be with a company by the name of W.E. Hall & Co., of Ordsall in Salford. Hall's main contract was for the delivery of reels of newsprint from Salford docks to the Daily express Printworks at Ancoats and the Daily Mirror at Thompson House, Withy Grove. Another firm that had the same contract was Frederick J. Abbots of Potato Wharf and the two companies compete, unbeknown to the bosses, in a rather dangerous way, for loading and unloading. The vehicles were loaded at the docks and each load was supposed to be roped and sheeted, but the trip was made with just a back chock roped in. If it rained a fly sheet was hastily thrown over and secured with sheet ties, not a rope in sight. The drivers were on a load bonus, the more loads the more money. I lost out in the bonus stakes simply because the older and more experienced drivers ran rings around this callow, naïve, relatively new driver. Consequently, this bonus system was the cause of the wages being high and health and safety low, if not non-existent. The vehicles and trailers were rolling write offs, and the way the drivers threw them round the docks was tantamount to a giant dodgem car arena. The units were KM Bedfords with a 7.63 litre diesel engine of Bedford's own design or the Detroit diesel. They were used to pull 33ft flat bed, semi trailers, loaded out to 32 tons gross. Abbots used Dodge 500 series units powered by Perkins diesel or Cummins.

Another driver working at W.E. Halls was a black guy I knew from the Railways a few years earlier, Des Perado, who had lost his license through drink driving. He didn't tell anyone, parked his car up at home, bought a bike, rode to work, got in the wagon and carried on with the job as if nothing had happened until he got his license back. I stuck it for a few weeks but no amount of money could compensate for the procedures resorted to by both employer and employees and I left whilst I was still of sound body and mind and got my fourth job of 1969 at Kendal Milne, which belongs to the House of Frazer group, delivering furniture to customers that had bought items from the Deansgate store and needed a home delivery service. The garage cum warehouse was situated on Oxford Road near Whitworth Park. The job entailed working with a crew of two porters. The vehicle I drove was a BMC with the angle plan safety cab, and was of typical pantechnicon design with a Luton over the cab. If a night out was required and part of the delivery was beds, mattresses would be thrown onto the Luton and the Luton became a bedroom for the night, and the night money became beer money.

When we delivered new furniture the customer would ask us if we could dispose of their old and no longer required accoutrements and trappings, be it a 3 piece suite or a bed or wall units or a dining room set of table and chairs. We would say that really we shouldn't and that it was more than our jobs were worth, this would prompt the customer to offer an inducement of cash for the removal of the second hand furnishings and equipment, to save them the problem of disposal of the said used goods. We would then load the used furniture onto the van and immediately take it to the nearest second hand furniture store and sell it on. This way we got paid twice for the same thing, making a handsome cash profit to enable us to ease our way through this life. As with most driving jobs, there was always a fiddle of some sorts to complement or supplement or maybe compensate the low wages one earned. I didn't last long at Kendal's, a couple of months at most, because of the multi drop aspect and the way some of the well heeled patrons of Kendal's looked down their noses at mere manual workers.

My fifth job was as a drayman/driver for Holt's Manchester Brewery on Empire Street, Cheetham. Holt's beer is a strong but cheap brew that had an individual aroma. After completing a mid morning delivery to the Lamb Inn at Eccles, I and the rest of the dray crew went into the bar for a complimentary drink and to secure the Landlord's signature for the delivery. As we entered the bar the Landlord had just finished cleaning the lines and had pulled a half pint of the golden nectar which he was holding up to the light. He said 'Look at that, clear as crystal.' He then thrust the glass under my nose and said 'Smell that bouquet.' I winced and the publican carried on 'Do you know that aroma is unique? It can be compared favourably to cunnilingus. Once you've gotten over the smell you've got it licked.'

Overall, the job was quite uneventful, punctuated by bouts of drunkenness. My time at Holt's only lasted a few weeks and I left before I became a dedicated sot.

I then got a job with an Eccles based general haulage company called Storey Brothers. This was my sixth job that year. Their main contract was working out of British Steel in Trafford Park., carrying Railway bogies and axles all over the country. Drivers would start at 0600hrs, drive to British Steel, load up, chock and secure the load and then book on. It may have been 0800 or 0900hrs or so when the loading was finished and the notes received, but according to the log book the driver had only just started. Drivers at Storey Bros were paid from a separate time sheet that bore no resemblance to the hours shown in the log book. This practice allowed the driver to get to most parts of the country and back in the day as the company wanted the wagons back for loading the next day, illegal though it was.

There was a tale told of a Scottish guy that worked for Storey's who having loaded in the late afternoon, took his vehicle home and kicked off at 0300hrs ran up to Aberdeen, tipped, ran back to Glasgow and by then feeling rather tired slept for a couple of hours between his sheets and then ran back to Manchester.

It was whilst working for this company that I managed to seize up the engine on an old wooden framed, fibreglass cabbed, 'A' series ERF with a 200 Cummins, something I had never done before or never done since. I had loaded at British Steel one morning, made out my log and proceeded on my way to Huwood Mining at Team Valley Industrial Estate at Gateshead. It was a midsummer's day with soaring temperatures and as I approached Ferrybridge on the M62, I thought ' Jesus, this cab's getting hot,' I had both windows open to give a cross draught to keep myself cool, that was 1960's air conditioning, and then the inevitable knocking started. Now as any good driver does, I'd checked the oil and water prior to starting off that morning. I pulled onto the hard shoulder, dropped the trailer and phoned the gaffer who sent a wrecker and a spare unit so that I could continue with the load. When the wrecker arrived with the spare unit on suspended tow, the mechanic took the radiator grill off to reveal the radiator in all its glory. It stood there, still simmering away, steam coming out of the various cracks, but all that was there were the radiator stand pipes, not a cooling fin between them. This, of course, absolved me of any blame and called into question the maintenance procedures. The mechanic and I dropped the spare unit off and I coupled it up to the trailer and I helped him put the broken down vehicle on suspended tow before continuing my journey to Team Valley. I finally got unloaded at Huwoods's at about 22.00hrs. Because Huwood's was the type of company it was and worked on a rotational shift pattern, I was able to avail myself of their canteen and showers. Once tipped, it was too late to book any lodgings for the night and so I ended up sleeping across the engine and both seats in a quiet corner of Huwood's yard. Not the most comfortable night out I'd ever spent, but I, once again could use their canteen and washing facilities the following morning. After washing and breakfasting I returned to the Eccles yard and the spare unit was returned to the driver that usually drove it and I was then left hanging around the yard doing mundane jobs whilst the engine of my ERF was rebuilt. After a couple of days I told the foreman I was leaving, so I waved bye-bye to Storey's and went home to consider my options. Thus my sixth job of the year came to an end.

I then heard of a vacancy for an artic driver at Oswald Inghams in Newton Heath, Manchester. Oswald Ingham was s small fleet operator with a mixed bag of vehicles. I was allocated a Guy Big J with a 200 Cummins and set to work collecting and delivering containers nationwide with occasional nights out, but if one was loaded at the end of the day an early start would be expected and a trip from Manchester to Southampton and back in a day was the norm. On other days one could be sat in the Container base or Freightliner's for hours on end, or just running local. The money was not much good for the hours put in and there was no way to boost the paltry income one received so, after a few weeks, I called in at the transport office of the Co-operative Society on

Briscoe Lane, Newton Heath in Manchester, to ascertain if their were any vacancies for class one drivers, and sure enough there was. I returned to Ozzie's yard, parked the vehicle up, and told Ozzy what had transpired, said my goodbye's and started my eighth situation of the year at the Co-op the next day.

WHAT'S AN ANGUS DUNDEE

The Co-op job was fairly well paid for easy work and consisted of mainly local deliveries to shops and depots with just the occasional night out. The furthest South we went was Milton Keynes and the furthest North was Carlisle and the Scottish border. The vehicles used were Ford Custom cabs pulling 33ft flat bed single axle, semi trailers and it was mostly rope and sheet work, except for the bacon and butter runs when box vans were used. The nights out only occurred if you had a number of drops around the Midlands area.

The loads were all palletised and after offloading an equal amount or more of empty pallets would be put onto the flat bed of the trailer. These empty pallets or at least any surplus amount would then be sold at the nearest pallet yard on the return journey. Obviously the pallets could not be sold after every trip or suspicions may have been aroused so one had to use ones common sense. The selling of pallets is a regular money making scam for drivers and numerous pallet traders have opened up on motorway service areas and industrial estates to accommodate this fiddle and ensure the drivers can enhance their salaries and enjoy the finer things in life that unearned income can provide.

During the couple of months I was at the Co-op, one of the other drivers, a young fellow by the name of Stan Delone, was watching me finish off the roping of my load. I was in the process of tying an Angus Dundee at the rear of the trailer. The Angus Dundee or Scottish Star as it is sometimes called is a method of tying off at the rear of the trailer by threading the remaining rope through the already tied crossed rope at the rear and applying a dolly to pull everything in, nice and tight. Stan said 'What do you call that knot, then?'

'It's an Angus Dundee,' I replied.

'Will you show us 'ow ter do it?' he asked.

'Course I will,' I said and proceeded to do so.

At first he couldn't get the hang of it. One day he drove into the yard while I was there. He got out of his cab and shouted over to me 'Laurie, come and have a look at this Aberdeen Angus on the back of me load.'

I had visions of a huge Scottish bullock roped to the rear end of his trailer.

Another time one of the drivers lost a near side front wheel whilst travelling down the M6. He heard the clunking and felt the wobbling as the nuts became looser and the studs made the stud holes larger with the vibration. He had the sense to pull onto the hard shoulder and as he came to a halt the near side of the cab dropped suddenly as the wheel came off and rolled a few yards further and came to rest, harmlessly on the grass verge on the far side of the shoulder. It could have been worse, it could have come off whilst he was travelling at 60mph, in the centre lane and maybe jump the central reservation and plough into an oncoming vehicle, causing fatalities and utter chaos. The results could have been catastrophic and I have heard of such cases. The driver involved was sacked despite the union's efforts to save his job.

The checking of wheel nuts along with tyre pressures and condition and oil, fuel and water, lights and lenses and various other components contributing to the roadworthiness and safety of the vehicle is part of the daily checks expected of a driver. The reality is that drivers do not carry torque wrenches and pressure gauges. The time allocated by most haulage firms to do such checks, in these days of time sensitive deliveries is nowhere near the time needed, especially with 6 axle artics. The companies will not pay an extra half hour as this is seen as non-productive work, and if one is seen to be taking too much time one will be pressed to move on. Even so the responsibility rests with the driver.

BACK TO THE RAILWAYS

I left the Co-op at the start of 1970 and returned to the Railways, whose transport sector was now National Carriers Ltd., at Liverpool Road goods depot. It was all rope and sheet bulk loads from wood pulp for papermaking to whisky for merry making. It was easy and quite well paid work with overtime and bonuses, although there was no obvious fiddle except the occasional odd few pallets to sell.

Liverpool Road had its own bonded warehouse where Granada Studios Tour now stands and foreign vehicles made regular deliveries, German mainly with wagons and drag, but also other nationalities. Besides the railway staff the bond was manned by Her Majesty's Custom & Excise. It was at the bonded warehouse, one day that a barrel of neat Jamaican rum rolled off the loading dock and burst open. Before the Custom's men could get to it three or four drivers scurried forth as if materialising from thin air and filled their brew cans with this molasses like liquid and it was shared out in the mess room to be watered down at home.

AFORE YE GO

One day I loaded 14 pallets of whisky, from the bond, onto a 28ft semi trailer, for onward delivery to an air freight agent at Manchester Airport. I sheeted the load and roped it up. Unfortunately, there was a tear in the canvas sheet on the near side, rear corner of the load. I placed a corner board over the rip. Corner boards had to be used to avoid crushing the boxes which contained the whisky. The boards we used on the Railway were about 2ft long and consisted of two laths of wood joined together by two strips of canvas which were fitted along the sides of the cargo forming a right angle of protection where the ropes would pass over the load. After loading and securing the consignment, I made my way towards Manchester Airport. I was travelling up Princess Parkway (A5103), towards Wythenshawe when a car drew along side me. The car slowed down to keep pace with my vehicle. The driver blew his horn and I looked down to see the passenger holding up, at the open window, 2 bottles of whisky. I noticed that the box was on the back seat. The occupant of the passenger seat in the car then raised the two bottles a little higher and shouted 'Cheers, mate.' Then the car sped away with me too surprised to even get the license number.

At the nearest place of safety I pulled over to check my load. The corner board over the hole in the tarpaulin had fallen away, exposing the gap from where the case had fallen, but the board was still held, though only barely, by the rope. It was patently obvious that a box of 12 bottles of whisky had fallen off the load. How many Bottles had survived the fall I didn't know. What I did know was that at least 2 bottles had escaped and found comfort on the back seat of the car speeding away from me and that I was a full case short of a full load.

I undid the ropes and sheet ties, pulled the sheet back and removed the top 2 layers off the suspect pallet. I then re-stacked the boxes leaving a hole in the third layer down and finished off with a complete top layer. To anyone looking at the pallet it seemed to contain its full complement of boxes and unless the pallet was broken down no one would be any the wiser. I then re-sheeted and roped the load, this time placing the corner board under the sheet and covering it more securely. I then continued on my way to my delivery point.

I reached my destination, stripped the ropes and sheet off the load and allowed the fork lift truck operative to commence with the unloading whilst I folded my sheets and wrapped my ropes. Upon completion of his duties, the stacker truck operator asked for the consignment notes which he duly signed as complete and undamaged. Once I had his signature on the notes I hurriedly threw the ropes and sheets onto the flat bed and without bothering to tie the sheets down, scampered to my cab, started the motor and beat a hasty retreat before I was found out. Nothing more was heard of this incident and I suppose the recipient of the load, after signing for it, and then finding one box short, knew he had no redress.

THE AMAZON

Local haulage companies sent their vehicles into the yard at Liverpool Road to pick up their own consignments, or for groupage. It was mid way through 1970, while working at this rail terminal that I came across my first *'lady'* trucker. She pulled into the yard driving an 'A' series ERF, 6 wheeler powered by a 120 Gardner, and she had come to collect 10 tons of 45 gallon drums of oil. I think the company she worked for was called Consolidated Transport or something similar. She climbed out of the cab dressed in an ill fitting boiler suit which had probably been tailored for Goliath. The lady herself was of Amazonian proportions standing close to 6ft and weighing in the region of 15 stones, and had long, blonde, greasy hair, tied back in a pony tail. As I and my workmates watcher her make her way to the office, moving like an Olympic weight lifter, driver Tom Bowler, a Salford lad, was heard to utter 'Bleedin' 'ell, look at that, ya wouldn't know whether to fuck it or fight it.'

We watched her load up, hurling those 45 gallon drums around as if they were empty. She roped the back end in using barrel hitches, she then threw her sheets onto the load and proceeded to rope and sheet her consignment, asking none of us mere men for help. Tom Bowler piped up, 'Did ya see the way she chucked them bleedin' barrels around, I'll tell ya what fightin' 'er's out of the question and I'm glad I'm happily married.'

When she had finished the load her sheets were nice and tight and were secured over the head and tail boards to ensure no ingress of the elements. All her dollies were at the same height along the load. The ropes were so tight that one could've played a tune on them. It was a rope and sheet job any man would have been proud of and that a lot of men could not have aspired to.

SOME PEOPLE JUST DON'T HAVE WHAT IT TAKES

The NCL; vehicles at Liverpool Road grossed out at 20 tons and were all TK Bedford's, but they still had the quick release Scammell coupling, although this was of no concern because my main aim was to use NCL; as a stepping stone to Freightliner, at the Longsight Terminal, via an inter company transfer, though to facilitate this I first had to move to Oldham Road Good's Depot where they had 32 tonners with fifth wheel couplings. An added bonus was that the rate of pay was higher for driving the heavier vehicles.

While I was working at Oldham Road, in the autumn of 1970, a young lad, Hal Avago, who had just personally paid for private lessons and passed his class 1 test, got a start. He had obviously heard that class one drivers earned astronomical wages. He knew nothing but the basics about transport and transport law or the hours required at the workplace to earn a living wage and less about driving but he was given a chance to prove himself. On his second day the foreman told him he was to do a Carlisle trunk. The young lad said 'I've never been to Carlisle.'

The foreman said 'Do you know how to get to the M6?'

The youth replied 'Yes, I think so.'

To which the foreman said 'Right get on the M6 and run it right to the end and you're at Carlisle.'

The lad got his unit, coupled it up to the trailer and set off. About 3½ hours later there was a phone call to the depot, it was the young driver and he said 'I got on the M6 and ran it all the way, I'm at Watford Gap and I can't find this Carlisle anywhere.' The vehicle and driver returned to the depot where Mr Avago was reprimanded and the trailer was sent to Carlisle on the night trunk to arrive better late than never.

The same lad, a few days later, was given a run to Bromborough and ended up at Bromsgrove. When he returned to the depot the foreman was waiting for him to give him a public dressing down in front of everyone. Hal got out of his vehicle and started 'I'm very sor……….'

'Shut up, you thick useless idiot,' said the foreman. 'Christ, Avago! If you had to go to the dentist's it would be to have a bloody wisdom tooth put in, but you'd probably end up at the chiropodists anyway. If you had twice as much sense, you'd be a soddin' half wit, now get in my office and wait for me, I'll sort you out later,' which he did by issuing a severe reprimand.

A couple of weeks later, while shunting, Hal ran into another truck in the Oldham Road depot, through his own stupidity, causing extensive damage to both units, although no one was injured. At his de-briefing about the occurrence the foreman asked 'How fast were you travelling at the time of the incident?'

'About 10mph.' was the reply.

'And what gear were you in?'

'I was in my uniform.........'

He was taken off the road and kept in the depot as a porter/loader while his case was reviewed. The management came to the conclusion that Hal was surplus to requirements and an industrial liability and he was given notice and his services were dispensed with.

PICKFORD'S, BRS AND FREIGHTLINER

After the 2nd World War when the Labour government came to power in 1945, part of their manifesto was for the nationalisation of inland transport. This was followed, in 1947, by the transport act which received Royal Assent in August 1947. The trading name for this new nationalised transport system was British Road Services (BRS). BRS stayed in state ownership for 34 years 1948 - 1982, and at its peak had a fleet of over 40,000 vehicles and 1,000 depots and a staff of over 75,000.

Pickfords, which was part of the nationalised transport system, goes back to the 17th century when the family was engaged in the business of mending roads. A quarry was owned by the family and stone was moved by teams of pack horses. Rather than return to the quarry empty, the horses would carry goods for others on a hire for reward basis. This established Pickfords as probably one of the earliest carriers.

The Pickford family was based in Adlington, South of Manchester and later moved to neighbouring Poynton. In 1816 the company, after coming close to bankruptcy, sold out to Joseph Baxendale but retained the Pickford name. In 1934 the company was taken over by the 4 main Railway companies and in 1947, under nationalisation, became part of BRS, but still, to this day, retains its own identity as the largest moving, storage and relocation company in the world.

BRS, consisting of numerous transport and allied companies including Pickford's later became part of the National Freight Corporation which included National Carriers Limited (NCL), Railfreight and Freightliner which were in house road hauliers for the Railway.

It was in the year of 1830, on the 22nd November that container transport was introduced by Pickford's Carriers in an agreement with The Liverpool and Manchester Railway Company. Although the containers used at the time were not the ISO twist lock type, they were certainly the forerunner of all modern container transport.

FREIGHTLINER LONGSIGHT

Freightliner was the container arm of British Rail and I started at Longsight Freightliner Terminal early in 1971 driving 32 ton gross vehicles. The fleet consisted of Guy Big J's powered by Cummins V6 200, Seddon 32: four models with either the 220 Rolls Royce Eagle or the AEC., AV690 and AV760 diesels with AEC's straight 6 gearbox and ratchet handbrakes. These last 2 engines and gearboxes were specified only for BRS., and Freightliners. Nowadays 4 and 6 wheelers have these engine ratings and more. The trailers we pulled were 20, 30 or 40ft skeletal, twist lock trailers.

The container trains came in overnight, from London or Glasgow and were tipped and reloaded by a pair of mobile cranes which straddled the lines. There were Freightliner depots dotted around the country. There were 2 in London 1 at Stratford and another at Willesden, then there was Birmingham, Felixstowe,

Holyhead, Leeds, Liverpool, Glasgow and another one was opened in Manchester at Trafford Park and a few others.

Longsight, like other Freightliner Terminals, was home to the transport sector of London Brick, a company that chartered rolling stock to bring up from London full trains of flat bed containers loaded solely with their product.

Safety, on the Railways, was paramount but now and again things will and do go wrong. Early one morning the train had a green signal and someone blew the whistle for the train to go. Unfortunately one of the straddle cranes was still working, having lifted a container off a truck and was at the point of depositing it on to the train. The train moved forward pulling the crane over, it landed on the containers on the slowly moving, laden train. One of these containers held 2 brand new Rolls Royce cars which were written off. Another was full of bonemeal which started a small Anthrax scare. Also a tank of Toluene di-isocyanate (TDI), was ruptured. TDI is a chemical compound used in the car industry and is used for hardening foam for car seats. It is also a very dangerous substance, if inhaled it crystallises on the lungs causing lung collapse and it is carcinogenic. I delivered the stuff to the Dunlopillo factory in Hirwaun, South Wales and was required to wear breathing apparatus whilst off-loading.

The train was stopped, the emergency services were called. Because of the TDI, all the houses on New Bank Street, opposite the terminal had to be evacuated until the Fire Service gave the all clear. Rolls Royce staff turned up and threw sheets over the cars so that the newspapermen, who had also arrived, couldn't photograph them, but not before someone had stolen the Sprit of Ecstasy from each of them. Specialists in special clothing came to test the bonemeal, which was later declared safe.

The crane driver, Derek Fellover, a man of very few words, escaped with minor injuries and as he clambered out of the toppled crane, and down to floor level, he dusted himself down and said the immortal words 'What the fuck............?' The Health and Safety Executive was called in and a major enquiry undertaken. Oh the joys of working on the Railways.

The idea of the Freightliner terminals was that massive tonnage would be carried hundreds of miles by train and be delivered locally by truck, but sometimes a container would miss the train and have to go by road. Most of the drivers did not want distance work so I and one or two others volunteered for most of the long jobs.

One afternoon I was given a job to Holyhead, on the Isle of Anglesey. I was given the job about 16.30hrs and I only had about an hours running time left and the container had to catch the 07.30 sailing for Ireland next morning, so I loaded the box and started off for ....home and pocketed the night out allowance. I set off the next morning at 03.00hrs and poodled off while the roads were clear. Everything was going all right until I approached Conway, as dawn was breaking. Just prior to Conway, on the old coast road, was a long lay-by, about 100 yards or more, and waiting there were the Traffic Commissioners accompanied by the police.

One of the Ministry men waved me in, so I pulled in and ran the full length of the lay-by. These were the days before tachographs, and my log book was not filled in due to the fact that I was running bent. I looked in my mirror and saw the Ministry man walking the 100 yards or so down the lay-by, holding his clip board in one hand and shaking his other fist at me and looking somewhat pissed off, so I stretched across the cab and started to fill in my log book on the passenger seat. There was a rat-a-tat-tat on the door; I carried on doing my log sheet. There was a louder rat-a-tat-tat on the door. Still I hadn't finished. There was then a loud banging and a shouted demand of 'Open this bloody door!' by this time my log book was up to date so I opened the door and proffered my log book to the irate commissioner who said with a wry smile and a hint of sarcasm, 'I don't suppose there's much point in looking at this swindle sheet, is there?' and handed it back to me, knowing in his mind that I was on a fiddle but unable to prove it. By then his compatriots had arrived at the vehicle, and they went over it with a fine toothed comb. By this time I was sweating and worried about catching the 07.30 sailing. Finally they gave me the all clear and a stern warning and sent me on my way. I reached the Freightliner Terminal on Holyhead docks with about 15 minutes to spare. The box was off loaded and transferred to the ship and I let out a great sigh of relief and promised myself I'd never pull another stunt like that again. Well, not until the next time.

Running bent was something most drivers did at one time or another in the days of the log book. Most drivers only ran bent for their own benefit to get home and profit from the subsistence money. Drivers that ran bent for the gaffer or to make the company more money were frowned upon. A lot of companies got a reputation of being cowboy outfits, although in all fairness this was not always justified. A typical joke going around at the time was about a multi millionaire whose young son's birthday was approaching, the father said to the son, who had almost everything a child could wish for 'Well, son, it's almost your birthday, what would you like for a birthday present?'

The son replied 'Gee, Dad, the one thing I'd really like is a cowboy outfit.' So his dad bought him BRS.

WOOLWORTH'S AND MORE FREIGHTLINER

Freightliners was okay, but I developed itchy feet and by this time my family had grown and I had two young daughters, born 15 months apart, one in October 1968 and the younger in August

1969. They were called Sharon and Tracey respectively. More of the filthy lucre was needed and I thought it was time for a move, so I searched the inter company vacancy lists for a new challenge. This was found in a vacancy for a long distance class 1 driver on the Woolworth's contract based at Castleton, Rochdale. I decided that, instead of fluctuating between local work and distance work and jobs that were a mixture of distance and local work, I would go tramping which entailed going to work on Monday and returning home on Friday night or sometime Saturday. The job was fine and the wages reasonable. The basic pay was the same as at Freightliner but more hours could be worked and the Woolworth's contract had a bonus scheme which raised the overall earnings, plus a little could be saved from the subsistence money. The down side of being a young father on distance work is that I and others like me miss their kids growing up. We are unable to attend parents' nights at the kids' schools. There is no evening story telling or good night kisses or quality time with the offspring except at weekends, but sadly that was just one of the many constraints of the job.

One night, in late 1971, not long after starting at Woolworth's, I was stranded in Carlisle waiting for a return load. I had parked up in the NCL yard and was walking down London Road, looking for a bed for the night. The first B&B I came to had a vacancies sign in the window so I knocked on the door. One of our brethren from north of the border opened the door, he had wild, bushy ginger eyebrows that gave the impression of 2 hairy caterpillars doing battle across his peepers. Upon his head was a Tam O' Shanter, from the bottom of which protruded bright, ginger hair. He wore a tartan shirt and green, plaid trousers. He was a consummate caricature of a Jock.

I said 'Do you have low terms for lorry drivers?'

'Aye,' he replied 'ye're a load of 'airy arsed thieving bastards. 'noo' awa' wi' ye,' and he closed the door. So, somewhat shaken,

I departed. The next establishment, upon whose door I knocked, was a regular transport house and I secured a room for the night. I related my tale to other drivers in there whereupon I was told that if I had stood my ground and knocked on the door again I would have found out that this was the Scotsman's idea of a little joke and I would indeed, if one had been free, have gotten a room there. Now that's what I call a perverse sense of humour.

It was around about this time that the company name changed again becoming the NFC, The National Freight Corporation, consisting of NCL, Pickford's, British Road Services (BRS), Railfreight, Freightliner and an assortment of other allied companies. The vehicles used on the Woolworth's contract were the same mix as at Freightliners, with the exception that the Seddon's were now the 34:4 models. They were all day cabs; the policy as far as was possible was to buy British.

The Woolworth contract had two types of deliveries. One was for shop and store deliveries, the other were depot deliveries, and suppliers' collections. I was put on shop deliveries at first but used what bit of seniority I had to move onto depot deliveries and collections. Some drivers are born shop delivery men that thrive on multi drop work, but I prefer bulk loads, down the road with 20 tons, unload, pick up 20 tons at a collection point and on to the next delivery destination and so on. Both sides of the job entailed being away 4 or 5 nights a week; it was just a matter of choice.

There was a driver at Woolworth's by the name of Geoff Nichollson, with whom I would be re-acquainted years later at British Telecom. At the time in question we were both sent to load at a company in South Wales. By the time we were both loaded we only had enough time left to run to a local digs whose name or identity I won't disclose other than to say it was once a bakery prior to it becoming a truckers digs. Generally it was a good and usually clean digs with fresh bed linen and I and other drivers stayed there regularly.

On this particular night Geoff and I were allocated a twin bedded room and had retired fairly early to necessitate an early start the next morning. At about 0100hrs in the morning I was awoken by a loud shout. I sat up and turned on the light and saw Geoff whacking his bed with one of his boots and shouting 'FUCK OFF! TAKE THAT YOU BASTARDS, FUCK, FUCK, FUCK!'

I said 'bloody 'ell Geoff what's up?'

He turned round to look at me and in the dim light of a single 40 watt bulb, made worse by the way the shadows fell, he looked like something out of a horror film with swellings and red weals all over his phizog and about his body. He would have made a very credible Mr Hyde. I got up and went over to his bed and saw his sheets were spattered with red blotches where he had battered to death, a number of bed bugs. I moved my bed as far away as possible from Geoff's who by now had gotten dressed, he said 'I can't make do with this, I'm goin' to my cab and kippin' in there and I'll see the owner in the mornin' for my money back.'

Geoff went to his cab and I took the chance of getting back in my bed. I slept all right and wasn't bothered by any bugs. Upon arising the next morning and after a shower, I met Geoff who had come back in for a shower and breakfast and to discuss some terms with the owner. His face, in the cold light of day and after a wash did not appear as horrific. The swellings had subsided somewhat and he had applied some TCP that the proprietor had given him. After a lengthy, whispered conversation during which the proprietor was heard to implore, numerous times 'Pleeease, keep your voice down.' They came to some amicable arrangement concerning costs and we left to carry on with our jobs. Not many of the Woolworth's drivers used that accommodation after the story of Geoff and the bed bugs had spread around. Luckily the bad digs were few and far between.

Whilst working at Woollies a mate of mine, Bob Slayer, was made redundant from his job as a bus driver. He used part of his redundancy to obtain his Class 1, and I got him a start at Woolworth's by telling my boss, Jim Carner, that he had took to artics like a duck to water. On the Monday that Bob started all the other drivers, me included were in the depot waiting for our loads. Jim told Bob to get in the shunt motor and start on a bit of trailer shunting and gave him a trailer to take to the loading bays at the rear of the warehouse. These bays were in such a position that the driver had to back in on his blind side and Bob appeared more like a fish out of water. After about 20 minutes Jim said to me 'Where's your mate, Bob? Go and see what he's up to.' I went round the back and there's Bob pouring in sweat with the artic tied in knots. I said 'Get out Bob, I'll back it in for you, it's just a matter of practise and experience.'

Just as I had backed the trailer in and gotten out of the cab and Bob was winding down the landing legs Jim appeared round the corner and he said 'Well done Bob I was just testing you.'

The job called for the use of 20ft, 30ft and 40ft trailers; they were all box trailers with roller shutters. The 20 and 30 footers were for stores that had limited access and the 40ft's for tramping. When the 20 footers were dropped on the loading bay at the home depot, there were two additional stabiliser legs at the front of the trailer that had to be lowered before loading could commence, this was because the stacker trucks ran straight into the back of the trailers off the loading bays and with such a short, single axle trailer, once the stacker had passed over the trailer landing legs with a heavily laden pallet the trailer could take a nose dive and the single rear axle would come off the floor. Bob Slayer, being still quite new to the game forgot, on one occasion, to lower those extra stabiliser legs. The loader didn't check and he ran his stacker truck into the vehicle to deposit a pallet at the bulkhead. As he passed over the landing legs the trailer started to tip. The stacker gathered a little momentum as the trailer continued to tip forwards and it crashed into the bulkhead, crushing the pallet and driving the forks through the front of the trailer. The trailer was righted by another fork lift and the one in the back of the trailer was extricated from its ignominious position. No one was hurt and the only damage was to the front of the trailer which was later sent for repair, and of course, to the pallet and its load. After a brief enquiry both Bob and the loader received disciplinary notices.

It was the winter of late 1972 when I was given a load to deliver, to the NCL; Woolworth's depot in Glasgow and a collection from a company in Edinburgh. I had my night out in Edinburgh. At the time I was using a left hooker Volvo 89, sleeper cab with a night heater, on hire from a Manchester rental company, so I slept in the vehicle in the NCL yard in Edinburgh. Normally Woolworth's drivers would park up at Portobello near Leith and book into one of the transport digs there. The next morning I did the collection and headed on back to Manchester down the A702 Biggar Road which joins the A74 near Crawford. The weather was treacherous; snow had fallen on top of the already icy roads and had been compacted by passing traffic.

Approaching Biggar on a slight descent, doing about 5mph., I looked at the wagons on the other side of the road which were climbing and they were virtually crabbing to keep traction, when all of a sudden, a figure appeared in front of me shouting and waving his arms about like a wailing banshee. He didn't realise, at that time, how close he came to his own demise. I tentatively touched the brakes and steered into the kerb to help bring my vehicle to a halt in a straight line.

Before I could say anything this animated Caledonian shouted in clipped sentences 'Ye've got ta help. There's a Cortina jest gone off the rood. It's doon yon ditch across the way.' I climbed out of the cab and made my way, somewhat cautiously, across the icy road surface to the ditch, closely followed by Jock and sure enough, down an embankment and about 6 feet below me was a Ford Cortina on its roof. The door pillars were crushed into the roof making it impossible to open the doors. The driver obviously thought it was too dangerous to drive and so tried flying instead. I went down to the car, followed once again by the Scot. I could see the lone occupant frantically kicking and banging on the windscreen and shouting to be freed, whilst the Scotsman stood nonchalantly smoking a cigarette near the ruptured fuel tank. I shouted at the trapped driver of the car to hang on and I told the 'numpty heed' native clansman to stub out his ciggy away from the fuel and then went back to my truck and got the winding handle used for winding the trailer's jockey wheels down. Thus armed, I returned to the stricken vehicle and with a few hefty blows succeeded in smashing the windscreen and with the help of the Scot, pulled the trapped individual out. After ascertaining his physical state, which was okay apart from a couple of cuts and bruises, although he was badly shaken. I said 'Who are you? What's your name?'

He replied 'My name's Hymie Barber and I'm a rep for a well known razor blade company.'

Without thinking I said 'Well that's the closest shave you've ever had.'

He responded, in a somewhat sullen tone I don't think that's very funny.'

The Scotsman who had flagged me down and helped in the rescue of this traumatised rep picked up on the humour and said 'Ay noo laddie, Dinna' get stroppy with ye mon. He jest sa'ed ye life so ye can carry on in this cut-throat business.'

There was a Milk Bar just down the road, so I and the

Scotsman helped Hymie there. I then got in touch with the company for whom he worked. After buying him a hot sweet drink and wishing him good luck, I said goodbye to him and the Scotsman who had helped me. I made my way back to my vehicle, fired her up and went on my merry way, very slowly and carefully. I reached the A74 at Crawford and was much relieved that the gritters had been out and I continued my journey a little faster and in relative safety, and I never heard another thing about the close shave incident.

Not long after the episode on the Biggar Road, I heard that there were vacancies at the new Freightliner terminal which had opened in Trafford Park. The old Trafford Park rail shed was demolished in 1969 to make way for this venture which was completed around 1971, about the same time the Manchester Container base opened. Once again I applied by way of an inter company transfer and for the second time in my career, in the early part of 1973, I became a Freightliner driver. Shortly after the opening of Trafford Park, Longsight was deemed one too many terminals in Manchester and was closed with the transfer of some of its drivers. Those that didn't transfer either took the redundancy or early retirement.

At the Trafford Park Freightliner terminal was a driver who had transferred from Deansgate to join this new venture. He was of Irish descent and was called Joe O'Heeney and he knocked around with Knocker, Stuart Onigbanjo, Dusty Rhodes and I. Joe, who had just become a driver when I started at Deansgate, had thick greasy, mousey coloured hair and oily skin. Because of this, the large amount of dust and grime that was forever present in Railway yards and loading bays seemed to attach itself to Joe. So much so that Stuart once said 'Look at Joe, he only has to clock on and he's covered in shite.'

Joe was an excellent driver but like anyone else he made mistakes. Whilst at Freightliner he was once given a container to deliver to a company in Barnsley, Yorkshire. As one drives through Penistone on the A628 towards Barnsley, there is a low arched, railway bridge with the warning 'HIGH VEHICLES GET INTO THE CENTRE OF THE ROAD.' Joe approached the bridge and pulled into the centre of the road. Just as he was about to enter the bridge a car coming the other way was close to the centre of the road coming straight for Joe's vehicle. By virtue of self preservation and instinct Joe forgot about the arched structure. He took evasive action and pulled back into the inside lane and found himself firmly wedged beneath the bridge. The car, apparently also took evasive action but carried on going. Luckily Joe was unhurt on this occasion and there was little damage to the container as it was more of a friction collision than a sudden impact. The Emergency services were called out, the Health and Safety Executive were notified and as is usual with accidents concerning Railway bridges. The Railway engineers were summoned to the site. All rail services using this line were either diverted or cancelled until a thorough investigation had been carried out at a cost of thousands of pounds. Joe found himself the recipient of a reprimand for the incident; although once his vehicle was freed from the structure he was able to complete the delivery and return to the terminal.

Joe recently lost the sight in his right eye after an accident with one of the custom's handles on a container door. The handle was, apparently, very stiff and as Joe applied the necessary pressure to release it, it suddenly sprang free whilst he still grasped it, and being at head height it caught him forcefully in the eye causing much pain and blindness. Although the actual orb was saved the sight was lost permanently. His LGV license was revoked and at 60 years of age after a lifetime on the Railways he was medically retired.

The vehicles at Trafford Park were a mixture of old and new and were given a new livery of red as opposed to the old

Railway yellow. On my first day I was allocated a Seddon 34:4 powered by an AEC, AV691 engine coupled to a David Brown straight 6 transmission but this was soon replaced by a Leyland Marathon fitted with the 265 Rolls Royce Eagle engine with the Eaton, Fuller 4 over 4 gear box. After I had been at Freightliners for about 6 months I was asked to take a driver that had passed his class 1 and just transferred to Freightliner from Oldham Road Goods Depot, out with me for the day, to show him the ropes and report back on his driving skills. The new driver was an easy going Irish lad, whose name was Paddy O'Dore. He had never driven a Leyland Marathon or used the Eaton Fuller 4 over 4, constant mesh, air assisted, range change gear box before. He had only used synchromesh boxes and I thought to myself 'This is gonna be fun.'

I showed him around the vehicle, which was hooked up, loaded and ready to roll. I explained the shift pattern of this gear box, which is not the usual 'H' pattern. The shift pattern is of such that you go around the box in a clockwise square to change up, then pull up the air assisted range change button and round the box again, and the opposite way for changing down. These types of gear box also have a high and a low ratio reverse gear.

We set off to deliver the contents of the container with Paddy behind the wheel. To say he had a lot to learn would have been a prime example of understatement. I don't think he made a clean gear change on the outward journey, although his manoeuvring of a 40ft trailer around corners and his general awareness of the requirements of a HGV driver was up to scratch. The problem was that every time he missed a gear, he had a tendency to look down to find it and we drifted across the carriageway narrowly missing other vehicles whose drivers had to take evasive action when they realised that holding their hand on the horn was not having the desired effect. I don't know who was most embarrassed and afraid, Paddy or me.

On the return journey there was a big improvement with not as much cursing or crunching and grinding of cogs. When we finally returned to the yard and had the empty container removed, reversed the trailer into a parking spot and parked the unit up, Paddy asked me 'What de ye call dat gearbox again?'

'A Fuller's 4 over 4 range change' I replied.

'Oi know whoi dey call it dat.' He said.

'Why's that?' I asked.

'Cos it's Fuller fuckin' gears ye can't bloody well find.' He replied, with a grin.

I reported back to the traffic office that Paddy was a good driver, competent at reversing and just needed a little more experience with the constant mesh, range change gearbox. He stuck it out and finally mastered the Eaton Fuller's box.

After a few more months, I was allocated the first brand new motor I had ever had, a Volvo F86 of which a number had been bought, some with an automatic box the rest with 4 over 4 synchromesh, range change, one of which I was allocated. This was a total diversion for the NFC; to buy foreign vehicles, even though British vehicles were in decline.

The Volvo's were actually built up in a Scottish plant at Irvine and the main agent was one Jim McKelvie of Glasgow who set up Ailsa Trucks, in 1972, and who had once ran a substantial haulage fleet of his own. The Volvo 86 was a nice comfortable vehicle to drive, but with its rounded shape and expanse of glasswork, it was akin to driving a very large goldfish bowl, although it did offer panoramic views of the road and motorway network.

A FOOLISH DODGY NIGHT OUT

It wasn't long after I was allocated the Volvo F86 that I and 4 other Freightliner drivers were sent to the ICI plant at Billingham, just off the A19 North of Middlesbrough. We were to run up with empty 40ft containers to be loaded with 20 tons of Terephalic acid in powder form. I believe this product was used in the manufacture of fertilizer. The powder was loaded in 4ft x 4ft polypropylene bags with handles on each corner to accommodate the forks of the lift trucks which lifted them and drove off the loading bay directly into the back of the container and deposited them 10 down either side of the box, 20 bags at 1 ton per bag equals 20 tons.

On the day in question, besides the 4 Freightliner trucks, there were also 2 trucks belonging to Benson's Transport. Benson's was a local, family run haulage company from the Miles Platting, Collyhurst area of Manchester, but are nowadays located in Trafford Park. Benson's like many other local companies would regularly work out of Freightliner's or the Container base.

We all left the Freightliner terminal together and ran together. We all stopped at the Woodside Café on the A19 for breakfast and all rolled into the ICI plant in convoy, with me at the rear of the caravan of vehicles.

One by one the containers were loaded and sent on their way, until it came to my turn. I reversed on to the loading bay. The loading ramp was placed in position and then I was told that there was a plant breakdown and that I would not get loaded until the following morning. It was now mid afternoon.

Now this particular time, a Monday, I had come to work without any night out gear or any money, bar for a few bob, as I thought that I would be home that night, which would have been the norm. I phoned the Freightliner office and told the traffic clerk that because of problems with the plant I would not get loaded that day. The response was to tell me to have a night out and carry on the next day. Not wishing to seem unprofessional, I was too embarrassed to say that I had no cash or credit cards with me, or any washing tackle, not even a tooth brush. So I said I would have the night out, whilst contriving to get home and back again the following day.

Luckily one of the Benson's drivers was still waiting for his notes, so I left my truck backed onto the bay, locked up the cab and deposited the keys in the despatch office and got a lift home in the Benson's truck.

Getting home was the easy part. The Benson's driver dropped me at Birch Services, at about 1730hrs, from where I phoned my wife, who then picked me up.

I was back at Birch at 0530hrs the next morning, courtesy of my wife, once again. Billingham is approximately 2½ to 3 hours if you get a good run. I was waiting at the exit slip road and the first vehicle to leave the services stopped and I was offered a lift, but only to Hartshead Moor. After a fairly long wait at Hartshead I secured my second lift just as it started to rain. This time only as far as Ferrybridge Services. It had become a cold, wet morning so I went inside Ferrybridge Services and had a brew. When I returned to the exit a Newcastle driver on his way home stopped and offered me a lift to Dishforth roundabout at the junction with the A1 and the A168. This was before the A1(M) was built and lorries would have to slow down to negotiate the roundabout to the A168 which runs into the A19.

I waited at the roundabout for about ½ an hour; all the trucks seemed to be heading up the A1. The rain had increased in its intensity and it was now pissing down and bloody freezing. Rain was running off my head and dripping off my nose in a constant stream like a mini Niagara. I had my wet weather gear on but these coats are only of any use in a shower. After the constant soaking that I was subjected to on that morning, the weatherproofing had given up its integrity. I was soaked to the skin.

Eventually a truck came onto the A168 and pulled up. The driver was going to Sunderland. I clambered in, shivering and wet, and was grateful to feel the cab heater. I thanked the driver who asked where I was heading and offered me his flask. I poured a cup of steaming hot, sweet, milky coffee and explained my situation. This driver was good enough to drive off the A19 and into Billingham where he dropped me at the ICI gates. When I exited his cab, I left behind in the vinyl passenger seat, a little puddle of water as a parting gift, I had been that wet when I had gotten in.

Luckily no one from my home depot had phoned the ICI plant to enquire of my whereabouts. My truck had been loaded, sealed and pulled off the loading bay. It had been loaded since 0830hrs and it was now 1130hrs, it had taken me 6 hours to reach Billingham.

I went into the despatch office, picked up my keys, signed for the load, thanked the loading staff and went to my vehicle. I checked the motor over, fired it up, stuck it in gear and made my way, post haste, back to Manchester. As I drove I was shivering violently, so as the vehicle warmed up, I switched on the heater and by the time I reached Wetherby, the shivers and the chattering of teeth had subsided and the steam had ceased to rise from my clothes, the numbness had disappeared from my muscles and bones and I was reasonably dry and warm.

I was amazed, when I arrived back at the Freightliner terminal, that nobody asked where the hell I had been until that time, which was then about 1500hrs. I went into the traffic office to pick up my night out money, expecting a court of enquiry and a ballocking. Nobody said a thing. The fact that there had been a plant breakdown 24 hours earlier sufficed to explain my elongated absence.

For the second time in my Freightliner career I promised

myself that I would never pull another stunt like that again and since then I have always carried the bare minimum for a night out, as well as some spare cash and my credit card.

BARBED WIRE AND ROPE SPANNERS

Other vehicles that came into the Freightliner fleet were the Ergomatic cabbed AEC Mandator with an AV691. 11/3litre diesel and the high cabbed Leyland Marathon powered by Leyland's own engine or the 265 Rolls Royce Eagle and the Guy Big J with the same power unit or the smaller 220 Cummins. All these vehicles had the Eaton Fullers 4 over 4 or 5 over 5 range change gearbox as opposed to the David Brown straight sixes or 2 speed axles of earlier vehicles.

The work was mainly local, but once again I and one or two others volunteered for any distance work that came up. One such job that I got was a 40ft flat bed container containing pallets of barbed wire which were to be delivered to most of the RAF camps along the East coast. Some camps took a pallet or 2; other camps took just a few reels. It took me from Monday to Saturday to do all the drops and the load had to be re-sheeted after each drop. I was treated to meals in the NAAFI and was generally well looked after. When the flat bed was empty, I attempted to fold my sheets, they were full of holes and rips because of the needle pointed barbs of the wire and were beyond repair and I eventually folded them into a rumpled and crumpled and shredded heap which I then secured to the flat bed up against the headboard. They had to be thrown away when I returned to Trafford Park.

Roped and sheeted flat bed containers often came in from Ireland. The Irish seemed to have a different method of tying dollies than the English. They served the same purpose, but whereas the English dolly is a quick release knot, the Irish dolly was somewhat more difficult to undo, so frequently the drivers favourite and preferred tool, the rope spanner would be employed. An ordinary spanner is used to undo nuts; a rope spanner is used to undo knots and goes by the more popular name of the knife.

I HATE COCKNEY'S

Not long after the RAF job, me and another Freightliner driver, Bill Sticker, were waiting for our notes in the office of OOCL, a shipping company, which was situated next to the Freightliner terminal and employed about half a dozen staff. As we waited, the entrance to the office burst open and a London driver made his entry like a sonic boom or a thunderclap. He was loud and full of the joys of spring, like your typical cockney sparrer 'Orwight my san, Ow yer doin?' He said to me 'You orwight mite?' he said to Bill. He then lifted the hatch, which had a sign on it clearly stating 'NO DRIVERS BEYOND THIS POINT.' He swaggered through to the office saying in a very chirpy voice to the office staff 'Orwight guys and gells, wanna cappa, where's the kettle? I could murder a cap a' cha meself, knar what a mean?'

Bill said 'Look at that bastard, I sure as hell hate cockney's'

'Oh', I said, 'My dad's a cockney.' which was true.

'Er..........well they're not all bad are they? he said, a little embarrassed.

The cockney located the kitchen, the kettle and the brewing gear and made everyone a cup of tea including Bill and me.

He then came back through the hatch to the driver's side of the counter and addressed the head clerk, 'Right, abaht this box I've cam' ta pick up.' And he handed the clerk his requisition notes. The clerk took the notes and as he read them a wide grin split his face and he said to the driver, 'I'm sorry mate but this isn't one of our boxes, these notes are for an OCL box and we're OOCL you should be at the Container base not here.'

The driver's face started to redden with embarrassment and he said 'Er....Bit 'f a ballock dropped, 'ey ....er, best fack orf then.........I feel a right bleedin' plonker now, knar what a mean,..........Orwight, see yas.' And he grabbed his notes back and left a little more subdued than when he entered and with somewhat less cockiness, leaving his 'cappa cha' on the counter, much to the amusement of the office staff and, of course, Bill.

THE CASE OF THE AMPUTATED FINGER

A couple of weeks later, 3 drivers, me included were told to pick up a 20ft Merzario tilt container each. Merzario being an Italian shipping line which brought a lot of uncut Marble to the UK and loaded back with whichever commodity was needed. Tilts being continental soft skinned containers i.e. a metal frame with stanchions with wooden slats between them and a hardwood floor and normal container doors. The side was reinforced plastic sheeting, not unlike a Tautliner and the roof could either be steel or a continuation of the curtain sides. Tilts are used on all types of transport on the continent. We were then to make our way to a company called Diamond Refractories in Stourbridge, Worcestershire, 12 miles South of Birmingham, to pick up 20 tons apiece of firebrick destined for Italy.

We left the terminal at approximately 08.00hrs in a three vehicle convoy. In the lead was a guy named Jim Craque followed by a guy named Jack Boote and me taking the tail end. We arrived at Diamond Refractory's yard approximately 3½ hours later, having stopped at the Hollies Transport Café on the A5 at Cannock for breakfast. We trooped into the despatch office where we were told that we would have to strip the tilts. We complained, somewhat bitterly, because there were two loading bays available that we could reverse onto and the loading could be affected by the stacker trucks running straight into the back of the containers with the pallets, thus negating the need for strip down.

The despatch clerk dismissed this notion and reiterated, in a no nonsense tone, that it was his desire that the tilts be stripped. The three of us started to strip down Jim's box first. We'd undone the security wire and the lacings and pulled, via a rope, the side curtains onto the roof. We'd pulled out the wooden slats that fitted between the metal stanchions that gave the container its rigidity. These particular stanchions had not been removed for some time and were solidly rusted in place and no amount of kicking, pulling and pushing or shaking would move them. The stacker truck driver suggested that he put his forks under one of the holders for the wooden slats and attempt to lift the stanchion out thus. Jimmy clambered up onto the bed of the container to steady the stanchion as it came free. Unfortunately he held the stanchion above the pocket that the stacker driver had chosen to position his forks. As the fork lift operative fed power to the hydraulics and started to lift, the stanchion being so well fast, the whole caboodle started to lift. After 4 or 5 inches the forks slid from under the receptacle and as the trailer dropped that few inches the forks came back into contact with the stanchion, above the wooden slat receptacle, raggedly severing Jim's left index finger at the lower knuckle.

Immediate first aid was administered and an ambulance called. Jim and the severed digit were taken to the local infirmary where the detached finger was reattached, although after that it was of little use and became a purely cosmetic instrument, useful only for pointing. When the hullabaloo had died down, Lo and Behold, Jack and I were told to reverse onto the loading bays where we were loaded without incident and in less time than it would take to strip one tilt. One of the bosses from the Manchester Freightliner Terminal brought another driver down to take over Jimmy's truck and this same boss waited at the hospital to take Jimmy home.

I relate this story to depict how some traffic office employees and clerks suffer from megalomania, bloody mindedness and sheer stupidity in equal amounts in their efforts to try to impress their superiority over us mere drivers. Jim Craque, by the way, made a successful claim and recovery and although he was taken off driving duties, remained on the Railways at Trafford Park Freightliner terminal as a shunter on the lines within the terminal until he retired at 65.

THE BLACK PANTHER

A rather strange thing occurred in 1975, whilst I was working for Freightliner, Lesley Whittle, a 17 year old heiress had been kidnapped, from her home in Shropshire by Donald 'The Black Panther' Neilson. This young lady had been left £82,000 in her father's will. The Whittle family ran or maybe still run a larger private coach company based in Kidderminster and Highley in Shropshire. The police were called in when a ransom note demanding £50,000 was received by Lesley's brother Donald.

I was loading out of Heinz Foods at Kitt Green, Wigan, and was in the process of roping up when I felt a tap on my shoulder. I turned around to be confronted by 2 rather tall gentlemen in suits. Like any other plain clothes policemen, they stood out for what they were, like the proverbial sore thumb. There were plenty of other drivers nearby that heard the following conversation.

'Laurie Driver?' one of these suited gentlemen enquired.

'Yes' I replied 'What can I do for you?'

'We're making enquiries into the disappearance of one

Lesley Whittle and think that you may be able to help us in our enquiries. Could you accompany us to our car, if you please?'

'Well yes, I suppose so, though I don't see how I can help you.'

'Let us be the judges of that, now come along.'

I was marched off towards the unmarked vehicle, but enough drivers had heard the exchange, and I heard little asides and saw drivers whispering to each other and pointing.

As it happens, it appears that I once worked for a company that employed Neilson, albeit the Black Panther worked in another part of the country and I was just being eliminated from police enquiries. No more, no less.

Sadly, Lesley Whittle, who was held captive in a 60ft drain shaft for 52 days, died from strangulation. Neilson received 4 life sentences in July 1976, for this and other offences, including the murders of Post Office employees and the robbery of sub post offices.

OUT OF THE ORDINARY

In the course of working for the Railways and on container work I have carried, what I considered to be, some unusual and exotic commodities. I have carried numerous canisters full of bull's semen for the artificial insemination of cows, but like humans I should think they would prefer the real thing. In my early Railway days I have driven and escorted a number of young exotic beasts to the Belle Vue Zoo. Whether or not these animals were the result of artificial insemination I know not, though I wouldn't like to try it on a tigress, nor would I like to be responsible for extracting the semen from the male, British companies have exported wine to France, and I have picked up loads of Vodka from Warrington destined for Russia.

Whilst working at the Trafford Park Freightliner Terminal I was on one occasion sent to a factory, in North Wales, to load 20 tons of firelighters in a 30ft box. Nothing unusual in that you may say. When the load was completed I went to the despatch office to sign for the load. I noticed that the final destination was Saudi Arabia, one of the hottest countries in the world.

Another time I had to pick up 20 tons of Dolly Blue from the Dolly Blue Factory at Backbarrow in Cumbria on the A590. For those too young to know, Dolly Blue was a whitening agent which looked like a little wooden doll wearing a white skirt. Dolly Blue was made from Caustic soda, sulphur and synthetic ultramarine blue amongst other constituents. It was added to the water of the wash tub (dolly tub) to whiten linen.

The firelighters, so I was informed, were used by Bedouin tribesmen to light fires in the desert at night, when the temperatures dropped dramatically during the hours of darkness. I have also been informed that Bedouins and Arabs in general used the Dolly Blue to whiten their traditional long garment known as the Jalabea.

I have even collected plastic chopsticks for export to China. The only reason I can think of for this is that they might be cheaper to make out of plastic, ship out and deliver them in China than it is to make them in the Orient out of traditional materials.
Vimto is shipped out to the USA, home of Pepsi and Coca Cola and also to the Arab States. It is even shipped to India and China where it must substitute for tea and even to Japan the home of sake.

REACHING THE PINNACLE

I now considered myself a fully fledged trucker. I could rope and sheet, use chains and tensioners and restraining straps. I'd carried long loads, wide loads, heavy loads, light loads. I'd carried steel, timber, concrete, meat, including hanging beef, worked on flat beds, box vans, curtainsiders, tilts, trombones, carried containers on skeletal trailers, done long distance, mid distance, short distance, worked off docks and ports, had nights out, cabbed it, stayed in transport digs, used multi-range, constant mesh gearboxes, gate change boxes and two speed axles. I had a comprehensive knowledge of the national road network. I'd done multi drop, bulk loads, tipper work, I'd pulled single axle trailers, tandem axle trailers, tri-axle trailers, four in lines, and I'd driven 4, 6 and 8 wheeler rigids on a multiplicity of jobs. I'd been to towns and villages my family had never heard of. I knew my way through and around most of the major cities in Britain including London, Birmingham and Glasgow. I was a seasoned trucker. I had learnt the game.

CHAPTER 4

CAFES, DIGS AND TRUCKSTOPS

BEFORE the advent of the sleeper cab, long distance hauliers had to book into digs for their nights out. The Parsimonious drivers would cab it in the corner of a lorry park by sleeping across the seats and engine cover with newspaper up at the windows. Cafes with lodgings above them proliferated on the major trunk routes such as the A5 and A1 and most towns had lorry parks for overnight parking. Good digs were easy to find in the 1960's and '70's, they were cheap and the food was good and plentiful, linen was changed daily. Of course there were bad digs but these were only used in desperation or, of course, if you didn't know of their reputation.

Since the opening up of the motorway network a lot of these cafes and digs have long since gone to be replaced by the Truck stops whose sole purpose seems to be to get every last penny from the driver. They are, in my mind, overpriced, utilitarian, poor excuses for the once traditional transport café and accommodation.

Tubby's on the A5 was one of the best cafes as was Nelson's near Towcester. Nelson's has been extended and re-named The Super Sausage. Others on the A5 that still thrive are the Hollies at Cannock, which still has digs and mammoth food portions, and the Watling Street Café at Junction 9 off the M1, though the lodgings at Watling Street no longer exist the food is still good, and there is a pub a couple of hundred yards up the road, the Horse and Jockey, where food is available and occasionally an exotic dancer would perform, Jack's Hill Café and accommodation at Towcester still thrives and has done since 1968.

The A1 being the major trunk road in Britain, running from Edinburgh to London, boasts numerous cafes , although as on other roads a lot of them no longer exist. Amongst those that still flourish is Kate's Cabin near Peterborough, The Barton Lorry Park just off the A1 at Barton near Scotch Corner, The Quernow Café which caters for sleeper cabs only but still provides good grub. Londonderry Lodge on the old A1 near Leeming aerodrome still provides good accommodation and comestibles at a reasonable price and is still a truckers favourite.

The Silvertown Motel at Silvertown Way in London E16 near the East India docks was used by drivers using the docks or Tate & Lyle sugar plant. The rooms had two sets of bunk beds; the food was good and plentiful. The owners employed a Marshall to park the vehicles in such a way as to maximise the room available. This employee would have the early starters to the front and the late runners to the back and would have you so close to the next vehicle that you had to be a contortionist to get out of and back into your cab.

Amongst those that no longer exist was Micklefield on the old A1 between Ferrybridge and Wetherby whose death knell tolled with the opening of the new M1 link road as was the case with a number of others along the A1 when stretches were turned into the A1(M). There was The Jungle Café on the A6 at Shap where it was said that the proprietor would keep a pair of dry boots by the fire for those truckers that had become snowbound on the old Shap Road, which was notorious for such things during the winter months. The Jungle Café closed not long after the opening of the M6.

The Coatesgate Café and accommodation block at Beattock

on the old A74, was known as the Quarry caff because it was situated opposite Beattock Quarry. It was a good café and the accommodation was good but it was forced to close its doors when the new A74(M) opened. Morley's Café on the A1 at Markham Moor was a family owned place which supplied good digs and food, but has been taken over and in its place is the Markham Truck stop.

Some towns and cities in Britain had streets near lorry parks where most of the houses had been turned into transport digs. Manchester's Hyde Road at Ardwick was one such place, though the big Victorian town houses that served that purpose have long ago been demolished.

Carlisle's London Road had a lorry park at one end and the houses were a mixture of transport digs and ordinary tourists B&B accommodation although most would accommodate a trucker if there was a spare room.

Oystermouth Road in Swansea was another such street where some of the properties were either B&B's or transport digs, but as I remember it the parking was on a piece of derelict land. There were many more major municipalities that saw the need for decent, cheap accommodation for transient truckers, and some truckers would travel that few miles more to stay in their regular lettings. Darlington had a large council car park and it was only a short walk across the park near the town centre where there were numerous streets with houses to pander to truck drivers needs. Lincoln is a nice town with a spacious lorry park near the river and plenty of transport digs within a few minutes walk.

Some cafes have been going for years; Londonderry Lodge was established in 1952. The Redrock Motel at Doncaster in 1962, and Chris's Café and Motel at High Wycombe in 1950. Motorman's Café at Marsden on the A62 has been going since before the 2nd World War and was established in 1938, and Graham's Transport

Stop at Bridgewater in the West Country has been around since the '20's. It would be foolish of me to try to mention here all the cafes and digs in Britain but I will mention some I have frequented myself that are worthy of note.

The Four Oaks at Rainham on the A13 was comfortable with good food but you had to book early to get a single room. The Kernel Transport Motel at Cheslyn Hay, Staffs, had mainly single and double rooms. It had a couple of snooker tables and a night club attached and a drivers' restaurant, but if the food there was not to an individuals liking there was a pub across the road that served food. Lincoln farm at Hampton-in-Arden in Warwickshire is off the beaten track but still does well, and as well as reasonable food and lodgings had, when I stayed there, strippers on a couple of times a week. The Quorn Café on the A6 between Loughborough and Leicester was a nice haven. The owner once fed and watered me by cooking me an individual meal when I turned up late after a breakdown whilst on the bacon run for the Co-op; I use the past tense because I don't know whether the Quorn is still trading. The Crawford Arms and the Heatherghyll, both in Crawford just off the M74 in Scotland are both good digs though they are different types of establishment. The Crawford Arms is not a pub as the name suggests, but is essentially a transport lodging house though tourists also stayed there, it is situated opposite the council lorry park and has single, double, triple and four bedded rooms and a well stocked bar. The Heatherghyll is a custom made transport motel with single and double rooms, with its own restaurant and bar and a spacious lorry park, but both serve the needs of the trucker admirably.

I have stayed at numerous truck stops including Carlisle, Penrith, Aberdeen, Alconbury, Wolverhampton, West Brom and Birtley. Some were taken over by BP, others were opened by BP. Carlisle Truck stop, I believe, was once owned or at least run by Geoff Bell who is a haulage man himself and runs a tidy fleet. I've stayed at the Alconbury BP Truck stop, and cabbed it at the Rugby and Wolverhampton BP Truck stops and also at West Brom BP Truck stop before its closure. These stopovers were all right when they first opened. The food was good, the accommodation was adequate some, even had *en suite* facilities. Then the overnight parking fees began to rise and the price of the food went up as the quality and portion sizes went down and they became a non viable proposition to the driver who was only on £7 or £8 per night out and whose gaffer refused to pay car park fees, and there are still a lot of those about.

Whether the proprietors knew anything about it or not the Truck stops became the hunting grounds for the local ladies of the night and drivers would be awakened to the offer of a blow job or a short time at whatever rate could be negotiated. For every ten drivers that turned down these offers there was always one willing to put at risk his health, his reputation or his marriage. Of course you could get these bothersome women on council lorry parks but it seemed to become more prevalent at the Truck stops especially those where there were more cabbers than those that booked rooms. These nighttime visitors are on the increase as more truck parks close down their sleeping accommodation as it becomes surplus to requirements.

As far as bad digs go, and before sleeper cabs had become popular, there was one, whose name I won't mention, by the Firth of Forth, Scotland. The food was good but the sleeping accommodation left a lot to be desired, it was above the dining area and was a massive dormitory with about 50 beds or more. There were no divisions between one bed and the next, not even a curtain. It was like an army barracks room, but with less space between the beds. Privacy was none existent and because of the noise generated by 50 or so snorers, the light sleeper would have no sleep at all. On the one instance I stayed there I watched the guy in the next bed to me lift his bed and put his boots under each leg so a bed leg was inside each boot.

I said 'What's all that about mate?'

'Well,' he said 'These are a brand new pair of boots and if I leave 'em out in the open it's a pound to a pinch of shit that they'll be gone in the morning and I'll have some other bastards cast offs.' He then lifted the other end of the bed and put his suit case handle under the leg.

I thought he was just a bit eccentric but as the digs filled up I saw others drivers do the same thing, so I thought, eccentric or not, they can't all be wrong so I followed suit. The noise through the night was unbearable. There was the occasional alarm clock going off every now and again through the night even though the early starters could have got the night warden to give them a shake. There were people stumbling around in the dark and all sorts of indescribable noises. I believe that the drivers that stayed there did so because it was cheap and a bed was better than sleeping across the engine and seats. Needless to say I never stayed there again. If I was in that neck of the woods I stayed at Stirling or Dunfermline or if time allowed I would run to the Dundee Tayside Truck stop or the old Perth Gaol House which had been turned into a truck stop.

CHAPTER FIVE
BRAINS AND MORE

GOOD-BYE TO THE RAILWAYS

IT WAS whilst working at Freightliner, Trafford Park Terminal in 1976, that 3 wagons from a new company in the Park pulled into the depot, the company was Brain Haulage, a well established company from Gray's, West Thurrock, Essex that was expanding and so had opened a depot in Manchester. There were already depots in Liverpool, Birmingham, Tilbury and Southampton and one was due to open at Linwood near Glasgow. To attract drivers Charles Brain was offering a guaranteed 50 hours and a rate much higher than local hauliers, with higher night out money and a fleet of mainly new, sleeper cabbed Scanias. It seemed like a driver's dream job.

As the three vehicles pulled up I noticed that the driver of the first motor was Andy Mann who had worked at Barratt's on the meat haulage. The second vehicle was driven by John Quill who had been a trailer boy on the Railways at the same time as me. The third by a guy known as DJ who it turned out was the shop steward for Brain's Manchester drivers. After a chat and a renewal of old acquaintances DJ got me an interview with the traffic manager, Hugh Gofar, and I was offered a job doing the same work as Freightliner's but for half again as much money and a couple of quid more night out money. Being somewhat pecuniary minded and forever chasing the elusive well paid situation of employment I handed in my notice and started at Brain's a week later. I was put on spot hire working for all the major shipping lines working out of Freightliner and the Container Base and Manchester International Freight Terminal (MIFT). We ran to all the major ports in Britain but mainly to Felixstowe, Greenock, Bristol and Southampton as well as inter-depot work, and averaged between 3 and 5 nights out per week. We sometimes ran three or four of us together to the same destination.

Brains ran as a closed shop and as such I had to cancel my membership to the National Union of Railwaymen (NUR), and join the Transport and General Workers Union (TGWU). If you weren't a member of the T&G you didn't drive for Brains, and one was required to carry, at all times, one's membership card. I thought that this requirement was fine until one day I joined the queue at Seaforth Docks at Liverpool to off-load a container for an outward bound ship. The Scousers are renowned for their militancy in the workplace and Seaforth was no exception.

As I waited in a long line of trucks I noticed a fellow Brain's driver walking along the line of trucks and stopping at each one to talk to each driver. Every now and then a truck would pull out of the line, turn around and leave the docks. The chap responsible for this situation was one Al Astic, a Brain's driver and member of the National Executive of the TGWU. He was from the Liverpool depot situated on Sandhills Lane off the Dock Road and he was in the process of doing a union card check. He reached my vehicle and I said 'Good morning Al, what can I do for you?'

'I'd like to see your union card, please.'

I fumbled through my pockets and came to the realisation that I had not got my card with me. 'I'm sorry Al but I seem to have left my card at home, but you know that I wouldn't be driving a Brain's motor if I wasn't in the union.'

'I cannot accept any excuses,' he said ;'You'll have to turn your motor round and get off the docks.'

'But Al,' I said 'We work for the same company, you know that I'm a union member, don't turn me round on a technicality.'

Mr Astic would have none of it and said 'If I let you on I'd have to let every non card carrying driver on and I can't make any exceptions, sorry, you'll have to leave.'

We argued the point for a while but common sense would not prevail and I had to leave the docks. I took the container round to the depot in Sandhills Lane where it was transferred onto another trailer and one of the Scouse drivers returned to the docks with it. I was loaded at the depot with a container for Manchester.

TOUPEE OR NOT TOUPEE

One of the drivers at Brains was a guy named Al O'Peesher; he was as bald as a coot but wore a toupee to cover up his shortcomings. The wig was a Beatles' style and was fairly long and to Al's mind was undetectable and he thought that no one knew he work a syrup. In fact like most wigs it was totally obvious to all and sundry but as they say, ignorance is bliss. One day, I, DJ, Andy Mann and Al O'Peesher went to load up at Nicholl's Vimto factory in Wythenshawe and run down to Bristol. We all ran together and parked up at the Avonmouth Motel near the docks. We booked two double rooms, DJ and myself in one and Andy and Al in the other. We had a couple of pints and retired to bed. The next morning DJ and me were at the breakfast bar, pondering the dehydrated, culinary delights under the red tinged heat lamps above the victuals on display when Andy came in, he was in paroxysms of laughter. I said 'What's so funny?'

He replied 'I woke up and looked over at Al in the other bed, his rug had slipped round the side of his head, honestly, and I thought he'd broken his bleedin' neck.' Then he almost doubled up with laughter again and laughter being infectious it caused DJ and myself to join in. We had just stopped laughing when Al walked in with his hairpiece reset and that set us off again, much to his bewilderment.

WIVES, LOOSE WOMEN AND GIRLFRIENDS

On the day I started at Brains there was another new starter, a Middle easterner by the name of Mustapha Fuq. He was a nice enough lad but suffered from a very highly charged libido. He was married to an English girl and had two children, but when he was down the road, all thoughts of his family were forgotten and he would attempt to chat up any and every girl in any pub in any town in which he happened to be, so long as they were white girls. He ended up with regular girlfriends in Bristol, Greenock, Northampton and various other regular stopovers.

There was a time, about 2 months after I had started at Brain's when me, DJ and Mustapha, who had anglicised his name to Mike were in Felixstowe, on a Monday night after loading earth moving plant in soft top, tilt containers at Fiat Allis near Stamford, off the A1. We had parked up for the night at the Routemaster, gotten ourselves mopped and stoned and changed into mufti and went into town for a pint or two of the Suffolk brew. We were in one of the pubs when we noticed a couple of the London based Brain's drivers chatting to a bouffanted, peroxide blonde, buxom lass in a mini skirt, low-cut blouse and high heeled boots.

Mike asked DJ 'Who's dat sexy beetch wid de big teets dat de cockerneys a' tockin' to?'

DJ replied 'I believe her name's Jackie, she's a bit of a nympho so the Londoners tell me. In fact the term used was, she's had more prick than a second hand dartboard, and another of the cockneys said she's got more fingerprints on her arse than they've got in Scotland Yard. Apparently she has a particular penchant for truck drivers.'

I'd never heard of her or seen her before but DJ carried on. 'I'm told that she shags like a rabbit and some of the cockneys have had gang bangs with her, personally, I wouldn't touch her with a barge pole, let alone my cock.' he said.

'Spake for y'ursel' said Mike, 'I'd flirt it one.' With that statement he went over and joined the Londoners and their floozy.

As we were talking the two cockneys and Jackie, the woman of easy virtue, walked out of the pub followed quickly by Mike. Me and DJ finished our beers and went after them to keep an eye on Mike.

'Don't rush' said DJ 'apparently she goes down to the beach where it's a bit quiet and lets whoever wants it have it.'

When we reached what was the scene of activities the trollop was on all fours with one of the cockneys banging away at her doggy fashion while the other cockney and Mike stood by watching. Suddenly Mike pulled his cock out pulled a Johnny on and dropped to his knees in front of this strumpet and stuck his bell end into her mouth. Every time the cockney thrust forward from the rear she went forwards onto Mike's knob moaning in pleasure.

Me and DJ decided voyeurism wasn't exactly our cup of tea and we certainly had no intentions of joining in, so in disgust we turned away and went back to the pub. About 30 minutes later, Mike and the cockneys came back with their *'fille de joie'* in tow and continued to drink and chat as if nothing untoward had happened. Apparently this wanton scrubber would go with any driver from any company, irrespective of age or caste. She never charged anyone and the only proviso was that a condom must be worn. Mike was a regular participant whenever he was in Felixstowe. He is now divorced.

Whilst on the subject of casual sex, there was a driver, Steve Priapus, from Brain's Southampton depot who had a problem keeping his cock in his pants whilst away from home, his indiscretions cost him a dose of gonorrhoea. He was at his wits end but must have had some suspicions of his own. He went home one weekend and confronted his wife. He shouted at her, told her he'd been faithful but had ended up with a dose and that he must have gotten it off her. She, in turn, broke down and confessed that while he'd been away she'd had a number of affairs. They became yet another statistic amongst divorced truck drivers.

Mike and I tipped and reloaded for London the next day. DJ loaded for Scotland and we bade him goodbye until the weekend. When nighted out in London the Brain's drivers from the outlaying depots would make for the ramp on Kingsland Road, Shoreditch which was at the Southern end of the A10. The ramp was so called because the entrance to the lorry park, which was situated on Railway land, was up an incline which took one to the land above Shoreditch and which carried the line into Liverpool Street Station. There were usually 3 or 4 or more Brain's drivers parked up on the ramp on any given night plus drivers from many other firms from all over the nation.

The usual plan of operations once parked up was to get ones washing gear and towel and walk over to the gentlemen's washroom at Liverpool Street Rail Station, pay the attendant and give him a tip, get oneself sluiced off and return to the lorry park for a change of clothes. Once changed, we would take ourselves to one of the many Greek or Maltese Cafés around the area. After our repast we would take a walk around the Bethnal Green Road area and try a couple of the East end pubs.

On this night Mike and I parked up the ramp it was unusual that amongst all the other drivers, there happened to be just the 2 of us from Brain's parked up there. Mustapha or Mike as he preferred to be called was from the Eastern end of the Mediterranean and as such ate quite a healthy diet. Apart from the kebabs he loved he always carried with him, or kept in his cab, numerous pieces of fruit.

We were, this particular night, walking along the back streets around Bethnal Green Road, getting close to closing time, looking for a different pub to try when Mike spoke just as we were passing a pub from which loud music was issuing. What I heard was 'Do you fancy a meander in?' so I walked through the door followed by Mike. Once in the pub he tapped me on the shoulder. As I turned around he was holding out his hand with a tangerine like fruit clasped in it which he was offering me. What he had actually asked was: Did I fancy a Mandarin? I really should have known better. Mike's limited English didn't stretch to words like meander.

A lot of the pubs had strippers on and this was one of those. There was one stripper that did a number of different pubs in the area in one night. This particular disrobing artiste was known by the soubriquet of Slack Alice, and one of her props was a bowler hat and she was performing in that very pub that same evening. I had never seen her act before although I had heard about her from other drivers.

Alice started her act as any other stripper does by doing a very amateurish erotic dance while slowing removing various items of attire. When she had stripped completely, except for the bowler, she would place a beer bottle to one side of the stage, stand over it and slowly lower herself onto it by squatting down. The neck of the bottle would enter her vagina, where, by what I think must be very good muscle control, she would stand up again, walk across the stage, squat and deposit the bottle on a tray which was situated on the floor at the other side, she would then take a bow for applause. This act was accomplished without the use of her hands.

That however was not the finish of Alice's talents. She would walk amongst the customers wearing not a stitch and getting groped as she walked by. She would approach a table and lean over until one of her nipples was dangling in some punters beer. She would then offer the dripping tit into the mouth of the said punter. She would then return to the stage and remove the bowler hat and place it on a table. People would throw coins and notes into the hat until it held a reasonable amount of cash.

Alice would then select some young, handsome, half pissed, punter, which let me off the hook on all counts, and invite him onto the stage. Mike at this time was doing his best to catch the attention of Alice without any luck. When she had made her choice and gotten him on the stage she would undo his belt and flies and drop his trousers. She would then grab hold of his flaccid or semi erect member, give it a couple of jerks to stiffen it up, roll a condom on, drop to her knees and proceed to perform the act of fellatio on the young fellow. After a couple of minutes the recipient of this oral massage would shudder visibly and grab hold of Alice's head and make a couple of late thrusts. She would then pull his knob from her mouth and with finger and thumb, dangle it towards her audience to show that the condom's bubble was full of sperm. She would then jump to her feet and run through a door at the back of the stage leaving the somewhat bewildered bloke on the stage with his trousers around his ankles and a filled up condom on his cock. Whether the blow job was performed at each venue I didn't know, but I was later told it was just a once a night finale, and I am sure that sooner or later an arrest would turn out to be the conclusion of her act.

Alice would, a couple of minutes later, reappear, fully clothed, once again, and walk back through the pub, valise in hand and disappear into the night. The bar staff would then start to clear the pub.

Most long distance trampers of my time were married quite happily or lived over the brush with their partners and didn't stray. The unmarried or uncommitted tramper could do as he pleased, whether he had a regular girlfriend or not and there was always the married driver that liked to score and put another notch on his trouser belt whenever he could. The number of offers that we drivers would get from prostitutes just after some money or lonely women just after some attention was quite unbelievable, especially to someone like me who had not been blessed with classic good looks. Midnight knocks upon the cab door, when parked up for the night, became a nuisance to me but a looked forward to pleasure for the likes of Mike, besides, my cash was too hard earned to waste on such frivolities.

The wives of these long distance truck drivers knew what they were taking on when they got married or accepted the situation if their spouses moved from local work to distance work, to attempt to forge a better life for the family. Most of these wives who were left at home were, to all intents and purposes, one parent families until the week end. They had to bring the kids up alone, tend to the housework and home management and maybe hold down a full or part time job, plus a multiplicity of chores that their semi absent husbands took for granted. Most of these wives are paragons, 100 carat diamonds.

It is true that there was and is bound to be the occasional woman who cannot survive without her hubby and will seek pleasure in the arms of another, but for each of these loose women, there are helluva lot more that believe in fidelity and the family and besides, with all the work they had to do, they were probably too knackered for extra marital affairs.

GRAFFITI AND A PUNCH UP

The day after the evening in Bethnal Green, Mike and I parted for different tipping points in London. Once I was unloaded I was sent back to Felixstowe. I arrived at the port in time to be unloaded and reloaded, which left just enough time to pull into the Routemaster. Like lots of other drivers on container work, we at Brain's, spent a lot of time at Felixstowe. In one of the shipping line office waiting rooms, the management put up a graffiti board so that bored drivers could jot down their thoughts, instead of defacing the walls, whilst waiting for their notes. There were the usual salutations to various football clubs, MUFC, R GR8., SHEFFIELD BLADES ARE SHARP, etc. the mediocre, such as BE ALERT……..WE NEED LERTS, the crude, such as RING*******FOR GOOD SEX, and, ALL BRAIN'S DRIVERS ARE WANKERS, or EAT SHIT, A BILLION FLIES CAN'T BE WRONG, or alternatively, EAT AT JOE'S CAFÉ, A MILLION FLIES CAN'T BE WRONG. Amongst all this dross there was the odd witticism like, CRAZY PAVING ISN'T ALL IT'S CRACKED UP TO BE or I'D GIVE MY RIGHT ARM TO BE AMBIDEXTROUS or DYSLEXIA RULES K.O. and I USED TO BE INDECISIVE, BUT NOW I'M NOT SO SURE or GIVE ALL MASOCHISTS A FAIR CRACK OF THE WHIP.

The sheet on which these thoughts and opinions were written was changed periodically, and fresh thoughts and opinions would be written down and so the cycle continued.

It was this very night, in the Routemaster, in Felixstowe that a fight broke out between one of the Brain's drivers from London and one from Manchester. The initial argument was over a game of poker in which accusations of cheating were bandied about. The argument soon developed into pushing and shoving and before long the first punch was thrown. This soon developed into a free for all between the Manchester drivers and the Londoners. It was on this night that one of the Manchester drivers, one Niall Pummeller, earned himself the nickname of 'Rocky' because of his undisputed pugilistic skills. He waded in and flattened 3 or 4 of the Londoners in as many seconds, with as many blows. This show of pure aggression and fearlessness brought the scrap to an abrupt halt as people tried to get out of the way of this seemingly mad man from Manchester. After the cessation of hostilities, I am only too glad to say I was on the same side as Rocky. There were one or two black eyes and bruises to members of both the battling factions, although there were no serious injuries. Everyone that had been involved chipped in to pay for breakages, the pot from the poker game was thrown in and apologies were made to the proprietor and bar staff. This was done to convince the guy in charge not to involve the police, and so things were smoothed over.

A RUDE AWAKENING

There were usually a number of Brain's vehicles parked up at the Routemaster Motel and Truck Stop at Felixstowe. Some would have just arrived at the port and were waiting to go in on the following day. Others would have been waiting on the docks for most of the day and having finally gotten their containers and not having much running time left, would pull into the Routemaster to spend the night.

A couple of weeks after Rocky's fight night there were 8 of us from various depots parked at the Routemaster. From Manchester there was Myself, DJ, and Andy Mann and the assistant shop steward Barry Hyland. There were 2 London drivers, 1 from Southampton and 1 from Birmingham.

We were all parked up in a row against the perimeter fence. There was a gap between my vehicle and Andy's that was just wide enough to accommodate another vehicle, but only just. The drivers from London, Southampton and Birmingham had already gone inside the motel for their evening meals and we Manchester drivers decided to follow them.

Whilst we were partaking of our repast a Brain's driver from Liverpool, one of a pair of brothers called Smith that both worked for Brain's made his entrance and joined us. 'Orright fellas?' he asked and we all replied in the affirmative.

Andy asked 'Where have you parked Smiffy?'

'Between two of the fleet by the fence, Lah, there was a gap just wide enough to get in, it were tight like, but I gorrit in.'

'Sod me Scouse,' said Andy 'you won't have left me much room to get into my cab, it's a good job I've only had a salad for tea.'

The Liverpudlian responded 'I'll tell you worr'll do Lah. I'll go an' move it an' darr'll give you a bit more room to gerrin' your cab; burrit seems a shame to spoil such a nice line up o' Brain's motors. It'd make a luvvly phota dat, wunnit?'

'No, leave it now, Scouse; the lorry park'll be nearly full by now. I'll struggle for one night and use the passenger door.'

We all finished our meals, got showered and changed. Those that wanted a room booked one and those that decided to cab it did just that. It happens that the only two to cab it were Smith the Scouser and Andy. The Scouser failed to mention that he was going to hit the road at 0500.

The next morning, Scouse fired up his motor at 0500 and started to pull out. The rear, near side twist lock had not been locked into place and thus protruded, sticking out about 6 inches. As he pulled forward and started to steer to the right, the back end of the trailer swung out to the left. If it had not been for the protruding twist lock handle everything may been alright. Unfortunately, the projecting handle made contact with Andy's cab at the rear of the sleeping compartment and as Scouser continued his manoeuvre and because of the camber of the yard, the back end of his trailer started to lift Andy's cab and push it sideways as the twist lock dug deeper into the metal cab. As this Merseyside buffoon continued and completed his turn the twist lock handle popped free, dropping Andy's cab suddenly and flipping Andy out of his top bunk as neatly as a pea from a pod.

Andy awoke in bewilderment, sprawled between the seats of his cab. He soon recovered his composure and disentangled himself from his sleeping bag. He quickly wound down his window to shout after the rapidly departing Liverpudlian who was now accelerating towards Ipswich apparently oblivious to what had happened. Andy got dressed and exited his cab to survey the damage and by now we had all been awoken by the noise of rent metal groaning trailers and shouting. The damaged cab had a tear along its side starting as a deep gash and finishing at the drivers door as a diminishing scratch.

The incident was duly reported and when the Liverpool driver was asked for his account of what happened he said he knew 'bugger all about it.' The workshop at Brain's Manchester carried out the remedial work and the incident was not mentioned unless a number of Brain's drivers were together and then the story grew in the telling.

JACK KNIVES AND CAR TRANSPORTERS

DJ, myself and Rocky were sent, one day, in the middle of the winter of 1976/77 to a chemical and pigment company in Stallingborough near Grimsby to load 20 tonnes apiece into 20ft containers for Felixstowe. I was last to load and made arrangements to meet the other two at the cattle market at Stamford, Lincs, just off the A1. It was about 17.20hrs by the time I had loaded and being midwinter it had turned dark around 16.00hrs. I realised that there was no way I was going to make it to Stamford that night and thought I might make Morley's Café at Markham Moor on the A1. I headed off towards Brigg along the old A18. The M180 wasn't constructed then and the route was through Brigg onto Scunthorpe and over Gunness Bridge and down to the A1. This was a better route than the seemingly more direct and shorter route down the A46 through Market Rasen and Lincoln. Besides we were paid by the mile as a bonus. Unfortunately, as I approached the village of Wrawby where the B1206 joins the A18, a car cut me up and caused me to brake suddenly. Black ice had formed in the freezing conditions and I experienced for the one and only time in my driving career, the sheer terror of a jack-knife situation. As I braked my wheels locked. I looked into my rear view mirror to be greeted by the sight of my trailer swinging round, at what appeared to be great speed, to greet my cab. The vehicle that caused the problem was gone as quick as it had appeared and by the time my trailer had completed its uncalculated response to my braking action and collided with my unit to spin me 360 degrees. I was the only vehicle on that stretch of road, thank goodness, and thanks also to the fact I wasn't pulling a 40ft trailer. Things happened so fast that I didn't get the number of the vehicle that cut me up and I doubt that anything could have been proved one way or the other if I had.

When the trailer made impact with the unit it pushed the rear corner of the cab in, flipping the window out, leaving me with a nice line in air conditioning. The overall damage was not too bad, but I was pretty shaken up and made for an old transport café just through Brigg on the A18. I reached the café at about 1830hrs. there was a couple of overnight trucks on the lorry park but the café was closed although the toilets were unlocked and there was a public telephone so I could at least get a wash and phone the Manchester depot and home. I found a piece of planking which, with the help of some rags and old newspapers and the assistance of the two drivers that were parked up for the night, I filled the gaping hole where the rear corner window used to be. Luckily the vehicle had a night heater, so I got into my sleeping bag and slept as best I could. Next morning when I awoke the café was open so I attended to my toilet needs and went inside for a very satisfying breakfast. the topic of conversation inside the café was of the Brain's Scania with the rearranged bodywork.

When I finally got to Felixstowe, Rocky and DJ were still there and knew all about my little mishap, via the jungle telegraph, and I was christened 'Jack the Knife.' I was loaded back for Manchester so that the damage to my vehicle could be assessed and repaired. I spent a week working in the Manchester depot yard with a crane driver, slinging the chains for container lifts and helping in the loading of containers on and off Brain's and other contractors trailers. When my allocated vehicle came out of the repair shop, I was sent with another driver by the name of Joe Kerr to load out of a local engineering company in Trafford Park for onward delivery to Felixstowe, with loaded 40fts for export. The route we took was down the M6 and M1 and along the old A45 through Northampton to Cambridge. The A14 by pass now runs from the M6/M1 junction, through to Felixstowe. We were following a car transporter through the many villages that dot this route, Higham Ferrers, Kimbolton, Great Staunton and St

Neots etc. These villages were not built to allow the passage of 50ft vehicles through them. The villagers, obviously, did not want us there and we, obviously, did not wish to be there, but this was the main route through to Huntingdon, Cambridge and so on to Ipswich and Felixstowe. In this respect by pass roads like the A14 are a blessing.

The car transporter that we were behind was of the articulated type whereby the trailer extended over the cab of the prime mover to allow an extra car to be carried. The problem that arises with this type of vehicle is that when taking a corner and the cab turns, the trailer is still facing forwards. This problem, latterly, has been alleviated by the use of close coupled, draw bar trailers, whereby the car loaded atop of the prime mover is now an integral part of that prime mover, and as such turns when the prime mover turns.

On the day in question, whilst negotiating a rather tight corner in one of the many villages along this route, the driver of the car transporter must have had a mental block for a moment. Either that or he was concentrating too much on what the back end of his trailer was doing and misjudged the proximity of the forward overhang to the row of cottages, or he may have slid on ice. There was a loud shout of 'WHOA, STOP, BLOODY 'ELL!' but it was too late, there was a loud crunch. The upper part of the trailer had become embedded in the corner of one of the quaint, timber framed cottages, of which these villages consist, causing extensive damage to the property, the trailer, and the lead car on the trailer. Because the emergency services had to be called to the scene, nothing much moved through the village for the next few hours and diversions were set up. Joe Kerr and I, because we were directly behind the transporter, were totally caught up in the aftermath. There was no place or room to turn an artic around and so we were unable to go anywhere. We had to wait for the transporter to be extricated from its, somewhat, inglorious position, and for any debris to be removed before we could resume our journeys. We made it into Felixstowe with minutes to spare and parked up at the Routemaster.

AN OLD GEORDIE TART

Early next morning I got a quick turn round and was loaded with a container for Newcastle upon Tyne and I left Joe Kerr in Felixstowe to await orders. It transpired that later in the day I pulled onto Washington Service Area for a dinner break. I'd brewed a mug of tea from my flask and just started a sandwich that I had bought earlier, when a black, customised, long wheel based, Transit camper van pulled up by the side of my Scania. The Transit had tinted windows all round an emblazoned down the side in bold script was the legend 'PASSION WAGON.' I looked down out of curiosity and as I did so the passenger window of the van, slid down. There sat a grey haired lady with her hair tied back in a bun, looking distinctly like a retired school mistress. She smiled up at me and proceeded to undo her blouse. She had no bra on and a massive pair of blue veined, stretch marked breasts flopped out. They looked like 2 white, Hessian sacks, each containing a large melon in the bottom. The old lady arranged herself so as to be facing me in her seat, hoisted one of these pendulous mammaries and started tweaking its strawberry coloured nipple, as if she were twisting the tuning dial on a transistor radio. It was then that she spoke in a broad Geordie accent, saying 'How'd ya lake to get your gob around that, canny lad?' she then lifted her skirt, revealing thread veined, flabby, dimpled, well battered, pasty white thighs and started to rub her crotch saying 'Ya can shag us in the back of the van if ya wanna. I usually ask a fiver, pet, but if ya let me boyfriend watch us while he jerks hisself off, ya can have it for noot. If ya dain't want a shag, lake, I'll gi' ya a good gobble, but'

As she was telling me this a bespectacled, old gent leaned across her and smiled up at me, he was already pulling steadily on his erection.

I said 'I'm sorry love but I'm not interested.'

The old lady, she looked like and probably was someone's granny, said 'Whay ay, ya bugga, ya can do us doggyways while I'm gan doon on him if that's what ya want, but.' She said nodding towards her companion, who was still tugging on his tosser.

'Sorry, I've told you, I'm not interested.' I reiterated.

She persevered offering all kinds of sexual favours until I said 'Look love, you're puttin' me off me butties, if you don't bugger off I'll phone the police.'

'Fuck ya' she said 'ya doon't know what yar missing. Ya never heard of in praise of owdah women? Well sod ya, ya fuckin' wanka.'

With that they reversed to the truck that had pulled in behind me. I watched through my mirrors and after a couple of minutes the driver, a guy of about 60, got out and got into the Transit which made its way to a quiet corner of the Service Area. After about 15 minutes the trucker emerged from the back of the Transit, adjusting his attire, and made his way back to his truck. The Transit continued to pull up at various trucks and proposition the drivers, but the only one I saw take up the offer was the guy in the truck behind mine.

The old couple were still cruisin' the Service Area when I pulled away with my dignity and tackle intact.

INCEST

The following week I had picked up an empty 20ft container from OOCL's depot in Trafford Park. I loaded out of a fancy goods warehouse in Cheetham, the Jewish quarter of Manchester for delivery to Greenock docks. When I reached Greenock my working hours were almost expended and so I cabbed it on the dock road overnight, and went into the docks early the next morning where I was at the front of the queue for unloading.

While I was waiting for the straddle crane to lift my container, another vehicle from Manchester arrived and joined the line. It was a middle aged guy that I knew, called Ivor Dickinson, who worked for a rival company of Brain's. His nickname was Incest, quite obvious if a little thought is employed. He too had loaded at the fancy goods warehouse directly after me, the day previous.

I watched in my mirrors as he tentatively climbed out of his vehicle like an incapacitated monkey. As he struggled down from his cab his foot slipped from the bottom step, he fell on his arse, looked around him, as you do, to ascertain that nobody had seen his mishap. He quickly sprang to his feet and proceeded to hobble over to my vehicle as if he had two clubfeet which were giving him some difficulty. When he reached my truck I said 'Good Morning, Incest. I thought you'd a' made it last night. What happened and why are you walking like you've got drawing pins in your boots?'

'You wouldn't believe it.' He said, sitting on a capstan and taking off one boot and sock and showing me his foot. All his toes except his pinkie were swollen and various shades including purple, black and blue amongst others tending to a yellow hue.

'The other one's the bleedin' same' he continued. 'I ran outa' time near Paisley and I saw this pub with a bloody great big car park with a couple of local tipper wagons parked on it, so I went inside and asked the landlord if I could park up there for the night. He said if I bought a meal and 'ad a few drinks I could park up on his car park next to the other trucks and he would make me out a £6.00 parkin' ticket, so that's what I did. In the middle of the night I woke up burstin' for a piss, so I got outa' mi sleepin' bag wi' just mi jockey's on. I opened the passenger door, it was bloody freezin' and snowin' like fuck, so I stood on the edge of the passenger floor well and pissed out into the night. When I'd finished I tucked old Percy back in mi jockey's and slammed the door shut. Unfortunately mi tootsies were over'angin' the floor well and I trapped 'em between the door and the floor. It's a good job there was no one else about 'cos I screamed blue murder and swore like a bastard trooper. I was frightened of op'nin' the door in case mi bloody toes fell off. I finally summoned up the courage and opened it. Mi toes were throbbin; like hell an' still are an' now they've gone all the colours of the bleedin' rainbow. I've 'ad' 'ardly any soddin' kip 'cos I'm in bloody agony. I've swallowed half a dozen Paracetamol pills but the pain won't go an' it's givin' mi some right gyp.'

'You'd better go to the local hospital then.' I said.

'Sod that' he said 'I'll see if I can get a box back for Manchester and go to mi local 'ospital.'

When Ivor returned to Manchester and went to his local hospital his feet were X-rayed and there were no broken bones. He had suffered severe contusions and severe embarrassment as he told me the next time I saw him and he had returned to a normal mode of perambulation.

TA-TA TO BRAIN'S

Brain Haulage was becoming one of the biggest and best known companies in Britain with over 300 Scanias running. Charlie Brain also had a fleet in Saudi Arabia. The company even got a mention on Radio 2 by the presenter, the late Ray Moore, who had a nice sense of humour and said on his show one day, 'On my way to work today, three of these Brain Haulage trucks passed me, what I want to know is where do they get all those brains from and where do they haul them to? There must be a great demand for Brain's.

At the time Brain Haulage was held in the same esteem as Eddie Stobart is today and was equally as big. The yard in Trafford Park had become too small as the Manchester fleet grew and so a new and larger yard was acquired at Sharp Street, Worsley. All the drivers, including myself, thought they were in the land of milk and honey and that they had got a job for life with good pay, good vehicles, good night-out money and decent gaffers, but after 2 years, rumours of difficulties within the company started to fly around. The difficulties may have arisen during the driver's strike of 1978. Charles Brain granted his drivers the rise that was required but insisted that we strike with our brethren. The strike lasted only a few weeks before we returned to work.

We drivers should have known something was amiss when Hugh Gofar found pastures new and went working for a rival container haulage operator, followed shortly by his assistant. DJ convened a meeting to discuss what to do next and even arranged a meeting with the other depots and then went down to Grays to speak to Charles Brain who assured everyone that everything was alright and that the company was quite solvent and healthy. Then came the first redundancies and I and Mustapha being the last ones in, at Manchester, were the first out. DJ who had to deliver the news, said he was sorry he'd gotten me such a short lived job.

It seemed that Brain's grew too quickly and relied solely on container transport instead of diversifying. In essence, Charlie Brain had all his eggs in the proverbial single basket. Other companies such as Abbey Hill Transport, besides running containers, had a car transportation section and other companies filled in the lean times with general haulage on flat bed trailers which were also fitted with twist locks. Brains had no flat bed trailers, all Brain's trailers were skeletal trailers capable of carrying containers only and therefore allowing for no diversification.

DJ told me of a guy he knew and who he had worked for, in Rhodes, Middleton, who was always taking drivers on. The company he knew was a scrap metal business that also did general tipper work. DJ said 'You'll be all right, I used to work there and there's plenty of hey-diddle-diddle.' (Fiddle). I went to see the owner of the scrap metal company who told me 'All the on road jobs are taken at this time and the only job I have going at the moment is driving an 8 legger tipper around Agecroft Colliery and power station, tipping coal and slag and running ash to Thermalite on the same site. The pay is union rate. It's a week in hand and I'll bring your wages to Agecroft every Friday afternoon. You can put as many hours in as you want, but don't forget to book them on your time sheet. The operation is solely within the confines of the Agecroft complex, but the job's yours if you want it.'

I replied 'O.K., I'll take it and thanks.'

'Right' he said 'Be at Agecroft at 7 0.clock on Monday morning.'

And with that I bade him good day.

The job at the power station, colliery was literally the pits. I had taken a cut in basic pay but that was better than being out of work and I could fatten my pay packet by booking excess hours without working them. The on site wagon was an old road going vehicle, running on red diesel that was siphoned, via a hand pump, from a 45 gallon drum which was refilled weekly. Engine oil was obtained by the same method and it was a toss up whether the vehicle used more oil than diesel. That knackered old 8 legger had out-lived its usefulness as a haulage truck and had been demoted to the rank of pit pony and a pit pony on its last legs at that. After about 3 weeks tipping ash at Thermalite, for the manufacture of breeze blocks, I got talking to a local Jewish hauler, named David Ailion who had a contract with Thermalite. He offered me a job delivering breeze blocks, on a 4 wheeler flat bed, to local building sites. I took the job but only stuck it for a couple of weeks. I thought there has to be something better than hand-balling 2, ten ton loads of breeze block per day.

Within the next 18 months to 2 years Brain's Manchester operation ceased and all the drivers were finished. It wasn't long after that the whole Brain's company folded.

My next job around early 1979 was with a Middleton based company called Fashion Express. Fashion Express had a contract with Richard's Shops, a women's clothing outlet. My job was to trunk a load down to London, tip and reload and return to Manchester the same day. My starting time was 0900hrs so that I would start my trip after the rush hour had subsided.

Twenty odd years ago there was not the same volume of traffic on our roads as there is today. Even so, London and back in a day with tip and reload was a bloody good day's work. I had to do it every week, Monday to Friday.

The route I took was onto the M6 down to the end of the M1, down Hendon Way to Swiss Cottage, across to Chalk Farm Road and Camden Street and Hampstead Road and into Richard's Shops Depot which was situated to the rear of Euston Station but was inaccessible from Marylebone Road. The round trip was 430 miles. 2150 miles per week and 25,800 miles in the 3 months I did the job. This would equate to well over 100,000 miles in a year.

The load consisted of hanging garments in a tandem axle 40ft trailer. The motive unit was a 7 litre Volvo F7. There wasn't a lot of weight involved but when one takes into consideration the high mileage and the type of driving required a higher specified vehicles was needed for the job.

Upon reaching Richard's shops London Depot I would

reverse onto the loading bay and take my statutory 45 minutes break whilst the Richard's shops staff unloaded and reloaded the trailer. This took between 45 minutes and 1 hour. When I had finished my break I would complete the necessary paperwork, close and lock the trailer and head back to Manchester returning to Middleton at approximately 1930hrs, where I would fuel up before clocking off.

It was pedal to the metal driving, both ways, praying that there were no hold ups or breakdowns or crashes. It was a white knuckle ride. I was speeding on the 'A' roads and running flat out on the motorways, shouting, to no avail, at other drivers to get out of my way. It was the only way the job could be done in a day.

I left after 3 months because the owner had introduced an extra collection to the job. This collection would be done after reloading at Richard's Shops and only consisted of a couple of cartons to be picked up at an industrial estate off Hendon Way, North London, but the job was so tightly scheduled that this extra pick up could mean the difference between running bent and running straight. I now considered the job too much. My nerves were shredded; I was becoming a danger to myself and other road users. I had had enough, I was permanently tired and going about my duties like an automaton in a zombie like state. I was running bent to line the pockets of the gaffer, which I resented. I was paid a fairly high rate, but not high enough for the effort put in. The job was having an adverse effect on my health and on my temperament and home life, and the extra collection was the final imposition, so I looked for pastures new with decent pay and a more sedate pace of work.

Whilst I was sat at home, one day perusing the situations vacant in the local paper I received a phone call from a guy that ran a stall at the fruit and veg market which had relocated from its old site at Smithfield to a new site on Ashton Old Road at

Openshaw in 1973. How this fellow had heard of my plight I have no idea but he offered me a job driving a Cummins powered, old Seddon 32:4 pulling a 40ft flat bed tandem axle semi trailer that he had bought second hand. I told him I would give it a try and he told me to meet him at the market at 0600hrs the following morning. I turned up bright and early next day and was greeted by my new boss who gave me the keys to his pride and joy. He had had it serviced and given a new paint job. There were 2 new sheets neatly folded and tied down against 2 stacks of pallets. My job was to go to Salford Docks to pick up 20 tons of Arabian potatoes and deliver them to Liverpool, Edge Lane, fruit and veg Market.

When I arrived at the dock I discovered that the job was not as straightforward as I had been told. The potatoes were lying on the quayside on the shippers over sized pallets from which they had to be transhipped onto the pallets on my vehicle. This also was not as straightforward as it seemed. After being in the ship's hold for God knows how long, these potatoes were starting to soften and go mouldy and so I had to separate the good from the bad, the wet from the dry. Approximately 4 hours after I had started to load and having handled about 40 tons to get a decent 20 ton load, which was all handball, I started to sheet and rope the load. When the roping and sheeting was finished I climbed, with great difficulty, into the cab. I had started the day as a fit man, who visited the gym whenever time allowed, now I had severe back strain. I had pulled muscles I didn't know I had and every bone in my body ached. I drove to the market at Liverpool where I expected to be unloaded by a stacker truck. It was not until I had stripped the ropes and sheets from the load that I was told by the stall owner that there was just me and him to unload and yes, you've guessed, it was all handball. By the time I was unloaded it was about 1400hrs and I couldn't stand up straight, so I hobbled, bent over like a creaking old man to the nearest telephone and phoned my boss. I said 'I'm tipped at Liverpool…….' but before I could explain my position the voice on the other end of the line said, 'Good, could you nip back to the docks for another load for delivery to Liverpool in the morning?' I replied 'No it's not good. Could you nip to the market and meet me at your stall in about an hour and have my day's wages with you? My back's achin' and near broken and you can get some other mug to do your donkey work. You don't need a driver, you need Superman.'

THE MOTORWAY BUILDER

When I said goodbye to the market trader, work had started on the M67 motorway which joined the A57 from Denton to the A57 Glossop road and the A628 Woodhouse Park road at Mottram. The company that had secured the tender for this job was Pickavance of St Helens, and they were advertising for 6 and 8 wheel tipper drivers to work on site, as well as grader drivers and machine drivers of all sorts. The pay was well above the national average for lorry drivers, and there was the opportunity to work 7 days per week to further increase the remuneration package, so in my quest for more spondulicks and greater wealth I signed on for Mr Pickavance. By this time my knowledge of tippers was greatly improved and the site was mainly a dry working area.

There was a quarry at the site with a rock crusher and the tippers loaded there with which ever grade of stone was needed at the time. There was also a workshop with a team of mechanics to keep the vehicles running. The job was twelve hours a day, seven days a week. This was allowed, but not compulsory, because we never went off site. All the vehicles ran on red diesel which was available on site. The majority of employees within the site, no matter what job they were employed to do, were either Irish or of Irish descent, with just a smattering of local lads. This ratio was the norm on road building projects or any other civil engineering jobs.

I was given an old split windscreen AEC Mammoth Major, *circa* late 50's - early 60's to drive. All the vehicles were of this vintage or a little earlier, all had cracked windscreens and multiple body and cab scars and they were worked until they expired or until no amount of on-going maintenance could resuscitate them. They would then be cannibalised to keep other trucks running. I'm sure that beneath the M67 there lies the LGV; equivalent of the elephants graveyard where lie numerous chassis and cabs of vehicles that outlived their usefulness and expired on the job.

The need for onsite workshop soon became evident. One particular day I was following an AEC Mercury down a steep decline to a tipping point when a bloody great lump of rock fell off the side of the load of the truck in front. This rock, which had somehow evaded the crusher, landed directly in my path causing me to brake violently. The wheels locked and being on an ungraded roadway of loose shale on a steep decline I slid forward. My speed, initially, increased and then the vehicle abruptly came to a halt as I hit the boulder. The seat mountings snapped under the strain and the seat and I shot forward. My lower body stopped when my midriff squashed against the steering wheel but my upper torso carried on, stopping when my head hit the windshield. This caused the loosely held windshield to break free from the perished rubber seal and tumble to the ground in front of the now stationary vehicle. I climbed out of the ancient cab to survey the damage. My head and upper torso were bumped and bruised and my midriff ached but apart from that I seemed to be OK. The truck had suffered slightly more than I. The offside wheel pointed forwards in line with the vehicle whilst the near side pointed outwards at an angle of about 45 degrees. The track rod had succumbed to the stress of such conditions and was bent to a ridiculous angle, and the bumper was practically destroyed. The tow truck was sent for and the damaged vehicle was towed back to the workshop. Within a couple of hours it was repaired, or rather bodged up, and back in the fray, earning its keep once more. The same cracked windscreen was refitted using a new rubber seal and a length of steel girder had been welded to the chassis to replace the bumper.

My time at this particular occupation was bout 3 months in the summer of 1978. For the last month I was put on water bowser duties. The bowser, which was of the same age as the rest of the vehicles, was an old split windscreen AEC, KV model with the Elliptical radiator grill. It was the only vehicle that was taxed, albeit, as plant. It was an old road tanker fitted with a spray mechanism and was used to spray the local roads and the roads within the site to keep the dust down, due to complaints from local residents. I soon got fed up of working seven days a week and so decided to sign on, for awhile, with an agency, although with the money I had earned I could have taken a month's sabbatical.

The M67 motorway was completed and opened, without any further assistance from me, in September 1981.

AGENCY WORK

The agency, I signed on for, made all kinds of promises, as agencies do, about regular work and blue chip companies but the work was intermittent and mainly the kind of jobs nobody else wanted. I found out, at the time, that no matter how much experience one may have, the agency driver is treated as a pariah and viewed as someone who can't get a proper job.

I was sent, by the agency, to a well known logistics company in Trafford Park, where I was given the keys to a unit which was already coupled up to its trailer. I was checking it over when I spotted that the off side mirror arm was broken along with the actual glassware. I went back to the transport office to report the damage. There were a number of drivers there who actually worked for this company, and as I was reporting the damage one of these drivers, a youngster of about 21, muttered, 'Fuckin' agency drivers, waste o' bleedin' time.'

'What did you say?' I demanded angrily.

'Er, I was only jokin' mate.'

'Well, keep your fuckin' jokes to yourself, anyhow, how old are you?' I asked.

'Nearly 22.'

'How long have you held a Class one?'

'3 months.'

'Well listen to me, tenderfoot,' I said 'I've been driving artics for 15 years and I've done more miles in reverse than you've done forward, so button your lip.' It was then that the yard Marshall and shunter, an old driver nearing retirement age, spoke up 'He's right yer know.' He said to the youngster. 'I watched yeh pull yer motor out before an' I watched the back end of your trailer wipe his mirror arm out. Now yeh know what yer'd done, but yeh thought yer'd put the blame on an innocent agency driver. I was gonna report it meself, but now yer've dropped yersel' in the shite yer've saved me a job. An' as far as I'm concerned, yer'll never make a driver while yer've got 'ole in yer arse.'

The youth was summoned into the office for a reprimand and to complete an accident report. A new mirror arm was fitted and I continued with the job, but I thought what a good job that the yard Marshall had witnessed the young whippersnapper commit the transgression and I hoped he, the young un', would get his comeuppance. Young drivers weren't like that in my day, I thought. A considerable amount of modern young drivers are nothing more than motorway jockeys. Take them away from the motorways and the adjacent industrial parks and they're lost. If they are diverted off the motorway for some reason or another, such as a major accident or the like, one sees the nearby lay-by's full of inexperienced young drivers with road atlases open across the steering wheel as they consult them to find a reasonable diversion along the 'A' roads we elder statesmen of the road take for granted.

Whilst working for the agency I was sent to a company that delivered to various sports equipment shops nationwide. I was given a Scottish run to do in a tired out, dilapidated old Leyland Riever, 4 wheeled box van. This pooped out old vehicle had about twenty drops on board.

Any driver worth his salt knows how to get to most major towns and cities in the UK without the use of a map. Finding the actual address in the town is, however, a different problem as no driver can possibly store, in his head, the encyclopaedic knowledge of every A-Z of all the conurbations in Britain. Bearing this in mind, this job that I had been allocated worked out at a 3 day run, i.e. 2 nights out. I had town maps and directions for most of the drops but not for all. One that I had no map or directions for was a little retail outlet in Perth. Before I left the depot with this run, I was told that the Perth drop was close to the large B&Q Warehouse and that if I found that, then I should find the shop.

When I reached Perth, and was close to the area where the shop was located, I decided to ask for directions. I pulled into the side of the road and waited for a male pedestrian who was approaching. As he got close to my vehicle I got out of my cab, with notes in hand, to apprehend him. He stopped, upon being confronted by yours truly, and I asked 'Excuse me mate, do you know where the B&Q is in Perth?'

He responded 'Och nay mon, but I ken where the two E's are in Dundee.' And walked away.

I managed to find a more amenable local and thus found the B&Q and the small sports shop for which I was searching. I made my delivery and continued to my next drop. I completed the run without further incident.

My next assignment for this agency was a job with a company in Ardwick. The company was called Curry's Transport and was based on the site of a former company also called Curry's who specialised in the collection from farms and delivery to retail outlets, of eggs. I had delivered to them, years earlier, whilst on the Railways. They had always given the driver a dozen eggs as a gratuity to stop the driver from pinching his own, although this perquisite did not stop the dedicated thief that liked large omelettes and egg custards.

The Curry's that by this time occupied the site, which was originally the site of St Andrew's Church, Ardwick, was a general haulage outfit that did a lot of groupage work for Ireland. They also had the contract for the MAKRO Cash and Carry Warehouses, nationally, which, after a few weeks on general haulage and groupage work, I was offered. After about 3 months of working like a donkey on the MAKRO contract, starting at all unearthly hours and running maximum hours every week for poor pay, and generally working myself to a frazzle, I was offered the job permanently at the same rate as the agency paid. Because of the work load and high turn over of drivers, combined with no increase in wages, I declined.

After Curry's I was sent to a company in Bury that specialised in the delivery of stationery to offices all over the North-West. I was given an old clapped out 4 wheeler and told that I had 25 drops around the Merseyside region. All the drops were in town centres and a lot of these offices had no loading bay or delivery entrance. The deliveries were made off the main road through the front door. This meant parking on double yellow lines or double parking, which in turn led to arguments with traffic wardens, police officers and the staff of which ever office one happened to be delivering to. I was continually told to move on or risk a parking ticket or a charge of obstructing the highways.

The staff in the offices thought I was their personal shelf stacker until I told them in no uncertain terms where that responsibility lay and that once I had gotten their stuff through the front door it was no longer my responsibility.

By the end of the day I was at the end of my tether and just about ready to blow a fuse. I had managed to get 20 of the 25 drops completed and I returned to the depot. Waiting for me, with a face like a slapped arse, was the transport manager. He was fuming and the minute I got out of the cab he laid into me. 'What the hell have you been doing and saying to my precious customers?'

'Hang on a minute.' I said 'I didn't know where any of these drops were, and your precious customers seemed to think that I was their personal pack mule........'

'You didn't have to abuse them and swear at them.' He interrupted.

'I didn't swear much or abuse them at all.' I replied 'I just did what a normal delivery driver does, delivered the goods onto their property.'

'Well that's not good enough. My drivers restock the shelves for my customers.'

'Well I'm afraid that that is not in my remit.'

'Not in your remit?' He reiterated 'I'll tell you what's not in your remit. Working here, that's what's not in your remit. You'll never work here again.'

Much relieved I said 'Honestly? Can I have that in writin' please?'

With that I locked up the cab deposited the keys at the feet of the irate transport manager, after he had reluctantly signed my timesheet, and went home. On the drive home I realised that I had hit on a wonderful solution for jobs I didn't like.

These are only a couple of incidences but similar things occur all the time on agency work. Irregular work, crap vehicles, shit jobs, no security, and poor wages. The office staff of these agencies, who incidentally, call themselves Employment Consultants, don't know their arse from their elbow when it comes to transport. The agencies dictate that Bank Holidays are part and parcel of the drivers annual leave allowance whilst they, themselves get 5 weeks annual leave plus Bank holidays. This is just another way the driver is discriminated against, and something MP's and the Government of the day should look into to ensure some equality as far as Bank Holidays are concerned, but they are too busy negotiating their own massive pay rises and securing their final salary pensions and taking their 3 months recess or sitting on different boards of directors, to think about the plight of the electorate. There is no philanthropy anymore in the job of an MP. It seems that the 'honourable' gentlemen and women of whichever political persuasion are in it for what they can get out of it by accepting junkets to far flung places in the guise of working trips, not to mention plain brown envelopes changing hands at clandestine meetings. All members of whichever party nowadays seem to have their snouts entrenched ever deeper in the money trough, as the expenses scandal as shown.

Working for agencies, now, is not quite as bad as it was, although the working practises are far from perfect. The holiday arrangements are no better and I like to think that if it wasn't for agencies most professional drivers would be in full time employment, on decent, regular wages, and with a pension to look forward to. Agencies are, at best, a necessary evil, and at worst, irresponsible, profiteering traffickers of misery in the labour market.

Agencies, being the type of businesses they are, hire drivers out on an *'as and when required'* basis. This means that the driver may work for a different company every day of the week, although in practice it makes sense to keep a driver at a firm for as long as possible. I have worked for up to 3 different companies in 1 week, conversely, I have worked at one company for a 6 month period.

Agency drivers are not in a position, as a lot of people think, to refuse work. There is a certain amount of choice but, quite obviously, the driver must take on a large percentage of the work offered, whether the job suits him or not, otherwise he or she will starve. At times and dependent on the time of year there is not always work available for the amount of staff the agency has on its books and drivers will be stood down for weeks at a time without pay. It is futile to sign on for unemployment benefit in these slack times as work may be offered at any time. A driver is at the beck and call of the agency and has very little choice as to his place of work or working hours and times.

Some of the firms I have worked for whilst employed by agencies include McVities Biscuits, Tibbett and Britten, Bibby Baron, Joint Retail Logistics, Iceland, Wincanton's, GKN Chep Pallets and most of the EXEL contacts including BMW/Rover, Princes Foods, Crazy George's which is now Brighthouse, Pirelli, Michelin, Daewoo and others, as well as small independent companies and many more large concerns. Most of these jobs were run of the mill and uneventful though 1 or 2 of them may be worth a mention.

Chep Pallets (GKN) was the first job where I drove a wagon and drag, which at the time were usually of the A frame type, with 2 articulating points and could be driven on a class 2 licence. When I went for the job I blagged them and told them I had bags of experience. I took the laden vehicle and trailer to a quiet corner of the yard and practised reversing the 'A' frame trailer. I wasn't very good and I have to say, after that experience, that I have the greatest admiration and respect for the drivers of these combinations. Luckily and because the majority of companies store their pallets outside in the yard, most of the places where I was sent to load or off-load, did so via side loading and there was very little requirement for me to reverse onto a bay. Lately most companies including Chep GKN are replacing their 'A' frame trailers with close coupled draw bar outfits that only have one articulating point and require a class one licence.

I was given a job, from an agency named Star, for a 0600 start at Iceland at Deeside Industrial Estate. To get to Deeside from Manchester for 0600hrs meant leaving home at approximately 0430hrs, which necessitated getting from my bed at 0330hrs. I arrived at Iceland's depot at 0550hrs. I was allocated my vehicle and trailer which held 5 drops around the Midlands. I made out my tacho, coupled up, did all my vehicle checks, and headed for the exit security gate. I gave my notes to the security guard who checked all the relevant details and returned them to me. The guard then went to the fridge unit at the front of the trailer to check the temperature. He returned to the tractor and said to me 'I'm sorry, driver, but your temperature is nowhere near low enough. I can't let you go. Turn around and go and park up in the trailer park and come back in about an hour.'

Now to say I was somewhat disgruntled, after getting up at 0330hrs to get to Iceland for 0600hrs, when I could have had an extra hour in bed, would be something of an understatement, but I had to do as the security guard requested. Because of the lateness of my departure, this day run, ran into a night out which I spent on Keele Services, and as I was not needed by Iceland the next day I received my full 8 hours for a couple of hours running time. I declined any further work for Iceland, not least because the travelling expenses the agency paid and the time lost made it a non viable proposition.

THE WORLD OF SCANIA

In 1979 while I was working for the agency, doing crap jobs for crap money, as and when the agency allocated me work and contemplating jacking it in, I heard of a job with B & W Motors, Scania Agents at Stakehill Industrial Estate, Middleton, which is now the West Pennine Scania franchise. B & W were a Wolverhampton based Saab and Toyota dealers who managed to pick up the Manchester Scania franchise. My job title was Demonstration and Delivery Driver. I applied for the position, secured an interview and got the job. The pay was abysmal but regular and better than the dole or the agency and I would soon find ways to increase my earning potential. The reason I got the job was because of my experience on Scanias, with Brain Haulage, once one of B & W's biggest customers and to be honest, if the pay had been half decent it would have been worth sticking it out.

The job itself entailed demonstrating to prospective customers how to use the various Scania gearboxes to achieve optimum fuel consumption, plus delivery and collection of new vehicles, collection of part exchange vehicles and working closely with the sales staff. Most of the time the vehicles were driven on trade plates.

In the top end of the yard was an old Scania Vabis, LB76 tractor unit which had been brought in as a part exchange vehicle. It was this model which in 1963 gave Scania their foothold in the UK. I decided to get the old beast started and give it a run round, on trade plates of course, and just out of curiosity. It took some messing about but it finally fired up with the help of one of the mechanics and a pair of booster batteries. I got behind the wheel and weighed up the gear change. To my surprise, there were two sticks emanating from the same collar on the cab floor. One stick was the main gearshift; the second stick was the splitter or range change, depending on which model was being driven. On this particular model it was a splitter and was reminiscent of the David Brown boxes of years previous which were known as 2 stick Brownies. It took me a good hour to master the gears and if it hadn't been synchromesh, I would certainly have rattled a few cogs with that two sticker.

It was whilst working at B&W that I got to know most of the local fleet operators and owner drivers such as Tommy Brierley of Swinton, Malcolm Woodhouse of Lancaster, S & J Bargh of Caton, Trevor Todd of Rochdale, Fagan & Whalley of Accrington, Baybutts of Burscough, Keith Watkinson of Keighley, Wally Thorburn of Liverpool and many more Scania operators.

One of the salesmen at B&W, a tight lipped, sour faced individual named Vinny Garr, was an opportunist and would try to strike the pecuniary advantage in any situation. Part of my job was to log in and store the spare wheels of the new vehicles. If a customer wanted an extra spare wheel Vinny would offer to get him one cut price. He would then requisition a spare from me, sell it to the customer, pocket the proceeds and say nothing to me. When I found out that I was being used to steal to line Vinny's pockets I pulled him in the yard, threatened him with a beating whereby he stuck £50 in my hand and said 'Say nowt and I'll not implicate you and I'll give you a cut.'

Thus I subsidised my meagre earnings. Tax free fiddles at times can be worth more than the legitimate wage. 'Vive Le Fiddle.'

Another of Vinny's fiddles was to ask me to remove the after sales, fitted air deflectors and body kits from the roofs of any second hand vehicles that came in with them. These he would sell separately and split the proceeds with yours truly. I even caught him early one morning siphoning diesel from vehicles that had been taken in part exchange. What he did with the spare money he made I don't know but he didn't spend it on clothes, he was the scruffiest salesman I'd ever laid eyes on. He wore an old fashioned yolk back, blue jacket that had seen better days but had not seen the dry cleaners. His shirts although fairly clean had frayed collars and cuffs and whichever tie he wore seemed to have the remnants of some long forgotten breakfast splattered upon it. He always wore brown shoes with black trousers and multi-coloured socks. He was hardly a picture of sartorial elegance and he suffered from a definite lack of colour co-ordination. He was the type of guy that if he was dressed in a Savile Row suit he would still look tied up like a sack of crap. I think he got the job because of an impressive CV and because the interviewer felt sorry for him, although what he lacked in style he made up for in sale acumen and proved to be a good sales person, despite his down at heel appearance.

There were three other salesmen that worked at B&W. Brian who talked as though he had a plum in his mouth was from a well to do family and could sell snow to the Eskimos. His wife had given birth, by Caesarean section, about a year previous and the couple were advised that any further pregnancies could be dangerous and would result in Caesarean delivery as the lady could not give birth naturally. When I started at B&W she was pregnant for the second time. Brian said to me, once we got to know one another 'If I had known the contraception would fail, I would have instructed the surgeon to put a zip in after the first child.'

There was Tony who was a bit of a smoothie and a lady's man. He knew Scania's inside and out and could sell central heating to the Devil. He started an affair with one of the ladies from the office, which broke up his family. The last I heard he was working for the Mercedes franchise, where, within no time at all he would know Merc's inside out. He was that type of person.

Lastly there was Bernard, a nice fellow, very laid back and with a very good track record in sales. He could sell a side of beef to a vegetarian.

One of the salesmen, Tony I think, took in from Keith Watkinson's of Keighley, a heavy haulage, three axles, double drive, V8 140, in part exchange for a new 141 heavy haulage tractor. The 140 was snapped up by a company in Exeter and I was to deliver it. The buyers company was on the Marsh Barton Industrial Estate, Exeter. I took the vehicle home so that I could get an early start the next morning. I left home at 0400hrs the next day and proceeded on my way. The only problem was that this being a heavy haulage unit, it was very low geared and in top gear would do no more than 40mph. It took me over 7 hours to reach Marsh Barton. I signed the vehicle over to the new owners and then started thinking about how to get home. As I was walking through the industrial estate I saw a van delivering to one of the companies there. On the door was the company name and its place of origin which happened to be Oldham. I went over and spoke to the driver who noticed I was carrying trade plates. He told me he had one more drop in Birmingham and then home and he would be more than happy to take me. We made much better time on the way back and even with the drop in Birmingham I was home for tea time and the van driver dropped me at the end of the street where I live. That is the sort of thing one driver will do for another. The trucking fraternity is a close knit bunch.

During the normal working week I had access to any vehicle in the yard and took advantage of the situation by using the vehicles as my personal transport to and form work, thus saving on travelling expenses. The man in overall command, one Spencer Francks, assumed I was taking the vehicle home in order to necessitate an early delivery the next day. This, on occasions, was the case, but the rest of the time I used the vehicles to make it easy for myself.

Spencer Francks lived in the Midlands, so when, one day, a vehicle had to be delivered to the Scania agents in Lutterworth, it was arranged that I set off at 0500hrs and meet Spencer there at approximately 0700hrs and return with him to Middleton. When I arrived at Scania, Lutterworth, Spencer Francks was there waiting for me. I signed over the vehicle and climbed into the passenger seat of Spencer's new Saab and we set off for Middleton. It had started to rain and was literally lashing it down as we hit the motorway. Visibility was just a few yards but little things like that don't deter the likes of Spencer who had complete faith in his vehicle and in his ability to drive like a maniac at over 100mph, in totally unsuitable weather. The rain water was running off the windscreen in rivulets which prompted Spencer to extol the virtues of the Saab's aero-dynamics, before finally turning on the wipers. During the rest of the journey we didn't talk much, my teeth were gritted tight. I closed my eyes as we weaved in and out of the traffic at insane speeds. I had one hand gripping the underside of the seat, the other gripping the door handle. My knuckles were white with the pressure. We arrived back in Middleton in just over an hour and I couldn't get out of that car fast enough. I made any excuse I could to avoid travelling with Spencer again.

On the trade plate deliveries and collections one had to be conversant with the method of bleeding the pump and/or the injectors of the Scania, as when the vehicles came off the boat from Sweden or from another franchise they had barely enough fuel to get them off the docks or out of the yard let alone to Manchester. There was supposed to be enough fuel to get the vehicle to the nearest fuel station, but this was not always the case so one would end up buying a couple of gallons and having to bleed the system to get mobile once again. The salesman or whosoever took me to wherever I had to pick up a vehicle always carried with them a 5 gallon diesel container, thus ensuring that I had the wherewithal to get to my destination.

I enjoyed working at B&W driving brand new Scanias every day and sleeping in my own bed every night and not having to get my hands dirty very often, but it became obvious that I could not afford to work for the rate at which I was employed. I approached Spencer Francks about an increment in my remuneration; he in turn expressed my plight to the owners. Spencer explained my working methods and indispensability to the sales staff and the company in general in shining prose. A small rise was awarded but not enough to dissuade me from seeking greener fields where the money tree might grow more fruitfully.

CHAPTER 6
SPECIALIST TRANSPORT AND S.T.G.O.

NOWADAYS since the demise in general haulage, most types of transport are specialist to a degree, and some companies have forged a niche within certain areas.

In the Lake District and close to marinas, canal basins and some ports, there are companies that have developed solely into boat and cabin cruiser carriers. They use specially constructed trailers to accommodate boats of carious sizes and are capable of carrying the longest of canal narrow boats. The trailers are usually of the drop frame type and a lot of them are also of the trombone type. They have to be of drop frame construction to accommodate the keel of certain craft, and of trombone constructions to take the longer vessels.

In the Peak District and a few other places where there are plenty of quarries, tipper fleets proliferate.

Beamish Transport from the North east are specialists in the transport of caravans on specially designed trailers and flat bed rigids, as are Burstwicks Transport of Hull who favour the idea of carrying 2 caravans on a rigid flat bed with a third being towed via towing hitch.

Allely's Transport from Studley, Warwickshire is another specialist haulier that specialises in the movement of railway rolling stock on low loaders.

Fridge work has become a specialist operation insomuch as the reefers cannot be used for anything else other than frozen or chilled goods. Not like the old insulated vehicles which were also used on general haulage. Even so the driver must be fully conversant with the workings of the motor that powers the refrigeration system and he must put in the correct fuel, ie, red diesel. It is also the driver's job to make sure the temperature is at the correct level for the goods carried.

With the advent of the ADR certificate and the Health and Safety at Work laws, chemical transportation has become much specialised, whether on flat beds, in tankers or in curtainsiders. The driver has to know the relevant legislation that applies to the cargo being carried, and be aware of the potential hazard, and be capable of taking the correct course of action if that hazard should materialise.

Drivers may have to take separate tests for auxiliary equipment such as vehicle mounted cranes such as the HIAB, or vehicle mounted Fork Lift Trucks such as the Moffat Mountie, or the Manitou Manilift. He may also have to sit examinations for his ADR license for the carriage of dangerous goods.

Vehicles with mounted cranes and mounted fork lifts are generally known as self loading trucks. The auxiliary equipment i.e., cranes can be mounted on rigid 4, 6 or 8 wheelers, either to the front or rear of the loading bed. Articulated vehicles may have the crane mounted on the rear of the tractor unit or to the front, rear or centre of the trailer, and the crane may be on tracks to enable it to run up and down the length of the trailer. The HIAB seems to be the most popular make of truck mounted crane but other makes include Atlas, Bonfiglioli, Palfinger and Cormach and all can be fitted with different types of equipment e.g; forks, grabs, buckets or a simple hook for use with chains or slings. These cranes are used in the delivery of a multiplicity of commodities such as Portacabins, bricks and blocks, timber, steel, plant etc.

The vehicle mounted fork lift is usually mounted to the rear of the vehicle. Other types of specialist trucks are the garbage truck with its hydraulic crusher, concrete mixers, fire tenders, logging trucks, car transporters, livestock carriers and fairground vehicles. There are mobile cranes with up to 10 axles that can weigh up to 100 tons as they stand and which have only recently come into the LGV grouping and until then could be driven on a car license, although, obviously a novice would never be employed to drive these mammoth machines without the relevant training.

Then there is the breakdown truck or wrecker, which many a lorry driver has been glad to see come over the horizon. Some wreckers, still in use, are old 2nd World War, American Diamond T's that were also used on heavy haulage. All these vehicles depend, in one way or another on a PTO (power take off) system. The last of the specialist vehicles worthy of mention are military vehicles which come in many and varied guises that a separate book could be written solely about them.

So even though these types of transport are of a specialist nature, the driver had to be multi-skilled. Not so when I worked at Freightliner carrying 20 tons of liquid Toluene Di-isocyanate in heated tanks to South Wales. The driver had no training; the only information was on the trem card on the back of the trailer. This gave limited information on who to contact in the case of an emergency, a couple of phone numbers and what type of chemical was being carried and its effects, whether it was corrosive etc.

Tanker drivers, especially those employed directly by the major oil and petrol companies, have always been classified as specialists and this was reflected in their remuneration. That was until these big companies decided to rid themselves of their in-house transport and put it out to tender. This resulted in drivers facing redundancy or taking a cut of over £100 per week in wages. Personally I never thought that tanker drivers were any better or any worse than any other haulage man.

Of course your true specialists in transport operations are the STGO, and heavy haulage groups, that allow the movement of large indivisible loads such as earth movers. Dumper trucks, farm equipment, steam turbines, Aviation and maritime equipment and Railway rolling stock and engines on the back of over length low loaders and drop frame trailers.

STGO stands for Special Types, General Order, and operates in three classes. STGO Class One allows carriage of equipment up to 65 tons gross, Class Two up to 100 tons and Class Three up to 150 tons. Anything over and above these limits, although still coming under STGO Category 3, is handled by companies such as Heanor Haulage, Bennett's of Wilmslow, Cadzow's, Allely's and Alsthom who move the Electricity Boards massive Generators and transformers using push and pull ballast motors and are subject to police approval and escort and are restricted to certain routes and times, although under new laws, most heavy haulage companies arrange their own escorts and have their own vans painted with hazard lines and with orange flashing lights and wide load markers. This is to free up more of our law enforcement officers to do some crime busting, though you'd never notice.

A couple of the biggest companies to undertake this kind of work were Pickford's and Wynn's who used the Cummins powered Scammell, ballast trucks on work up to 240 tons. Pickford's also used the Diamond T. Sunter's of Northallerton was another company employed on this type of work. Econofreight still has a heavy haulage arm. Most of the ultra heavy haulage companies used the big Scammell ballast tractors but others such as A.L.E (Abnormal Load Engineering) which was formed after the break up of Wynn's Heavy Haulage, use, amongst other vehicles, the German built Faun push and pull ballast tractors carrying GEC steam turbines up to and above 500 tonnes gross.

The routes for these extra ordinary loads are planned months in advance with teams of specialists being sent out to test the strength of any bridges that may have to be crossed and to check for overhead obstructions such as low bridges or telecommunication cables.

The British Army once used the might Antar, which was a descendant of the old Thorneycroft, as heavy haulage tank transporters, then Scammells and now these have been superseded by the American Oshkosh, which, in its British Army guise, is a 4 axle unit usually pulling a 7 axle low loader semi trailer.

On a lot of heavy haulage, when artics are used instead of ballast trucks, the Jeep dolly is used to give an extra Axle and thus spread the load. The Jeep dolly fits between the fifth wheel and the goose neck of the low loader, semi-trailer and is, in essence, a superimposed fifth wheel axle, and can be single axle or tandem.

Most commercial truck builders have a heavy haulage spec whereby close ratio gearboxes couple with 500 and 600hp, 14 or 16 litre engines are driven through a heavy haulage back axle or double drive in which both rear axles are driven. Each country has or had its own heavy haulage tractor manufacturer. In North America and Canada it would be Kenworth and Pacific respectively. Trabosa in Spain, Willemme and Nicolas in France whilst Germany has Faun and Titan. Another specialist manufacturer is MAN-OAF of Belgium, and of course, in England there is the world famous Scammell. A lot of these super heavies are custom built to individual operator's specifications.

At the lower end of the heavy haulage spectrum, though not

to be sniffed at, are Scania, Volvo, Mercedes-Benz, MAN, DAF, Renault and ERF who all produce heavy haulage units. Volvo produces a 16 litre, 610hp vehicle, which, though over specified, is used by some firms as a general haulage motor, generally as a flagship vehicle.

CHAPTER 7
BRITISH TELECOM AND ONWARD

IS THIS THE BEST JOB EVER?

WHILST working at B&W Motors I bumped into the husband of a cousin of mine, who told me he'd gotten the best job he'd ever had, working for British telecom. He told me that the night out subsistence money was about £25 per night. This was in 1980 when general haulage drivers were on between £8 and £10, per night out. He went on to tell me that the basic wage was well above any other haulage outfit and was based on a 37 hour week, as opposed to a 40 or 42 hour week, of course, transport being of the nature that it is, 60 hours was the average working week. This meant 20 odd hours at time and a half was usually worked, giving a very respectable and enviable top line. He also told me that there were, because of retirements and an expanding fleet, 4 vacancies for Class 1 drivers and to get myself down to the depot in Gorton and get an application form. Me being a man of mercenary outlook, and this being an opportunity to step into the high league of earners among the trucking fraternity, this is exactly what I did. I thought, at last I had not only found the garden where the money tree grew more fruitfully, I had found the orchard.

Being, as it was at the time, a nationalised company, coming under the auspices of the Civil Service, things moved very slowly at BT and I finally got an interview after about 3 months waiting. The interview was conducted by three gentlemen. One was the foreman, another the transport manager and the third a driver, John G, who also turned out to be the shop steward. After the interview I had to give a demonstration of my roping and sheeting capabilities followed by a road test. Finally I was told that I had secured the position subject to a medical. Another month passed by, I got a date for the medical, which I passed, and I was given a starting date. I finally started at BT, in January 1981, 5 months after filling in the application form. D.J. was still out of work after finishing at Brain's so when I proffered my resignation at B&W, I recommended him to Spencer Franck's and so myself and D.J. started new jobs on the same day.

British Telecom, at the time was going through some quite dramatic changes. In the run-up to privatisation the fleet colour had been changed from the Post Office Telephones dark green to the new British Telecom plc., yellow, although it would be a year or so before the company was actually floated on the stock market and shares would become available.

Upon starting at BT, the new recruits were measured for their uniforms and issued with a driver's handbook and loading kit which consisted of a hammer for nailing and a pinch bar for extracting nails, a number of restraining straps were also supplied, a bag was issued to keep this kit safe. After an induction day the new drivers were, initially, put on local work, taking empty cable drums to the local cable yards and bringing full ones back for the distance men to deliver all over the country, or delivering locally to the TEC's (Telecom Engineering Centres) with cable, concrete manhole covers and frames and cast iron manhole covers and frames and any other telecommunications equipment that may be needed. The 2 main cable yards were BICC at Blackley in Manchester and BICC at Prescott on Merseyside. Other suppliers of telecommunications cable were STC in South Wales, TLC at

Dagenham and Pirelli at Southampton and a few more smaller suppliers. The distance men loaded out of these depots when their deliveries were done, for ongoing delivery or to bring back to their home depot. Also the BT transport depots local to these yards loaded out of them for ongoing deliveries either local or distance.

The vast majority of the trailers were 40ft flat beds, although 1 or 2 Taut liners were making their way into the fleet, so the vast majority of loads had to be roped or roped and sheeted, depending on what commodity was being carried. The trailers which were brought in from Blackley and Prescott, for the distance men to take on delivery, were loaded with any amount of deliveries from 1 drop to 15 drops. Cable drums being of a circular construction and therefore capable of rolling had to be placed on chocks situated on the trailer these chocks then had a batten placed behind them and the batten was nailed down to prevent the chock sliding out, thus providing a safe and stable load. If the distance drivers finished in South Wales they would load out of STC, cable yard or Cwm Carn with telephones. If they finished down south or near London they could load out of the Crayford or Colindale depots or TCL or Pirelli's. If their last drop was in Scotland they would either load out of the Newhouse depot near Glasgow or load Telephone Kiosks out of the factory at Kirkintilloch. The majority of deliveries were to BT yards i.e.,TEC's and they always loaded for back home on Friday, thus ensuring their fifth night out.

THE 'V' SIGN IS NOT RECOMMENDED

Not long after starting at BT, and whilst still on local work, I was given a load with 2 drops to deliver to Liverpool and the Wirral. The vehicle I was to use was an old Guy Big 'J'. The trailer was fully freighted to maximum weight with steel and concrete manhole covers, which were secured by way of ratchet operated, restraining straps. After I had coupled up to the trailer I put the vehicle in a low forward gear and attempted to pull forward to ensure the coupling was secure. As I let the clutch out it started slipping. I went into the garage workshops to make out a defect report. I approached Keith McAnnic, the workshop foreman, and said 'Keith the clutch on this vehicle is slipping like hell.'

'We know about it.' he said 'Do you think you could run it for today and we'll get it in for repair tonight?'

'Well okay, 'I replied 'but if you get a phone call requesting the wrecker to tow me in, let it be known that I've reported it.'

'Fair enough, just give it your best shot.'

So off I went, doing my best to nurse that well worn clutch. I completed the Liverpool drop and headed for the Wirral via the Mersey Tunnel. When I arrived on the Wirral side of the Mersey and as I was approaching the junction for the A41 Chester Road I saw a vehicle approaching from my right, about 250 yards distant.

I was about to make a right turn and thought I had plenty of time to clear the junction before the approaching car was anywhere near me. I let out the clutch and applied some revs, the clutch slipped and would not pick up the drive to pull the heavily laden trailer. The cab rose in the air and came down with a resounding thump and the vehicle, finally, started to inch forwards. By this time the approaching car was upon me. The driver started blowing his horn continuously, a hand appeared from the passenger side window and started gesturing in a masturbatory fashion, and the horn continued to sound.

I shouted 'FUCK OFF!' and gave the 2 fingered salute and completed my manoeuvre. My vehicle slowly gathered some momentum. I looked in my rear view mirror and to my complete surprise I saw the same car that had bore down on me, now following me. The driver accelerated and passed me. He then stopped his vehicle, straddling the central white line. I had no way to pass him so I stopped.

The door of the car, a Mini, flew open and a denim clad leg terminating in a size 12 Doc Marten's boot appeared. This was followed by two huge forearms, reminiscent of Popeye's, 2 huge ham like fists gripped the door pillars and heaved. Pointing forwards, the next thing to appear was a bullet shaped, shaven head and then this huge Cro Magnon creature began to unfold itself out of the Mini. He or it wore a T shirt with braces over the shoulders which were adjoined to the half mast turned up denims the T shirt of this Troglodyte appeared about to split in the fashion of The Incredible Hulk. This terrifying apparition ambled towards my truck, dragging its knuckles along the floor.

Sat in my cab, getting more scared by the second, I reached for the 2lb, ball peen hammer, which is part of all BT drivers' kit, and gripped the haft tightly. I was too slow to lock the door, and I doubt if it would have made any difference if I had. The door was wrenched open and before me stood a 6ft 6ins albino gorilla with red, menacing eyes. This quasi Neanderthal snarled 'Get outa' dat cab so's I can fuckin' kill ya.'

Showing more calm than I actually felt I replied 'I'm quite sure your capable of doing just that, but if you want me that badly, climb up and get me and this 2lb, ball peen hammer'll make a nice round hole in your skull.'

'No one tells me ta fuck off while I'm out wit' de wife, now gerrout.'

'No way, man, I've a wife too and I'm sure she has no plans to visit me in the Arrowbrooke Hospital,' which is the local infirmary.

I tried to get through to this missing link and to explain the pros and cons of heavy goods vehicles and slipping clutches. I also belittled myself and apologised for telling him to fuck off, although I'm not sure he quite understood the concept of the apology. He finally realised, with his limited intelligence, that an impasse had been reached, and his lust to kill would have to be vented on some other poor individual.

He was still gripping the cab door and he opened it to its full width and with all the strength he could muster, which was quite considerable, he slammed it shut. The door closed with such violence that the window came out of its holdings and fell into the interior of the door and smashed into innumerable fragments.

The Great Ape walked back to his car, turned and snarled at me again and said 'If I ever see you out, you're fuckin' dead', and then proceeded to refold himself into the Mini. He did a 'U' turn in front of me and as he drove past he once again glowered at me. I thought should I give him the 2 fingered salute again, but discretion being the better part of valour I decided not to, so I smiled at him and went on my way. I had to pull into a lay by and have a brew and to let the shakes and cold sweats subside before I could carry on. I finished my deliveries and made my way back to the depot, dropped my trailer and deposited the unit at the workshops for a new clutch and a new window, glad that the day was over.

SAILING SHIP AND SHEETED LOADS

Sometimes the distance drivers would return to their home depot mid week to be turned around with a fresh load and out again for the rest of the week. This happened one week while I was doing a bit of trailer shunting in the yard. A bear of a man, named Ray Brookie, pulled into the yard with a trailer of cages, stacked 3 high, full of telephones from Cwm Carn in South Wales, for onward delivery to the Preston depot. He dropped the trailer and went into the office. He came out a few minutes later and came straight over to me to tell me I was to deliver the trailer on to Preston. I backed my unit, a Guy Big 'J' with a 200 Cummins engine, under the trailer, connected up, checked all the electrics, wound up the legs, released the trailer brake and pulled out of the yard thinking the load would be right, after all one of the senior men with years of experience had roped and sheeted it. I pulled into the main road, Gorton Cross Street, looked into my mirrors. I could not see anything approaching from the rear, not because the road was clear but because as my speed increased the sheets started to billow out from the sides of the trailer obscuring anything to the rear. At the nearest available point I turned round and returned to the yard where I undid the ropes and was in the process of tightening the sheets when Brookie came out of the office, into the yard. He spotted me re-doing the sheets and lashings and immediately stormed over to me. 'What the bloody hell do you think you're doing?' he asked with his usual bull in a china shop finesse, 'I've just run up from South Wales with that trailer.'

'More fool you' I said, 'I couldn't see anything through my mirrors 'cos of the sheets blowin' out all over the place. Whoever sheeted this needs bleedin' lessons.'

'I bleedin' sheeted it.' Said Brookie, 'and there's the bugger all wrong with it.'

'You're jokin, man, it was like the Cutty Sark under full sail goin' down the road.'

With that, Brookie marched off muttering to himself something like 'Cocky young bastard.'

Brookie and I never really saw eye to eye after that, although on numerous occasions we had to work together; Ray Brookie was a very brusque character, a bombastic man who thought he knew it all.

MORE ABOUT BROOKIE

Brookie was involved in a serious accident near Biggar on the A702, prior to my starting at BT., whilst returning from a trip to Edinburgh and surrounding areas. The Biggar road is notoriously bad during the winter months.

The accident happened about a fortnight before I actually started at BT, but on the day I started the vehicle involved was still connected to the winch on a low loader flat bed, in the depot and it was completely trashed. The cab was crushed and the area where the driver would have normally sat was pushed back to the fifth wheel coupling. The front wheels were well out of alignment and there wasn't a window left. It was barely recognisable as a Leyland Marathon, which it once was.

Because it was an induction day I didn't have much work to do and at break time, Ellis Dargue, the yard man, shunter and myself and the other new starters went to the canteen. Ellis went to the counter and the serving lady said 'Good morning, Ellis, what can I get you.'

Ellis asked 'Could I have caviar on toast?'

To which the lady behind the counter responded 'I'm sorry Ellis, but we're fresh out of bread.' This turned out to be a regular piece of badinage between Ellis and the serving wenches with Ellis asking for all kinds of exotic dishes and the canteen staff coming back with a witty report.

When we had all been served and were seated around a table I asked Ellis 'The guy that was driving that Leyland Marathon write off, is he dead or in intensive care or what?'

Ellis gave a sigh and a wry smile and said 'The driver of that wreck, Ray Brookie, had the smash last month, coming down from Edinburgh. He lost it on black ice, on a bend on the A702 near a little bridge and left the road and ploughed into a bloody great tree, but Brookie was unhurt save for a few scratches and bruises.'

'How...........?' I uttered.

'Well everybody here believes he bailed outa that cab before the impact, it's the only explanation and anyhow he's back in work and down the road again now. He must be the luckiest bastard I know not to be dead. I've travelled that road hundreds of times, winter and summer and never had a single incident, because, especially in the winter months, you have to have respect for the weather and the type of terrain and countryside you're operating in and drive your vehicle accordingly.'

If nothing else Brookie was a man of principle and a staunch socialist, union man and as such was totally against the privatisation of the Post Office Telecommunications industry. British Telecom plc, did not ring right with him, so much so that at first he steadfastly refused the free shares in the new company that all employees were to be awarded. It wasn't until John G persuaded him, with great difficulty, that if everybody refused the shares the company was still going to be privatised. Nobody within the company really wanted the privatisation but it was inevitable under a Tory Government. After his talk with John G, Brookie relented and took the shares.

In 1983 after I'd been at BT a couple of years and had progressed to distance work, there was an influx of new drivers. One of these was a young guy named Nobby McKeowan. Nobby had been a driver on distance work for a local haulier from Droylsden for 4 years and a driver's mate prior to that. He was a good driver, a competent roper and sheeter and knew his way about the country. One Monday morning, because of holidays and sickness, he was given a run to Scotland with about 10 drops on the trailer. When the deliveries were done he was to pick up a load of empty drums from BT's Newhouse depot for BICC, Blackley. Brookie started complaining about new starters getting distance work, even though he had a five nighter himself, he begrudged Nobby his chance of a good week. On the following Monday, all the drivers were in the mess room awaiting their loads, when Brookie came over to Nobby, feigning friendliness and said 'Hello Nobby, how did you get on with that Scotland run last week? Did you find it all right?'

'Funny enough, Ray,' Nobby replied 'I went right up the M6 past Carlisle, and I fell right into it.'

'Sarcastic bastard!' Brookie retorted as he turned about and left the room to howls of laughter from the other drivers.

CHAIRMAN OF THE BRANCH

In the year of 1983, with me being a bit of a leftie and having the plight of the working man at heart and being somewhat vociferous and outspoken in my views, I was put forward for and elected to Chairman of the Branch, Manchester Drivers (NCU), *National Communications Union.* The shop steward, as I mentioned earlier, was a good and devoted union man named John G, and the assistant shop steward was none other than Ray Brookie. The union and its objectives were things Brookie and I totally agreed upon. Brookie, also, was a true union man and despite his brusqueness of nature, did all that was required of him as a union official.

I remained Chairman of the Branch for 6 years in which time I attended the yearly Annual General Meeting (AGM), at the Winter Gardens, in Blackpool, as both an observer and a delegate. I was instrumental, with other union officers, in securing decent pay rises and fought for and got better working conditions for the workforce.

Each Monday morning, union officers were allowed an hour's facility time in which complaints were heard and outstanding business concluded. Management were consulted on any ongoing situations and minor problems were sorted out.

EVERYBODY OUT

There was only one industrial dispute of any consequence while I was Chairman of the Branch and this took place sometime in the mid 80's whilst the Manchester BT Transport was still being run from the Gorton depot. The dispute was about the usual things, i.e. money and working conditions and involved all BT staff nationally. Because the negotiations between the Union and Management floundered, industrial action was called for and this escalated into a full blown withdrawal of labour by the manual grades.

The transport yard at Gorton also incorporated the Gorton TEC and because the salaried, office workers and managerial staff continued to work this led to the manual workers being the subjects of a lock out from their place of work. Being a Union Officer I was required to picket the depot on each day of the strike.

After a few days picketing outside the locked gates of the TEC during this wintertime strike, tempers were becoming frayed. The pickets had gotten hold of an old oil drum to use as a brazier and we had a good supply of pitch pine logs from old telegraph poles, which burnt ferociously, but each morning the management team would turn up, remove the padlock from the gates, drive in and park their cars and then replace the padlock to keep us out. They would look at us through the gates with smug grins on their faces. Then the goading would start with remarks like, 'I hope you have a happy Christmas without any wages, and 'you stupid morons are standing out there in the cold while we go inside to work in the warmth of our centrally heated offices.'

We strikers responded by calling these strike breakers, blacklegs and scabs. When the goading and name calling had finished and the office staff had gone to their workstations, one of the pickets produced a Hacksaw and a tempered steel, heavy duty padlock, which could resist hacksaw blades or bolt croppers. The original padlock was sawn through and removed and the new one fitted. What started off as a manual workers lockout finished up as a managerial lock in. The office staff ended up leaving their vehicles in the yard and, with a host of profanities, had to scale the gates to escape. The padlock was eventually cut off with an angle grinder and a little more respect was shown to those of us on strike.

The strike did not last long before agreement and concurrence was reached. The manual staff got less than they wanted and the management had given more than they wanted, so all in all a fine outcome.

During the time I held the Chairman's post, Nobby McKeowan fell foul of the law, I think it was in 1987, and he was breathalysed, and lost his license, stupid as it was for a professional driver. A couple of years prior to this, another driver lost his briefs under the same circumstances, and the management kept him on as a yard shunter until he regained his license. John G. and I fought for Nobby on the same pretext and even took the case before the top management in London, but to no avail. We appealed, but the appeal failed and Nobby was sacked. I still cannot understand how the same management can come to such a totally diverse decision when there was an obvious precedent. Nobby, by this time, was newly married with a child on the way and it is cases of this nature that tend to breed the 'Them and Us' school of thought.

I became so involved that a lot of my time at work became devoted to union business, travelling nationwide for meetings with other union officers and managerial staff. The union, of course, paid all expenses such as night out subsistence, rail fares, taxi fares etc.

C.B. RADIO, GOOD BUDDY

After C.W. McCall had a hit record in 1976, reaching number 2 in the charts with Convoy, it spawned a whole new craze within the trucking industry and beyond. The craze was still going strong when I joined BT in 1981, and I and a few others had sets fitted in our Telecom vehicles.

One time, in the late summer of 1983, on a Friday afternoon when returning from a week working out of the Newhouse depot, myself and 2 other Manchester drivers were running back together. We were chatting away on the CB's. My handle was 'Yellow Bird' after the BT mascot, a yellow canary called Buzby. We were strung out over about 3 or 4 miles and I was in the lead. A couple of police cars were patrolling up and down the A74, which then was a 40 and 50mph road. The legal limits were 40 on single carriageway and 50 on dual carriageway. I was taking a bit of a chance and was doing around 50 on the single carriageway when I spoke to the other 2 BT drivers and anyone else on channel 1-9. I said 'This is Yellow Bird, all you other truckers that have your ears on, keep your eyes peeled for them Smoky Bears cruisin' up and down.'

A reply came back 'Yellow Bird, I take it you're the BT truck, registration so and so. Well I'm Smoky on 2 wheels and I'm sat right on your tail. Now you pull her back to 40mph and we'll say and do no more about it.'

With this revelation I took my clog off the accelerator and I hit the exhaust brake and pulled over a little to my left. As I did so I looked into my rear view mirror and saw Smoky on his motorcycle pull out from behind me. He overtook me near Beattock summit. As he passed he raised an arm in acknowledgement and I gave him the thumbs up. He had been sat directly behind me, out of view of my mirrors, for God knows how long, without my knowing.

As I approached Beattock quarry opposite the Coatesgate Café I saw 2 red and white Jam butty police cars and 1 police bike parked up by the lorry park. The officers were out of their cars and grouped around the motorcycle talking to the biker cop. He waved as I passed and I waved back and then immediately got on the CB to warn the other drivers coming down from Beattock summit that there could be a welcoming committee at the bottom of the hill and to pull their rigs back to 50mph, as this section of the A74 was dual carriageway.

Now this biker cop kitted out with CB on his K100 BMW was either on special duties just to warn truckers of the speed limit or he had already done his quota of tickets for the day. Alternatively he could just have been one of the good guys who realised that we truckers were just like him, ordinary guys just trying to earn a living.

The novelty of the CB radio soon wore thin with me. It is a great tool for passing on information about highway conditions and accidents and traffic flow but sadly, like most things it was open to abuse by idiots playing music over the main truckers channel and others using it as a dating medium.

A SPY IN THE CAB

When the tachograph became law in 1983, BT being classed as a public service or utility, like the Postal fleet, the Water and

Electricity Boards etc were deemed exempt from the 'spy in the cab' so we still ran on log books and adhered to the 1968 traffic act. Of course one or two or more drivers were still having their dodgy nights out, especially the Friday night after a week away. The manager of the Manchester depot suspected that these transgressions were taking place but old habits die hard. The gaffer, who was an ex driver, suspected that this was the case but was at a loss as far as proof was concerned. In his wisdom and because of his suspicions which were not without justification, he approached the higher management with the idea of implementing the tachograph. The union, of course, fought this move, but because of suspicions and the intimation of fraud and fiddles the tachograph became a permanent fixture throughout BT's LGV fleet sometime in 1986/7. The 1968 Traffic Act still applied as far as the drivers' hours rules were concerned but the 'black box', 'spy in the cab,' tachograph, was here to stay. Like our brethren in the general haulage sector we had to learn to live with it.

It soon became obvious that the tacho was not the instrument of the Devil that it was purported to be but could, in fact, benefit the driver. There was a case in one of the transport journals of the day of a fully freighted artic attempting to negotiate a roundabout and rolling over. I seem to remember that this was on the A59 near the Tickled Trout at Preston. Witnesses to the accident, in which the driver escaped with cuts and bruises, said the driver was doing 40mph when he went into the roundabout. Upon consulting the evidence contained on the tachograph disc it transpired the driver had approached the roundabout at a speed decreasing from 30mph to 12mph when he actually entered the roundabout, and the adverse camber had caused the wagon to roll. This scenario became known as slow roll over syndrome. So as can be seen, without the tachograph, and with just the reliance of eye witnesses, this driver could have been charged with various offences and might quite easily have lost his license through no fault of his own.

THE AMERICAN DREAM

Coming up to 1984, when I was 38 years of age, a suggestion was made, by one of the drivers, to go to Los Angeles, the City of Angels, for the Olympic Games. A few people showed an interest and saving for the holiday started in earnest, but one by one people started to drop off until there was only me, Nobby and another driver, John O'Reilly. We decided that we would still go, but not for the games. We would go to see the West Coast and the Grand Canyon etc., and see the American trucks and truckstops and to talk to and find out about the American truck drivers lifestyle. At the time I was the only one married out of the three, but my wife sanctioned it, knowing it was a lifelong dream, though my wife and I have been to the States numerous times since.

In mid year 1984 we 3 BT truck drivers flew to L.A, picked up our hire car and began to tour, taking in California, Arizona and Nevada. For the first week we travelled South from L.A, to San Diego. We took the coast road, visiting Long Beach, home of the Spruce Goose, the largest ever flying boat, designed and built by Howard Hughes. The original Queen Mary ocean liner is also moored there and is used as a floating hotel. We then went to Carlsbad, not to be confused with Carlsbad, New Mexico, Escondido and on to San Diego. From there we headed north-east through Bakersfield and on to Barstow which is on the old Route 66. On the day we approached Barstow it was close to midday so we decided to stop and feed and water ourselves. We spotted a small bar on Main Street and went in. At the bar stood a big man, in his stocking feet he would have been 6′ 4″. He had on a Stetson hat and cowboy boots with 3″ Cuban heels, which gave the overall impression that he was about 7′ 2″. He wore leather chaps over denim jeans, a denim jacket and a gunbelt and holster. We ordered beers and sandwiches and we got talking to the big guy. Foolishly I asked 'What do you do for a living?' He looked me up and down in an appraising kind of way and answered 'I'm a fuckin' cowboy. What else?'

I had the feeling that I wanted the ground to open up beneath me and swallow me up, but I continued 'I see you're wearing a western rig but the holster is empty. How come?'

'Well, lookee 'ere, buddy' he said 'We ain't allowed to carry firearms in public paces, but if you take a walk outside you'll see a 4 x 4 Ranchero out there, look inside and you'll see mah gun a sittin' on the dashboard.'

I went outside, saw the Ranchero and looked through the window. Sure enough lying on the dash was an old type Colt .45 Peacemaker Revolver. I returned to the bar and I said to the cowboy, 'Man, if you did that back in England the window of your Ranchero would be broken and that gun would disappear.'

Once again he gave me that up and down look of appraisal and replied, 'Man, whose gonna steal mah old gun? We've all got 'em around here, and if I stow it in the glove box the po-leece will rope me in for carrying a concealed weapon.'

We spent a couple of hours drinkin' and talkin' to the cowboy who told us all about ranch life with the round-ups on horseback as well as by helicopter and quad bikes, the cattle branding, herding cattle to the stock yards at the rail head, line riding, fence fixing, sleeping under the stars and all that romantic stuff, and the general life of a ranch hand, which we all thought were things of the past, but apparently the American cowboy is alive and well and living in Barstow, California.

DEATH VALLEY, THE MOJAVE AND THE HIGHWAY PATROL

From Barstow we went up to Death Valley where the temperature was in the 120's degrees Fahrenheit and in July 1913 reached an astonishing 134 degrees Fahrenheit. It is the hottest, driest and lowest area in the Western Hemisphere, sinking at one point to 282ft below sea level. From the Valley we went down through the Mojave Desert heading for Kingman Arizona. John was the driver through this barren, over-heated, desert landscape, and we barely saw any other vehicles, except the occasional long haul truck and odd traveller, until Nobby shouted, 'Slow down! There's Smoky Bear on the central reservation.'

We shot past Smoky doing about 75mph. He pulled on to the Highway and came after us. When he got close to us the blue light and the siren came on. John pulled onto the shoulder followed by Smoky. As the officer got out of his patrol car and came towards our vehicle, we were all looking back towards the police officer and we all saw him flick his holster open and adjust his weapon. John lowered the window to greet the patrolman and said 'Good morning, sir was I doing something wrong?'

'Yup' said the officer, 'You guys European?'

'Yessir.' Replied John 'We're from the UK.'

'Well do you fellas know what the speed limit is, here in the US of A?'

'Er, I believe it's 55mhp.' I said.

'That's right, the double nickel, 55 miles per hour' he replied and then asked 'Do you fellas know at what speed you were travelling?'

Again I replied 'it wouldn't be 55 would it?'

He grinned and said 'would you like to accompany me to my

patrol car and I'll show you on the Vascar that you were doing 75mph.'

We all got out and followed the officer back to his patrol car, where he showed us the speed on the Vascar speed equipment, which, indeed, indicated 75mph.

'Now, what we have over here, in the States' he said 'is on the spot fines and you fellas jus' happen to owe me 20 bucks.'

Our hands went into our pockets. The patrolman shook his head, still grinning, as he wrote out our ticket, and said, as he gave us the speeding citation and an addressed envelope for the California Highway Patrol, 'Naw, yuh don't have to pay me now, yuh can pay from your next destination, which is?'

'We're heading for Kingman, Arizona, then the Grand Canyon' replied Nobby.

'Well, yuh can pay me by post from Kingman or the Canyon.' He said 'then where you guys headin?'

'Well, we're having a couple of days in Vegas, then over to San Francisco and down to L.A. for our flight home.' Said Nobby.

The officer rubbed his chin and said 'you guys can pay me from Vegas, 'Frisco or L.A. heck, yuh can even pay me from England and I know I ain't ever gonna see my $20. now drive safely and have a good day y'all.'

And with that we parted, but we stuck by the double nickel for the next 50 miles or so, being overtaken by numerous long haul trucks whose drivers obviously knew the whereabouts of Smoky and his speed traps. After an hour or so driving in the Godforsaken landscape of the desert, with its salt flats, gravel basins and mountains, the pangs of hunger came upon us but all we could see in front of us was the long black ribbon, barren land and heat shimmer. There was the occasional stand of Joshua trees and we spotted the odd roadrunner but no Wily

Coyote, when, in the distance, a wooden building, with a red neon sign in the window, came into sight. As we drew closer we could see a modern pick-up and an old rust bucket of a Buick parked outside with the bonnet up. There was an old hound dog lying next to a rocking chair, on the stoop, with its tongue lolling out, in the shade of an awning, and there were a few long haul trucks parked around the back. We had gotten close enough now to read the neon sign which proclaimed 'Coor's Beer, Sold Here.' We pulled in, got out of the car and went into this solitary diner cum store and truck stop. Inside was a toothless, bald, 80 something year old man. As I entered I saw, on the counter, a jar of beef jerky, something I'd always wanted to try, so I asked the elderly proprietor 'how much is your beef jerky?'

'It's 10 cents a pull, son.' He replied 'by the way, you guys European?'

'Yes' I replied, offering him the money for the jerky, we're from Manchester, England.'

'Yuh know, man, in 1942 when I was in the US Marine' he said 'we docked at that little port yuh got o'er thur, Liverpool is it? Waall, we sailed down that thur Manchester Ship Canal and moored at a piss poor town called Salford. Is the Fox Inn still there?'

I couldn't believe it, we'd come 6000 miles and in the middle of the Mojave Desert we'd met an ex US Marine who knew the Fox Inn in Salford. We spent an hour or so talking to the old guy, who it seems had done a spell at truck driving, both as a company man and an owner operator. We had a bite to eat, which his wife prepared, and a couple of Coors.

While we were drinking our beers one of the truck drivers called over in a mock English accent 'I say old chaps, are you from jolly old England, what?'

I replied 'Yes we're from Manchester, England and before

you ask, no, we don't know the Queen and Manchester is a 4 hour drive from London. We're truck drivers, like yourselves, on vacation over here.'

The truckers laughed and beckoned us over to join them, which we did. We talked the usual small talk. Amongst this group of truck drivers was a man and wife team and because one doesn't see this type of partnership in England we talked to them at length. I asked 'What sort of journeys do you undertake? Are you on long distance or local work?'

The male of the duo replied 'we travel each and every which way, man, locals around here is anything within a 500 mile radius, but we're on genuine long haul. We live on the East Coast, not far from Richmond, Virginia an' we aint seen home for 10 weeks but we're headin' that way now.'

Nobby chirped in 'Bloody 'ell, that's a long time away especially when you're both away from the house.' The distaff side of the duo answered Nobby's statement 'well we've got a coupla' teenage kids that don't need no child minders anymore and they're responsible guys that look after the affairs while we're away, we contact them everyday to see how they and things are.' The husband picked up their story, saying 'Yeah man, we had to re-mortgage the home to buy this tractor unit we've got now. She's a Kenworth mid 70's model powered by the big Cummins. We work on traction only pulling trailers for various companies and agents, and if we didn't do this type of long distance haulage we wouldn't meet the repayments. But what the Hell, it's one helluva good life. My first tractor was an old White Road Commander with half a million miles on the clock. I drove that old rig on my own until my wife, Bonnie, there, passed her vocational license test 15 years ago and since then we've run as a team. Do you guys wanna come out and see the old gal? The truck I mean not Bonnie.

We replied in the affirmative and went outside with the couple to view their truck. The sleeper pod on this K.Whopper was huge and was fitted with a large bed, television and sound system, washing and cooking facilities, it was home from home.

The lady member of this duo was in her late 30's. Her hubby whose name was Rocky had held his truck drivers license for 20 years and was in his early to mid forties. They told us that their lifestyle was by no means unique in the States and that there were plenty of man and wife teams hauling the length and breadth of America. Indeed, most of the female truckers in the US of A are part of such a team, although there are a number of lady truckers running their own rigs or operating as company drivers.

After we had viewed the big Kenworth and praised the owners on its livery, content and condition we went back inside to finish our drinks, and then we bade the old timer and his missus, and the truckers goodbye and went on our way. We wondered and discussed how the old guy and his missus could possibly make a living, solely from passing trade, and truck drivers miles away from anywhere, in the middle of the desert.

We drove on in to Arizona and stopped at Kingman for an hour and then drove to and spent a night at a true western town called Williams. The town was named after a mountain man named Bill Williams and the locals affected western wear as an everyday uniform and a western steam trains runs daily to the Grand Canyon. Shoot outs are staged daily at the Railway station and the bars are replicas of Wild West saloons in which we sampled a number of the beverages on sale, indeed it was in Williams that I first tasted Jack Daniels Old No. 7, Tennessee sippin' whisky, for which I developed a liking. It seems quite absurd to see a number of big American rigs parked up and delivering in what is essentially a cowboy town, but like towns, villages and cities world wide, if it's in the shops, then a truck brought it.

THE GRAND CANYON AND HOOVER DAM

We set off early the next morning and went to the Grand Canyon, the 8th wonder of the world, where we spent almost a full day. The Grand Canyon is over 200 miles long and between 4 and 18 miles wide and has an average depth of 1 mile from rim to base and over vast millennia has been carved out by the mighty Colorado River. It is a truly awe inspiring sight, and is worth spending a week or two there to explore its rims and depths and all in between, with it's multi-coloured strata and vastness, and wildlife. We parked the car next to a tree which bore a sign which read 'Beware of Mountain Lions' but Mountain Lions aren't the only wildlife to be seen. There is the Rocky Mountain Mule, Deer, Bobcats, Bighorn Sheep and wild burros, these plus the smaller species such as bats and squirrels and mice etc., make a total of 67 kinds of mammal. There are also 220 different types of birds including Humming Birds, add to that the numerous species of reptiles and amphibians and you have a regular outdoor zoological gardens on a grand scale.

There are various trails which you can hike or travel down by donkey or pony to the canyon floor, where a new world awaits you. There are a number of Indian Reservations dotted in and around the canyon, and if one has the courage, there are organised white water rafting expeditions. We took a helicopter flight over the canyon which was a totally breathtaking experience. Unfortunately our itinerary did not allow us the time needed to see everything that the canyon had to offer.

We also visited the Hoover Dam, which holds back the waters of the Colorado River for hydro-electricity and irrigation and

Lake Mead which is Nevada's largest lake albeit man made. As we drove down to the dam viewpoint we followed two totally different types of transport. In front of us was a 1340cc Harley Davidson chopper with a mountain of a man astride it, wearing leather chaps over denim jeans, a cut off denim jacket over a T shirt and a Harley bandana on his head from under which flowed a mane of long, black, greasy hair. His bare arms were heavily tattooed. In front of the HD was a Cadillac de Ville. The de Ville, the Harley and our vehicle parked alongside each other.

We watched as the driver of the Cadillac struggled out of his massive, luxury machine. He was middle-aged, just over 5ft tall and almost as wide. He went to the back door of the Caddy and opened it. A woman of equal proportions clambered out. He locked the vehicle, grasped his partners pudgy hand in his own and they waddled off down the footpath, towards a burger bar, like a pair of overweight penguins, dressed in T shirts and tennis shorts, with trainers and sports socks. They weren't the least bit worried about the way they looked or apparently, about what anyone thought.

We got out of our car and I went over to talk to the Harley rider. I owned a GL 1100cc Honda Goldwing at the time. We talked for a while when I broached the subject of reliability of the Harley in general, which at the time was notoriously bad.

His response was 'if yuh can't fix 'em, don't ride 'em.'

As he walked away I couldn't help but notice a spanner sticking out of his back jeans pocket.

AMERICAN TRUCKERS IN VEGAS

After the visit to the Hoover Dam we left Arizona and made our way into Nevada and up to Las Vegas. We stayed in Las Vegas.

The Jewel of the Desert, with its glaring neon signs, and it's round the clock lifestyle, for 3 days, staying at the Tropicana Hotel.

Nevada legalised gambling in 1931, Las Vegas was just a small desert town in the Great Basin Desert when Meyer Lansky and Bugsy Seigel, in 1945, built the first casino cum hotel, with Mafia money. Their first undertaking was the Flamingo. Seigel was a former hit man who ran a number of crime rackets on the West Coast, including blackmail, numbers and narcotics. His venture into Las Vegas was to be his undoing. Costs for the Flamingo overran by millions of dollars. Much of the money came from Lansky and other East Coast crime bosses, and a lot of it ended up in Seigel's European bank accounts. Bugsy Seigel was gunned down in his girlfriend's Beverley Hills mansion on June 20th 1947 and Lansky's henchmen took over the Flamingo and during the next ten years opened hotels and casinos at a fantastic rate.

We were stood at the bar of the Tropicana Hotel on the first night, chatting and drinking and playing the machines, which are everywhere in Vegas, when this American voice said 'Hey, youse guys European?'

We turned round to face a denim clad guy wearing a baseball cap who looked about 40. Getting a bit fed up of this greeting Nobby said 'No, we're British, we're from Manchester, England. My name's Nobby, this is Laurie and this is John. We're truck drivers on holiday over here.'

'Well, mah name's Ted and ah'm stranded over at the King 8 Truck stop across the highway, waiting for a return load to Philadelphi'. Ah'm running a bit low on cash and Ah've just sold muh wheel trims to another trucker thur. Say, yuh guys, being truck drivers, yuh wanna come over to the King 8 for a drink?'

We discussed the offer and decided to go with our new found friend to the King 8. The lorry park was about 5 acres of hard standing and was almost full with Kenworths, Macks, Fords,

Peterbilts, Oshkoshes, Internationals, Whites, GMC's and even Canadian Western Stars. Western Star was once a subsidiary of White but set up an independent plant in Kelowna, British Columbia. There were other trucks I'd never heard of before.

We walked through the doors of the truck stop, which consisted of a motel, restaurant, games room, bar and like most other establishments in Nevada, a casino, to be greeted by a 20 stone security guard with a .357 Magnum, holstered on his hip, who bade us 'Good day boys, and have a nice time y'all.'

Ted led us through to the bar where he was greeted by a couple of other truckers whose acquaintance he had made earlier. Introductions were made and we joined their company which made 6 of us.

I said 'Right, what yer drinking?'

One of the American truckers, a guy named Scott, said 'Pitchers of Budd'll do.'

So John and I went to the bar and returned with 6 pitchers of Budweiser beer.

Scott looked at me, shaking his head and said 'First time in the States uh?'

'Yeah' I said 'How do you know?'

'Man' he said 'yuh buy one or two pitchers, get 6 glasses and we share it out between us. Gee, you English, man, yuh drives on the wrong side of the road, yuh bangs yer women in the wrong hole and you buys the wrong amount of beer.' He and the others started laughing, and realising our mistake, we saw the funny side of the situation, and laughed along with them.

When a bunch of truck drivers get together the talk invariably turns to trucks and the job and this occasion was no different. I asked Scott 'what sort of rig do you drive?'

'Ah'm an owner operator outa' Loosianni' he said 'Ah drive a

Pete, with a 500 Cummins, on traction only, but the repayments 're killin' me, but it's mah choice and Ah don't think Ah could be a company man.'

I turned to the other yank trucker, his name was Gary, and said 'what about you?'

'Ah'm a company man,' he said 'Ah drive a cab-over White with a big Cat engine. Man, yuh cain't beat that thur pussy power. I hail from Californ-aye-ay.'

'What about you Ted?' I asked.

'Ah'm a company man too, Ah've got an International with a Detroit Diesel giving 475bhp pulling two trailers,' he replied and then asked 'What about youse guys? What type of vehicles do youse guys drive?'

'Well' I said 'we all drive the same type of truck, which happens to be the British Leyland Marathon, powered by the 265 Rolls Royce Eagle.'

It went kinda quiet round our table and then Ted stood up and said to all the other truckers in the bar-room 'Hey fellas, come meet these here Limey truckers, man, they drive Rolls Royce's for a livin'.

We didn't have to buy another drink that night.

I asked our American truck driving brethren about the unions in the States and in particular about the Teamsters. All present had nothing but admiration for the Teamsters and what it stands for and their capability, by sheer weight of numbers, to bring the country to a standstill. They seemed to disbelieve the stories of corruption and bribery and the involvement of organised crime within the union. James Riddle Hoffa, born 14th February 1913 in Brazil, Indiana, disappeared 30th July 1975 was accorded God like status by our trucking acquaintances.

CHAPTER 8
THE TEAMSTERS AND OTHER UNIONS

THE TEAMSTERS

THE Teamsters Union was formed in 1903 by the amalgamation of the Team drivers International Union and the Teamsters National Union. The word teamster derives from the frontier days when wagons were drawn by teams of oxen and later by horses or mules delivering the commodities needed by the new boom towns of the West. They were used to haul lumber from the lumber mills to build these new towns.

The full title of the Teamsters is The International Brotherhood of Teamsters, Chauffeurs, Warehousemen and Helpers of America, abbreviated to the IBT, its membership is made up of mainly truck drivers and van drivers with the rest coming from allied industries. The Teamsters had, in 1998, 1.4 million members.

In 1907 Daniel J. Tobin, a Boston Teamster, took over the reins as President of the union and held that position until 1952. He helped the Teamsters grow by being less than charitable to other unions and by keeping a tight grip on the purse strings and the expenditure of union funds. In 1933 the Union started to organise the fast developing, long distance trucking industry, gaining contracts in the peripheral enterprises as well as the actual trucking.

Tobin's successor, Dave Beck, had problems concerning corruption and upon the findings of the Senate investigating Committee, the Teamsters were expelled from the Federation of Labour and the Congress of Industrial Organisation. This ostracism lasted until 1988 when the IBT was allowed re-entry.

Beck was jailed in 1958 for larceny and income tax violations. He was succeeded by the most famous or infamous President the Teamsters have had, depending upon one's point of view. This personage was J.R. (Jimmy) Hoffa.

James Riddle Hoffa was summoned before various Senate Committees concerning the finances of the Union and dealings with organised crime. He carried on a running battle with one of the Senators, there was no love lost between Hoffa and Bobby Kennedy. Kennedy was Chief Counsel of the Senate Labour Rackets Committee better known as the McClellan Committee. He was everything Hoffa hated - born into money, Ivy League educated, refined and good looking. Hoffa on the other hand was a pugnacious character who defined manhood by the way a man handled himself in a brawl, he believed the ends justified the means and only success mattered no matter how gained.

Hoffa himself was jailed in 1967, but held on to presidency until 1971 when he resigned and was succeeded by Frank E. Fitzsimmons. Under Fitzsimmons' presidency massive IBT contributions were made to President Nixon's re-election committee which paved the way for Hoffa's release. In 1975 while attempting to regain power in the Union, Hoffa disappeared from a restaurant parking lot in Bloomfield Hills, Michigan. His body was never found and in 1983 he was declared legally dead. It is generally believed that Hoffa was bumped off by the Mafia.

Numerous books and films have been produced documenting Hoffa's life but his demise remains a mystery,

During the 1970's and 80's a number of Teamster leaders were convicted of irregularities in the handling of pension funds and of accepting bribes from employers to stop strikes. The pension fund was yielded to outside interests to oversee.

Fitzsimmons died in 1981 and was succeeded by Roy Williams who was convicted the same year of bribing a U.S. Senator. He was followed as President by Jackie Presser in 1982. Presser was indicted in 1985 for embezzling union funds.

In 1989, with William McCarthy as President, the Teamsters settled a federal racketeering suit that accused officials of allowing known criminals to control and exploit the union. Following this Ronald R. Carey, a former New York parcel delivery driver and local Teamsters official was voted in as the Teamsters President. Carey barely won re-election in 1996, just beating James R. Hoffa, Jimmy Hoffa's son, into second place. Hoffa won the 1998 election to replace Carey and was re-elected in 2001.

It seems that the Teamsters Union is run on a closed shop basis and that if you are non union, you don't work. It also appears that the Teamsters, over the years have been riddled with corruption.

TRANSPORT UNIONS IN THE UK

In the UK the unions are fragmented with the Transport and General Workers Union being the biggest transport union. There is also the United Road Transport Union. A lot of big retail companies and utility companies are unionised with whichever union has the franchise. This means that the drivers have union representation but not from a dedicated transport union. The days of the closed shop were made illegal under the Thatcher

Government. Mrs T. did her damndest to kill the unions in the UK, resulting in a loss of power that I doubt will ever be regained and some people think rightly so.

Unions were originally formed to protect the rights of manual workers and to ensure that the said workers were not taken advantage of. This being the case the majority of unions have a member base that is a Labour voting working class base. Nowadays there are white collar unions that look after managerial staff and office workers and has a base drawn mainly from centre to right wing Conservative voters. Of course, the political affiliations of union members may overlap so that the Labour, Conservative split is not a yard stick by which to judge membership.

Most working class union members are of the belief that the wealthy company owners would like to see unions destroyed and a return to the days of *'The Ragged Trousered Philanthropists'* as written by Robert Trestle, in which the bosses ruled with an iron fist and children were sent down the mines and up the chimneys. Wages were low and hours long in order to swell the coffers of the bloated mill owners and mine owners and business men in general at the expense of the working man and woman. In the eyes of the Labour voter Margaret Thatcher only served to prolong these views.

As a union man and officer I would like to put to bed the myth that unions and management are forever at loggerheads. Obviously there are requests from either side that the other cannot acquiesce to, but these points form the basis of negotiation by which some common ground can be achieved. Both the unions and management want what is best for the company and the workforce, although the opinion of what's best may differ considerably between the two opposing factions.

CHAPTER 9
MORE AMERICA AND MORE B.T.

YOSEMITE, MOUNTAINS AND A FEW BARS

WE left Vegas a couple of days after our evening at the King 8 and headed back into California and up to the Yosemite National Park. We spent the night just outside Yosemite and had most of the next day in the park, looking in wonderment at the Giant Sequoias, in all their majesty. These giant Redwood trees can live for 3000 years and attain heights of over 300ft. We gazed at the landscape with its mountains and Yosemite Falls, the tallest waterfall in North America cascading 2425ft. We actually drove through one of the big redwoods that straddled the roadway, though you could not have driven an articulated rig through there. In the late afternoon we left the big Redwoods behind and drove over the Sierra Nevada Mountains to Modesto, where we spent the night. We arrived at our hotel in Modesto fairly late in the evening after fuelling up in the town.

The ride over the mountains was quite eventful because upon leaving Yosemite we realised that we may need some fuel to get us to Modesto. Now on the desert roads and over the mountains of North America, fuel stops are few and far between and with all the gear changing and the long hard climbs up the mountain roads and because there were 3 adults and all their luggage, fuel consumption was hardly frugal. By the time we reached the mountain road we had still not seen a fuel station, but by then we were committed. By the time we reached the summit, the fuel gauge needle was touching the red zone. I was the driver over this mountainous terrain and on the downhill run I knocked it into neutral and coasted, re-engaging gear on bends and any slight uphill gradients and any really steep downwards gradients, in order to conserve fuel. John, who is of a nervous nature, kept asking 'How's the fuel? Are we going to make it off these Godforsaken mountains?'

I replied 'We're really low John boy, we might have to park up at the side of the road and get some help in the morning.'

'No way, man,' he replied 'we'll get eaten by grizzly bears or cougars or something, or someone'll come along and kill us and steal the car.'

'No-one's gonna steal a car with no petrol.' Said Nobby 'an' I don't think there's gonna be a bunch of murderous hillbillies out looking for 3 Englishmen in a broken down hire car, an' I don't think wild bears and cougars have the knowledge to open car doors.'

These comments did nothing to assuage John's fears and he responded with 'Just get us off this Goddamn mountain, for Christ's sake.'

So I carried on coasting when I could, in gear when I had to, until the lights of Modesto came into view. There was a fuel stop on the edge of town and as I drove in the car started spluttering and died as I pulled up by the fuel pump. Since that day I have never let a vehicle, be it a truck or car, run below a quarter full.

After fuelling up we found our hotel, deposited our cases and went for a well earned drink in the nearest bar, our hotel being a dry establishment. We were stood at the bar having a beer or two when a fight broke out at the pool table between a black guy and a white guy. The black guy threw a haymaker which caught the white guy on the side of the head. He fell backwards into the pool table with such force that both his arms went out to the sides and smashed heavily onto the playing surface of the pool table. His watch flew off his wrist, through the air and landed in John's beer glass. The black guy stood waiting with his fists clenched. The white guy recovered some of his composure, pointed at his protagonist and said 'right motherfucker, Ah'm goin' ta mah pickup, get mah scattergun and ah'm gonna blow yore sorry black ass to kingdom come.'

The black fellow made to move towards the other fellow when the waiter cum barman ran between them and ushered the defeated fighter to a neutral corner, this being the car park.

The bartender re-entered after a few minutes with a scattergun cradled in his arms and declared 'Bob's gone home to sleep it off. Thar'll be no more entertainment tonight.'

John handed the watch to the barman, we finished our drinks and retired to our hotel. So, all in all, a very eventful day.

The following morning we drove on to San Francisco. We took in all the usual sites of 'Frisco' including a boat ride under the Golden Gate Bridge and around Alcatraz Island. We went to Fisherman's Wharf, Chinatown etc. We rode cable cars, watched the street mime artists and generally had a good time.

On the trip down to L.A., we called at Monterey Bay, Big Sur, drove the famous 17 mile drive, and went into Carmel where Clint Eastwood was Mayor. We found his bar, The Hog's Breath, and called in for a bite to eat and a couple of drinks. I went to the bar for some more drinks and engaged the barman in small talk.

I said 'Does Clint come in often?'

'Oh yeah man,' said the barman 'He comes in all the time.'

'Yeah?' I said questioningly.

'Yeah man, in fact he's in the back right now cleaning up and washing the dishes.' He said and then burst out laughing. In the words of the yanks I'd been suckered.

We left Carmel and continued South down the coast road through San Luis Obispo, Santa Barbara and Santa Monica and back into L.A., where we had a week to visit Anaheim home of the original Disneyland and Universal Studios, Newport Beach, Knotts Berry Farm etc.

It was while we were in Anaheim for our last week that we happened to be in a local bar, when we met a hippie guy named Gene. He heard us talking and asked 'Are you guys from Europe?' We explained to him that we were from Manchester, England.

'Manchester eh? Is that anywhere near London?'

'It's about 200 miles away.' I replied.

'Gee, that close eh?' he responded and then said 'Listen you guys, I can take yuh to a bar where they play English darts, if yuh wanna.'

'We've come near 6000 miles to get away from that.' Said Nobby.

'Well how do yuh fancy a biker bar?' he asked and continued it's only a short walk.'

We decided to go to the biker bar with the hippie. When we arrived there were numerous Harley's and Gold Wings lined up outside. We went inside, got some drinks and were challenged to a game of pool. John and I play snooker, so we took on the opposition and beat all comers. I was down to take a shot when I heard this guy behind me say to one of his compatriots 'Dese guys are European, man. Big bucks, man.'

I thought to myself 'Hello, we could have a spot of bother here.'

I took my shot and as I rose I felt a tap on the shoulder. I turned to be confronted by a broad shouldered, well built, crew cutted young man who said to me 'these guys yuh keep whuppin' at pool, man. Waal them's American gypsies man, and I think they may be out to rob yuzz. Now me and my buddies over there,' he pointed to half a dozen or so T-shirted, well built, cropped haired men, 'are US Marines. Now you need a hand, just holler and you've got it, man, in fact, fuck the pool, come over and join us.'

Mysteriously, Gene had disappeared, so we finished our last game of pool and joined the Marines. We had a good night. The gypsies moved on and we were invited by the Marines, who were stationed at San Diego, to visit their camp and avail ourselves of their PX Stores. Sadly, as we only had a couple of days left of our trip Stateside, we declined their offer. At the end of the evening we said our goodbyes and made our way back to the Travelodge, Anaheim.

For our last full day of recreation in Anaheim, before we flew home, after spending 2 days in Disneyland, I day at Universal Studios and a full day at Knotts Berry Farm Amusement Park and seeing all the attractions deemed necessary, we decided to spend a day lying in the sun and swimming at Newport Beach. We left the car at the motel and took a local bus to Newport Beach where we discovered mini-skirted, long legged waitresses serving drinks whilst wearing roller boots to skate along the boardwalk.

On the beach were the keep fit fanatics including joggers, volleyball players, even people playing that most English of games, cricket, but the strangest sight was the muscle bound, body builders, working out on the beach with an assortment of weights that they had brought along for the purpose. They were the epitome of the most egotistical, self adoring, show offs that I have ever seen.

We secured a fairly isolated spot on the beach and took it in turns to go swimming in the clear, cobalt blue Pacific, at last one of us staying on the beach to sunbathe and to guard our belongings.

After a couple of hours of swimming and sunbathing we went to a beach bar called Blacky's Bar. We were introduced to Blacky, the owner to whom we chatted whilst we had a couple of beers and a little sustenance, when John, who had been staring at the stuffed carcase of a huge hammerhead shark that was mounted on the wall, asked 'Say Blacky, where did you catch that bloody big hammerhead over there?'

'A hundred yards out where you've just been swimming.' Was the reply.

'Good Jesus, that's the last time I go in the bloody water.' Said John.

Blacky started laughing and said 'Ah'm just joshin' man, okay.'

The next day we deposited our hire car back at the Alamo Car Hire Depot at L.A. Airport, had our last look around Los Angeles and prepared ourselves for our return flight. We all agreed that we had had the most fantastic holiday of our lifetimes.

During our travels we had stopped at numerous truck stops and seen many and varied US trucks from plain day cabs to units with massive sleeper pods fitted with showers etc. Some of these heavily customised tractor units with the big sleepers must have been near 30ft long on their own. Most of the 53ft trailers had their axles set right to the rear and would be almost impossible to negotiate on general haulage on British roads.

Upon arriving home and returning to work we pinned our speeding citation on the notice board, feeling quite proud that we'd got away with it and wishing the British bobby was as easy going on motorists and truckers as his American counterpart.

A TRIP TO THE SHETLANDS

Shortly after the visit to 'The home of the Brave and the Land of the Free.' British Telecom moved its HGV operations from the yard in Gorton to a custom designed transport depot off Greengate, Chadderton. There was much more room in the yard and we now had a trans-shipping shed where vehicles could be stripped and loaded under cover. It was just after this move that BT purchased two specially constructed trailers, one for the Northern sector of the UK and one for the South. They were to be used by BT at sales shows and venues as backup for the sales team. The prime movers for these trailers were Dodges powered by Perkin's diesel, somewhat under powered but they had to do. Another case of management not consulting with the staff as to what was the right machine for the job.

The trailers were a wonderful piece of engineering and were 40ft, tri axle low profile, drop frames with their own water supply and waste tank, their own generator and electrical plug in lead and air conditioning. On the upper bed of the drop frame was a self contained kitchen with microwave oven and fridge and tea and coffee making facilities. The external sides of the trailer along the lower section opened up hydraulically giving an extra 7ft of floor space and ceiling on either side. The space between ceiling and floor was then filled with a series of glass panels, which were stored in cupboards in the trailer, giving an enclosed working floor area of approximately 33ft by 22ft. The trailer was loaded with telecommunications equipment. There were telephone systems, answering machines, modems, computers and all the latest technology of the day both commercial and domestic. This equipment was fitted to desks which were moved into their relevant position within the trailer which had numerous plug-in points around the floor. The trailer was now a mobile salesroom offering refreshments, ready for both the sales team and the punters.

I became the driver for the northern vehicle. Venues and shows were held locally and further afield. Down as far as Barnstaple in North Devon and as far up as Aberdeen, Elgin, Wick and even the Shetland Islands. Because of the air-con, which could be used, either as a heating or cooling unit, and the self contained kitchen, I used to take a camp bed with me and use the kitchen as my bedroom. It was like home from home, my own little bed-sit.

The job to the Shetlands was different to the sales jobs. The reason the sales trailer was sent up there was because a new digital exchange was opening at Aberdeen which would handle all the calls for Shetland, and this was a case of BT at its most philanthropic. The trailer became a classroom to enable the disenfranchised exchange workers a chance to learn new skills on the computers and other equipment to allow them to get alternative employment.

I was to take the vehicle over for a fortnight. The vehicle was based at the Northallerton depot and I had to get a train on a Saturday morning to Northallerton, then a cab to the depot where I picked up the vehicle, charged the water tanks, fuelled up, checked the vehicle over then left for Aberdeen to catch the overnight ferry to Lerwick. Driving up the ramp onto the ferry, the rear end of the drop frame grounded where the ramp came to an apex because of the low profile tyres and an incoming tide. A massive fork lift was brought from the dockyard to lift the trailers back end and give me a gentle push forward, freeing me from this embarrassing position.

BT had supposedly booked a single berth for me on this crossing, but when I found the cabin and entered there were two bunks and a suitcase on the top one. I got washed and changed and went for my evening meal followed by a couple of pints. Upon returning to the cabin, at about 22.00hrs, I found a drunken Scotsman lying in the top bunk. We made a bit of small talk but he was well in his cups, so I cleaned my teeth and got into bed. By this time the gentleman on the top bunk was well away in the Land of Nod. As I got into bed it started, the talking in his sleep, the talking ceased and the snoring started and vice versa, and all the time he was thrashing around like someone demented, which I'm sure he was. Needless to say I got very little sleep that night, but in the wee small hours I finally nodded off. When I awoke I was alone and I actually thought someone had played a monstrous joke on me.

We docked at Lerwick on the Sunday morning. I drove off the ferry, out of the docks and on to my rendezvous point, by the old telephone exchange. I spent most of the day setting the trailer up and getting everything working. I spent the first night sleeping in the trailer, but because I was to be on the island for a fortnight, I booked into a nearby B&B for the rest of my stay. On the Monday morning one of the BT staff met me. He had brought a hired minibus, which I was to use to pick up and return the tutors and pupils for the two classes per day that were to be held. I made them tea and coffee and there was light snacks of crisps and biscuits. The rest of the time was my own and I visited the Viking museum, went bird watching, spotting Artic terns, Great Skuas, Artic Skuas and Cormorants, Shags and Gannets etc. I also went seal watching and even watched the peat diggers. I booked on each morning at 07.00hrs and finished at 20.30hrs and was on stand by for 8 hours for each day of the following week-end, although in reality the time was used cleaning the vehicle, emptying the waste tank, re-charging the fresh water tank and a multiplicity of other small but necessary jobs.

When it was all over I stowed away all the computer and telecommunications equipment, removed the side glass walls of the trailer and packed everything up and secured everything in place. I closed up the hydraulic floor and roof, discharged the waste tank, I was then ready to leave the site and thus the Shetlands. I drove to the docks to catch the overnight sailing to Aberdeen. The following day I drove down to Northallerton, parked the vehicle up, got a cab to the railway station and caught the train back to Manchester and was back at home by the early evening.

My wages for this jaunt were approximately 4 times the average wage I normally cleared for a fortnight, thanks to the extended hours plus three week-ends with time and a half for Saturdays and double pay for Sundays.

A CHANGE OF WORKING PRACTICE

After the privatisation of British Telecom and at the start of 1987, cost cutting measures came into being and a trunking system was set up, and a number of Fodens with the S83 cab, fitted with 290hp Cummins were bought for use on trunking operations. This meant that deliveries were not carried out by the distance men but that fully loaded trailers were dropped at major depots for the local drivers from these depots to deliver. The distance men would then pick up another fully laden trailer and take it to its next destination. One could pick up a trailer in Newhouse for delivery to Crayford in Kent, so the nights out were still there.

Because it was 'pedal to the metal' driving, these Fodens were turning out only 4 or 5 mpg. In an attempt to better the fuel returns and become more efficient for the shareholders, a further cost cutting exercise in the guise of trailer change-overs was introduced. This meant the Newhouse drivers would change over trailers with the Manchester drivers at a pre-determined spot, this usually being Carlisle. The London drivers would change over at Birmingham. All the major depots, Manchester, Preston, Newhouse, Crayford, Colindale, Birmingham, Hereford and Northallerton set up day trunking operations, thus the distance men lost their nights out, whereas the local delivery men and low loader operators were still getting the occasional night out due to the number of drops on their trailers, or, in the case of the low loaders, the type of work being carried out and the distance involved. This caused a lot of animosity because the distance men had seniority over the delivery men and so demanded a share of the nights away. It took a lot of thrashing out, by the union and management, but there was resolution, of a kind, after a while.

By this time most of the established distance men were approaching retirement age, which was 60 at BT, some took early retirement and the younger element didn't mind sharing whatever work there was. It seems in the world of privatisation one cannot stand in the way of progress and profitability.

Like all the other depots Manchester had a couple of drop frame and low loader trailers. The low loaders, when I started, were of the 4 in line, knock out type. This meant that the rear axle was comprised of 4 equally spaced wheels on an axle which was secured to the rear of the trailer bed by two massive threaded pins. These pins had to be removed, the trailer jacked up and the back axle knocked out, then ramps fitted to enable loading from the rear. If the cargo could be loaded from the side, it would be, but if one was to load a mobile generator or another vehicle the rear axle had to be removed. Getting the axle out was easy but lining up and trying to re-insert it was a somewhat more laborious and tedious operation. To assist in the loading from the rear, both the low loaders and drop frames were fitted with a manual ratchet winch and cable.

When the time came for renewal of the low loaders the company bought state of the art, tri axle, 50ft King trailers with hydraulic goose neck and double hinged rear ramps and a powered winch. They even had solar powered power packs as back up. When laid our flat with both the goose neck and rear ramps down the overall length was 70ft. A mobile exchange or generator could be pulled on over the goose neck, uncoupled and the towing vehicle could drive off over the rear ramps, making the job much easier. I drove both types of low loader on various occasions on different types of work thus adding another string to my bow.

With the loss of the majority of the distance work, I ended up working out of the local cable yard and doing local deliveries and day trunks, with the occasional low loader or drop frame load thrown in, as and when necessary.

A TRIP TO THE HEBRIDES AND BACK

In the winter of 1987, I and another driver, Arthur Larkin, were given a two man job in a 4 wheeler, delivering computer equipment to Jobcentres and Benefits Offices around Scotland. It was considered a 2 man job because of the high value load.

Arthur Larkin was a Londoner living up North. He had a rather descriptive way of talking and as we were heading North towards Scotland, somewhere along the M6 where the inside lane was somewhat well used and deteriorated and had two deep grooves worn into its surface due to the constant passage of heavy goods vehicles, Arthur remarked ' 'Ya' could let go of the bleedin' handlebars in these bloody tram lines and the old bus'd steer 'erself.'

We were to go to the furthest drop and work our way back down. So our first drop was to be Stornaway on the Isle of Lewis in the Outer Hebrides. We made our way up to Ullapool where we caught the Caledonian McBraine ferry to Stornaway. We made our delivery to the Benefits Office in Stornaway but, because of the infrequency of the ferries, had to spend the night in Stornaway and catch the early morning ferry back to the mainland.

On our way down, from Ullapool, due to the drops we had on, we came down through Inverness, and Aviemore, Newtonmore and down through the Dalwhinnie Pass. Weather conditions were atrocious. Blizzard conditions prevailed and into the pass we were down to 10mph. As we slowly made our way Arthur said to me 'have you ever had that feeling you're all on your lonesome? There ain't no traffic coming the other way, I haven't seen another bleedin' vehicle for the last couple of miles.'

'Funny enough, Arthur' I said 'there's nothing behind us either. It looks like we're the only vehicle on the pass.'

'Somehow, I don't think we should bleedin' be here. They usually close the pass in white out conditions and I reckon that's what we've got here.' was Arthur's critical opinion.

There was a slight break in the weather when we were a couple of miles from the Dalwhinnie Hotel, at the bottom of the pass, when we glimpsed the massive spotlight of the police helicopter above us. We finally reached the bottom of the pass and stopped to be greeted by a welcoming committee of police and mountain rescue people. A police sergeant came over and said 'Och aye mon, where've ye bin?' We're waiting to close the snow gates to the pass due to the inclement wither, ye were getting' us werried.'

We had somehow got through at the top of the pass when we

should not have, but we were safely through and the authorities wished us a safe journey and sent us on our way.

The rest of the deliveries were in Fort William, Campbeltown on Kintyre, and a few drops in and around Glasgow. On our way down from Fort William we, with time running out, came to a village called Tyndrum on the A82 by the River Lochy. We parked the wagon near the village square, where there was an information board listing the local amenities. Amongst these amenities were the names of a couple of B&B's and the first one we phoned had vacancies. We drove to our accommodation and parked up outside. The house was used for tourists as a rule, but this being the depths of winter, tourists were, somewhat, thin on the ground and so Arthur and I had a single room apiece. The tariff wasn't cheap although it was worth every penny, and we got a little discount for the time of the year. The rooms were *en suite* the beds were comfortable with electric blankets. We were invited to dine with the proprietors who served us a three course meal. The first course being a thick Scotch broth, which normally, would have been sustenance enough. This was followed by a venison main course and we finished with a boiled pudding known as duff. After this repast, Arthur and I had to go for a stroll around the village to walk it off a bit. Upon returning and whilst we were watching the television and chatting with our hosts, the whisky bottle appeared and we were offered a single malt as a night cap. The man of the house had a full time job for a local landowner as a gillie, or gamekeeper whilst his wife ran the B&B. After the television, the whisky and the small talk, we retired to our rooms.

When we awoke the following morning, and went down to the breakfast room, we were greeted by the lady of the house, who laid before each of us, a steaming bowl of thick porridge oats, cooked as only the Scottish can cook porridge. This was followed by poached salmon and toast. It ran through my head, knowing the houseowners trade, that this salmon might be poached in more ways than one. We finished this epicurean delight, got ourselves ready for the elements outside, said our goodbyes and made our way to our vehicle, checked it out, started it up and continued down the A82 through Crianlarich to Tarbet where we picked up the A83 and headed for the second town called Tarbet at the head of Kintyre, and so down to Campbeltown. We made our delivery and parked up on the quayside and went in pursuit of digs for the night. We found some not far from the quay where we had to share a double room. We each had a shower and got changed and went down for our evening meal, watched a bit of tele' and then, at about 21.00hrs went out for a pint to what was the local fisherman's pub. We were enjoying our couple of pints when, at 23.00hrs the landlord came from behind the bar, locked the pub doors and returned to the bar. It was the first time Arthur and I had ever been to Campbeltown and here we were, the subjects of a lock in, without being asked.

At about midnight, voices could be heard outside the pub, and then there was a knocking on the door. The Landlord opened the door and a number of snow sprinkled fishermen clad in oilskins, woolly jumpers and sea boots came in, and a bit of a knees up ensued. Arthur and I struck it out until about 01.30hrs and then asked the Landlord to free us from the late night social gathering so that we could go to our beds. We left the pub to be greeted by a snowstorm so fierce we could barely see our way forward. We reached the digs and let ourselves in, compliments of a spare key loaned to us by the owner. There was no heating on and the household was freezing. The owner of the digs had been good enough to turn on the electric blankets on the beds and it was that cold that we left them on whilst we slept. The next morning we arose a little later than normal, performed our ablutions and went down for breakfast, which was your usual egg, bacon, sausage, beans, a fried slice, toast and a mug of tea. It looked lovely upon presentation, steaming away, but by the time it was on the fork and to the mouth it was merely lukewarm. I felt like an Eskimo in an Igloo and couldn't wait to get back in the wagon and get the heater going.

We finally left Campbeltown at about 10.00hrs and made our way back up Kintyre on the A83 alongside Loch Fyne, past Inverary, to pick up the A82. Then down to Dumbarton where we started the last of our deliveries around Glasgow, before we finally headed home after a fairly eventful week, but not before we had our final night out, for the week, at the Brock Truck stop North of Preston on the A6, which gave us a guaranteed 5 hrs for running in on the Saturday morning.

The Dalwhinnie episode wasn't the only time I was caught unawares by the weather. Later that same winter after the Christmas break I was given a trailer load of mixed goods to deliver to Newcastle upon Tyne. My return load was a mixed bag of empty cable drums for transhipment at Manchester. Once I had tipped and reloaded I set off down the A1 at a leisurely pace, as I was running a bit early, I ran down to Ferrybridge and joined the M62. The weather had been cold but bright and sunny all day. I reached Hartshead Moor Services some time in the mid afternoon and pulled in for a cuppa. I proceeded to brew up and have a Cadburys Snack; I then had a browse around the service area shop. After about a half hour had passed I started up my vehicle and pulled off the services and onto the motorway. I was approximately 40 minutes away from the BT depot. I was approaching the Huddersfield slip road when I came upon a queue of traffic and the motorway police. The motorway had been closed ahead due to heavy snowfalls across the Saddleworth Moors which rendered the motorway and local roads impassable. The police were diverting everybody off the motorway and into Huddersfield.

By this time the snow had reached Huddersfield and all

surrounding areas and was falling like an impenetrable wall. I was forced to park up overnight on Leeds Road in Huddersfield Town and look for accommodation. This I found in a little pub that did bed and breakfast and evening meal. I booked in, had a shower, a lovely evening meal and a few pints of Tetley's mild beer to wash it down.

The next day I arose about 07.00hrs, had my breakfast, paid my bill and ventured outside. To my complete and utter surprise the sun was coming up and there was only a little snow remaining. By the time I reached the motorway it was as if no snow had fallen at all on the roads. The adjacent fields and moorlands, however looked like a Christmas card scene, the sky and land almost blurring into one on the horizon, the telegraph poles and pylons standing stark against a wintry sky. The sun was low and bright yellow like a shining jewel hanging in the morning sky. When I reached the depot in Manchester, where no snow had fallen at all, it was to some disbelief, that I related my tale of the previous afternoon to the other staff. I had had to take a night out when just over half an hours run from home and with at least 2 hours running time left.

TRIPS TO IRELAND

BT also used to send vehicles and drivers to Northern Ireland. These were mainly vehicles of 7.5ton capacity, which were based at Manchester but worked out of BT's Monarch Factory at Leeds. Monarch, at the time was a new type of telecommunications system. They also sent trailers over, loaded with cable, concrete and ironwork and any other commodities that were needed. The Monarch men generally sailed from Liverpool, but the artics had to run up to Stranraer for the sailing to Larne.

I went over quite frequently, while there was still some trouble over there. Usually there would be 2 or 3 of us would go together or meet up at Larne. There would probably be one driver from Newhouse, one from Birmingham and one from Manchester. If we could all get in, we all used the same digs, the Curran Court, and normally went for a drink in Robbie's Bar in the town.

Wherever we delivered in Northern Ireland, be it Belfast, Newtownards, Londonderry or anywhere else, we were supposed to return to the secure lorry park at Larne.

I never saw any trouble during the times I was over there and the locals treated us well. I and other drivers were made welcome in Robbie's Bar and whichever digs we stayed in. Of course the fact that we were spending money was obviously a major factor.

The closest thing I ever say to trouble was one night when 3 of us were returning to the Curran Court after an evening drinking at Robbie's. we had just passed the police station, which had sand bags up against the wall and concrete barriers around it, when a car full of local youths came screaming down the road. The occupants of the car were shouting and swearing out of the windows and driving dangerously. Half a dozen well armed soldiers appeared from nowhere and stopped the offending vehicle. These soldiers must have been crouched in doorways and gateways or behind trees, because prior to them making their appearance, we had no idea anyone was about. We thought the streets were empty. It was as if they had materialised out of thin air, but we didn't hang around to see what transpired. Generally, though, the trips to Northern Ireland were a good crack, even though my wife was never happy about me going there.

I came across a taste of Irish humour the first time I went over. I was to deliver a load of cable to the BT depot in Newtownards and was on my way to the said depot. On the outskirts of Newtonards I pulled up by a little grocery shop and went inside to ask for some directions. I said to the proprietor 'do you know the best way to the British telecom Depot in Newtonards?'

'Ore ye drivin' a vehicle?' the owner asked.

'Yes I am' I replied.

'Well dat's the best way' he said 'it beats walkin' everytime.'

He had a little laugh and then pointed me in the right direction.

One week I went to work not knowing where I may be sent. It turned out that I had a number of drops starting at Bradford and Leeds and working up North Yorkshire and finishing in the Northallerton Depot where I did a trailer change over. I swapped my empty trailer for a trailer loaded with deliveries for throughout the North East. It was evening time by the time I'd done the change over and so I ran to my digs, which I'd booked from the Northallerton depot and parked up for the night.

After my tea and when I'd had a shower, I decided to phone my wife, which I did every night I was away. Part way through our conversation she asked me 'Where are you tonight?'

'Londonderry.' I replied.

'Oh no, they haven't sent you to Ireland again have they?'

I started laughing, realising what I had said. I was, in fact, at the Londonderry Lodge on the A1, less than a 2 hour drive from home.

IN MEMORY OF THE DEAR DEPARTED

Early in 1988, on a Friday night, a number of BT drivers met up at Micklefield Truck Stop on the old A1 north of Leeds. There was myself, Pete Gilly, Jonah, George Parrot and Marc Taylor a low loader driver. We had all booked in, gotten showered and shaved and met in the café cum restaurant for our evening meals. We discussed walking down to the Miner's Social Club in Micklefield village for a couple of pints and then back to the truckstop to watch the cabaret in the concert room and have a couple more pints before turning in for the night. We were about to depart for the Miner's club at about 20.30hrs when the lady owner of the truckstop came into the restaurant and asked 'Who's the driver of the Devereux's of Billingham from County Cleveland truck, registration such and such?'

There was no reply and the lady continued 'Well the vehicle has been parked up since about 4.0.clock. The curtains are drawn around his cab and he hasn't paid his parking fee.'

With that she and one of her minions went out to the said vehicle, followed by a few drivers. The Owner's assistant banged on the cab door. There was no reply. He banged again. Still no reply. The owner of the digs asked her aide to try the door of the cab to ascertain whether it was locked or not. Somewhat hesitantly he reached for the door handle and gave it a pull. The door sprung open. There was a brief silence then a high pitched scream emanated from the only lady present.

The curtains of the cab came to below the cab door window and the sight that came into view once the door was opened was of a naked pair of legs with trousers crumpled around the ankles. The upper part of the body and the head was slumped over the steering wheel and the arms dangled at the sides of the lifeless body. The driver was DEAD.

An ambulance and the police were called. The driver's company was notified. The body was taken away, interviews were conducted.

It appeared that the deceased, prior to the tragic event, had attempted to heat some water on a portable gas stove. Whether for a wash or a brew is unknown. He was in the process of getting changed out of his work gear and into something cleaner. It is assumed that the lighted gas had gone out and the cab became filled with toxic fumes causing drowsiness and then rendering the poor soul unconscious and finally depriving him of life.

We were told, at a later date, that the deceased was an agency driver and was only doing a couple of days for the company whose vehicle he was driving. This episode, of course, was the main topic of conversation in the digs for the remainder of the evening. Most of the drivers were somewhat subdued, the trip to the Miner's Club was cancelled and we all retired to our rooms early, mourning the cruel demise of one of our brethren.

A RATHER SERIOUS INDUSTRIAL ACCIDENT AND IT'S AFTER EFFECTS

It was while working at BICC at Blackley in the summer of 1988 that an unfortunately occurrence befell me. I was in the process of roping up a flat bed, semi trailer, fully laden with cable. BICC had an arrangement with BT that a section of the yard should be left clear as a roping and sheeting area. Unfortunately this agreement was not adhered to and the designated area was regularly used as a storage area for cable drums. For this reason I was roping up by the crane road. As I was putting the finishing touches to the back end of the trailer, tying off by means of double and treble dollies to ensure tightness and therefore safety. The rope suddenly snapped, catapulting me backwards, like a stone from a slingshot, off the footpath and down a 2ft drop on to the steel track of the straddle crane, upon which I landed heavily, pelvis first.

The impact and sudden intense pain rendered me unconscious for a while. I found out, some time later, that the crane driver had not seen the episode unfolding beneath him and was drawing ever closer to my prone figure lying across the track. Fortunately, for me, someone hailed the driver and prompted him to stop a mere couple of feet from my insensible form. I recovered consciousness as I was being lifted from the track, by a mixture of BT and BICC employees, to be deposited on the back seat of a car, to be taken to hospital. The car had been brought to the scene for that specific purpose, and belonged to one of the BICC workers. I was in severe pain and moaning audibly. Why an ambulance had not been called, I know not, and I never found out, and I was incapable of questioning the actions of the staff, who at the time, thought they were doing the right thing. I was ferried to the North Manchester General Hospital, which is only a few hundred yards from BICC's yard. The staff that had lifted me from the track were reprimanded for moving me before establishing the extent of the injuries I may have sustained. As it happened I sustained a pelvic fracture and some soft tissue, lower spinal damage, which necessitated my going on long term sickness.

I returned to work after 3 months sick leave, but this proved to be too early. The first job I was given was a load to deliver to Huddersfield, Bradford and Leeds. Upon reaching Huddersfield TEC and unroping the section of the load to be removed, I clambered onto the load to pull back the sheet to give access for the stacker truck. As I bent down to grip and pull the sheet a severe pain shot through my back. It felt as I imagined being stabbed would feel, cold steel delivering red hot pain, and I dropped to my knees and then fell face down, flat out on top of the load. The stacker truck driver watched this display and thought it was a show of histrionics, indeed, if it was, it would have been worthy of an Oscar. After a while the realisation that I was not jesting, downed upon him and he called for assistance. An empty pallet was put on the forks of the truck and raised to the level of the load. With assistance and some discomposure and looking and moving like Charles Laughton in his role as Quasimodo, I managed to wriggle myself onto the pallet and was lowered to ground level. A chair was brought out and I managed, with aid, to place myself into a fairly comfortable sitting position upon it. A hot drink was brought out to me, whilst my home depot was notified of the ongoing events. The home depot sent a car, in which I was to be taken home, in the car was a second driver to continue with the deliveries I could no longer do. I was firstly taken back to the Manchester depot where all the relevant forms were filled out. I was then taken home from whence I called out my GP for a home visit and another week on sick leave ensued.

After this further week's sickness I, once again, returned to work. This time I was given a load to Birmingham. Upon arriving in Brum, and whilst dropping my trailer I experienced the same excruciating, stabbing pain I'd felt at Huddersfield, and once again collapsed in a heap, this time by the side of the vehicle, where I was found by another driver, struggling to get to my feet, using the side of the truck as a climbing frame. I was assisted to the transport office, leaning on the other driver for support, and, moving, once again as if imitating Victor Hugo's bellringer. The Manchester depot was notified of my condition and arrangements were made to get me home. This time I was brought home in the Manchester vehicle, as a passenger, by a Brummy driver, who in turn was ferried back to Birmingham as a passenger with a Manchester driver. I was taken home and, once again went sick until an appointment could be made for me to see the company doctor.

When I finally received the appointment date, I went for the examination, hoping that the company medic would offer some universal panacea or the laying on of hands to affect a cure. Instead he told me of a degenerate disease and the slow worsening of my condition and, much to my surprise, recommended medical retirement. Within a month in June 1990, I was pensioned off and found myself out of work albeit still on sickness benefit, but with no viable means of earning a living. I received a lump sum and a pension of £300 per month, hardly enough to sustain both my wife and myself.

After the accident the union took up the cudgels on my behalf and set in motion a set of events and procedures to sue both BT and BICC for negligence and failure to protect an employee. I was put in touch with the union solicitors who gathered all the relevant witnesses and statements. They appointed a barrister and then began the long legal procedure. I did not realise how long these cases could last.

The powers that be were determined that I would not be a drain on Government resources and after a few weeks drawing sickness benefit I was sent for a medical. One wag at the medical board said they were going to give me an X-ray to see if there was any work in me. This was from someone who had never done a days manual labour in his life. How the numerous malingerers one sees, pretending to hobble along on sticks through the day and virtually bounding to the pub at night, get away with it I don't know. They must know the system intimately.

I was told by the very knowledgeable board of doctors that I was indeed fit for work of some kind, although not driving. I was signed off the sick and had to register as unemployed. After all those years striving for opulence and affluence I now found myself on unemployment benefit and no immediate prospects of bettering myself.

Within a couple of weeks the unemployment system had me signed up for an I.T. course in Business Administration and Information Technology, at the Manchester Chambers of Commerce and Industry. This was a 3 months course from which I graduated with an NVQ diploma at levels 1 and 2 and which, allowed me entrance into the Civil service at Administration

Assistant level, with earnings barely above subsistence level. This was in 1993 and I was on a basic wage of £7000 per annum. As an almost middle aged new entrant in the Civil Service, I was put on the same rate as an 18 year old and was being bossed around and told what to do by people half my age and with less than half my worldly wisdom and common sense. My dignity had been stolen away from me and I missed the tramping lifestyle, freedom and camaraderie of the trucking fraternity, not to mention the chance to earn something equating to a living wage. After 18 months I had had enough and left to take up employment with the Railways as a train conductor, for which there was a 3 months training period, which I completed successfully. I worked on the trains for a year or so, when the lure of the open road, well by now the lure of the somewhat congested road, started to draw me back. I felt fit enough to go back to a life of driving so long as there wasn't a great deal of hand-balling involved, so in 1998 I signed on with BRS Taskforce, an in-house agency that supplied drivers for all the EXEL Logistics contracts. I started on a part time basis gradually working up to mainly full time with days off when my back was playing up.

CHAPTER 10
TRUCKERS IN SONG, ON FILM, ON TELEVISION,

IN BOOKS AND MAGAZINES

BESIDES the Magazines for the truck driver that are printed in England such as Truck and Driver, Truck, Classic Trucks and Trucking, there are others that are aimed at the trade like Commercial Motor and one or two others. Headlight which is no longer published used to be the truck drivers Bible with plenty of helpful information about drivers hours and the like, but it lost out to the newer glossier magazines. There are one or two American trucking mags that make their way to this fair land by way of some importer or other, but not many and rather infrequently

There are plenty of books, in both hard back and soft back, about all aspects of trucking from light commercial to heavy haulage and taking in trucking on all the Continents. There are books about individual marques and individual companies. Books with comprehensive lists and specifications of trucks from all over the world, and there occasionally comes along a fictional trucking story to keep us entertained.

The truck driver has appeared on television, in movies and on record as a folk hero. In America he has replaced the cowboy as the romantic hero and saviour of many lost causes, rescuing maidens in distress, and saving bus loads of school kids from certain death and taking disabled orphans for a ride in his truck.

Firstly, on television, and I'll get the worst out of the way first. In 1979 there was a TV series about a trucker whose companion was a chimpanzee. The series was called *BJ and The Bear* and was about Billie Joe McKay played by Greg Evigan who drove a cabover Kenworth out of Milwaukee, Wisconsin. Why the chimp is called The Bear escapes me. It was classed as comedy which was the second mistake, the first being the series.

Once more on television there was a much earlier and far superior American series *Cannonball,* starring Paul Birch as Mike Malone and William Campbell as his mate Jerry Austin, which was my introduction to American trucking. It was highly stylised, for the day, and over romantic, but to a child in the 1950's when the world was viewed in black and white, it was compulsive and compelling viewing. Cannonball, the nickname of the driver of the bonneted, GMC, articulated rig, Mike Malone, and his sidekick Jerry, would save some family, individual or company from disaster be they financial or physical on a weekly basis. The theme tune went: *The rumble of the diesel, the shifting of the gears, name your destination, and brother he'll be there. Cannonba-a-a-all, Cannonba-a-a-all.*

The same subject matter was resurrected in a programme called *'Movin' On',* starring Claude Akins as Sonny Pruitt and Frank Converse as his co-driver Will Chandler, Claude Akins born May 25th 1926 died January 27th 1994, was a much renowned American character actor who had played in such diverse films as *Rio Bravo* alongside John Wayne, Dean Martin, Ricky Nelson and Angie Dickinson. *The Caine Mutiny* with Lee Marvin and *The Devil's Brigade* with Cliff Robertson and William Holden.

The series was first aired in 1973, as a pilot film called *In*

Tandem in which a 1973 Kenworth 925 was used. In the series a 1974 Kenworth 925 was used. The series ran for two whole seasons. The plots were somewhat far fetched, with the conventional K Whopper pulling 53ft tandem axle trailers round hairpin bends on cliff edge roads, rescuing all and sundry from whatever catastrophe had befallen them. The locations were fantastic making plenteous use of the great American countryside and truck stops and it was an easy on the eye series.

From what I can remember Cannonball was a company man and Sonny Pruitt was an owner driver, but the common thing about both series, that I can remember, is that neither was ever seen to deliver a load.

Around the same time Cannonball was being aired on TV a trucking film was released, directed by Howard W Koch. This film was *Violent Road* (1958). The main stars were Brian Keith and Efram Zimbalist Jr, with Sean garrison, Perry Lopez, Ed Prentiss and more. The film was classed as an adventure drama with Brian Keith as the leader of a truck convoy of desperate men hauling highly volatile rocket fuel over desert terrain in a race against time. It is a nail biting film full of tension that makes good use of flashback techniques. The film was also released under the alternative title *Hell's Highway.*

In the same vein as the above film as an earlier French production directed by Henry-Georges Clouzot in 1953. The film is *The Wages of Fear* and stars Yves Montand and Peter Van Eyck. Over 2 hours long it is about the transportation of nitro-glycerine to put out an oil fire in a Latin American outpost. Crazy risks are taken and it is a thrill a minute film with a final twist in the tale. The only down side for English speaking people is that it is a French Language film with Sub titles.

One film, *Hell Drivers,* shot in Vista Vision in the early 60's and direct by Cy Baker Endfield starring a spectacular cast including Patrick McGoohan, Stanley Baker, Herbert Lom and Peggy Cummins was the ultimate British trucking film. It co-starred Alfie Bass, Sid James, Gordon Jackson, William Hartnell, David McCallum and Jill Ireland. The story was about the trials and tribulations in the cut throat job of tipper drivers and the under hand practise of encouraging driver to drive recklessly for bonuses. Ex-con, Tom played by Stanley Baker, takes a job with this irresponsible outfit and is soon at loggerheads with foreman driver Red, played by Patrick McGoohan and the sparks soon begin to fly. It was down to earth, and totally realistic. The vehicles used were bonneted Dodges, probably the 200 series.

Duel starring Dennis Weaver and directed by Steven Spielberg was a Psychological thriller. The film was about a guy who goes out in the pursuit of his job and is pursued for no apparent reason by an articulated, tanker, conventional rig. The driver of the rig is never seen bar for his tan cowboy boots. I believe it was Spielberg's directorial debut and stands as a classic amongst trucking films.

Another film worth mentioning is James Szalapski's *Heartworn Highways,* from the mid 1970's. It was made in a semi-documentary style and is about country music but contains numerous shots and footage of big American rigs ploughing the highways and byways of America. It stars Guy Clark, David Allan Coe and Townes Van Zandt. It is an atmospheric film and totally out of the ordinary.

White Line fever named after the Merle Haggard song and starring Jan Michael Vincent who ultimately drives his rig through a massive, state of the art, glass building belonging to the villain of the film. Basically the film is about a driver popping little, white pills and running all the hours he can, because the rates are so low, to pay for his truck and keep his home and family together.

Robert Blake, born 18 Sept 1933, an American actor who began as a child actor in the *Our Gang* comedies and has made well over a hundred films and television shows, is probably most famous for his role as 'Big John' Wintergreen in the cult movie *Electra Glide in Blue* with Billy 'Green' Bush and the TV series *Baretta,* but he also played Jimmy Hoffa, the Teamsters leader in a made for TV film called Blood Feud in 1983. In 1980 he played a debt ridden truck driver called Charles Callahan in *Coast to Coast.* Blake was accused along with his handyman of the plotting and murdering of his wife Bonny Lee Bakley outside a restaurant in May 2001. He was released on bail of $1.5 million dollars after spending 12 months in jail. Robert Blake was found not guilty and acquitted and freed in March 2005. a later civil case at the court in Burbank, California, brought by Ms Bakley's children, found Robert Blake liable for his wife's death in 2001. Blake was ordered to pay $30,000,000 in damages to her children. This decision stands in stark contrast to the verdict in Blake's criminal trial in March when a panel of 12 jurors unanimously found Blake 'not guilty' of his wife's murder.

Jack 'Jack the Lad' Nicholson, born 22 April 1937, also portrayed James Riddle (Jimmy) Hoffa in the 1992 movie *Hoffa,* which was done in a semi documentary style and with Nicholson starring as the eponymous character.

Sylvester Stallone, born 6 June 1946, played a Hoffa type character called Johnny Kovac in the film *F.I.S.T.* (Federation of Interstate Truckers) based on a book by Joe Eszterhas, which in turn appears to be based on Hoffa's life. Stallone also made another trucking movie, *Over the Top,* in 1987, in which he plays trucker Lincoln Hawk who has been estranged from his wife and son for a number of years. The film centres around him trying to reunite his family and winning arm wrestling competitions in between.

Patrick Swayze of '*Dirty Dancin*' fame made a trucking film.

It was very much a mediocre affair called *Black Dog* and co-starring Meatloaf and Randy Travis as the villain and comedic relief respectively. The film was released in 1998 and was about a truck driver, Jack Crews (Swayze) newly released from prison for running a family down. He gets involved in gun-running for the Meatloaf character. The plot is full of holes and certain plot lines are left unexplained. One to miss.

One of the earlier trucking films I have come across is *Speed to Spare* made in 1948, starring Richard Arlen and Richard Travis with Jean Rogers, Nannette Parks and Ian MacDonald. The story is about a stunt driver, Cliff, (Arlen), who takes a job as a truck driver with an old pal Jerry McGee (Travis). Cliff makes an enemy of Pusher Wilkes (MacDonald), a trucker whose run he takes over. Pusher takes every opportunity to sabotage Cliff's rig causing several near fatal accident.

One of the earliest trucking films I have come by is *They Drive By Night* (1940). Directed by Raoul Walsh and starring Humphrey Bogart, George Raft, Anne Sheridan and Ida Lupino. This is a truly great film dealing with two brothers, Raft and Bogart trying to operate a freelance trucking business against the odds and against the mob and unscrupulous load agents. When the gangsters find the independents invading their business they plan to put them out of business by literally running them off the road.

Kurt Russell, born Springfield, Massachusetts in 1951 and best known for being married to Goldie Hawn, is one of those actors that made the transition from child star to male, adult lead. He starred in a trucking film of sorts with Kathleen Quinlan. The film *Breakdown*, made in 1997 and directed by Jonathon Mostow, is about a well to do couple who's brand new Jeep breaks down on a desolate stretch of Arizona highway. A trucker, played by J. T. Walsh, pulls up and offers to help by driving the wife (Quinlan) to a diner while the husband (Russell) stays behind to mind the

Jeep. From thereon in it is a well made, taut, suspenseful, thriller, about kidnap with the trucker playing the villain. Well worth going to see.

For light comedic relief *Smokey and the Bandit (1977)* starring Burt Reynolds and Sally Field as the Bandit and a runaway bride respectively. The film was directed by Hal Needham and also features Jackie Gleeson as Sheriff Buford T Justice. The Bandit is hired to run a Tractor and trailer rig full of beer across county lines pursued by the pesky sheriff. Highly entertaining and funny. There was a sequel *Smokey and the Bandit 11* plus *The Cannonball Run* but stick with the original.

Of all the trucking films the most popular must be Sam Peckinpah's *Convoy* (1978), starring Kris Kristofferson (Rubber Duck),Burt Young (Pig Pen), with Ali McGraw as the love interest and featuring Ernest Borgnine as the head Smokey Bear. The film, based on CW McCall's song of the same name is a romanticised version of the trucker's life style, although Peckinpah's direction and use of slow motion and aerial shots make it a visually stunning film. The song and the film were both instrumental in bringing the CB craze across the pond to Great Britain and spawning a new language about di-poles, twigs, Smokey Bear etc., and terminating in the phrase '10-4 good buddy' which doesn't sound the same without that American twang or Southern drawl. It also prompted Radio 1 Disc Jockey's Dave Lee Travis and Paul Burnett to put out the truly awful spoof record Convoy GB under the guise of Laurie Lingo and the Dipsticks. McCall's Convoy reached number 2 in the British charts with Travis's travesty reaching number 4, both in 1976.

CW McCall made other trucking songs including *Wolf Creek Pass*, which is one of the more humorous of the trucking songs, about hauling a load of chickens. The drivers red hot fire falls off the end of his cigar, down his pants and burns a hole in his sock, concentration is lost and they pass under a 12ft bridge when the chickens were stacked to 13ft 9 ins. 'It took the top off that load slicker than the scum off a Louisiana swamp.' Etc.

Trucking songs have been around as long as the trucks and drivers they portray. The earliest song of this genre that I have come across is *Truck Drivers Blues* written by Ted Daffan and sung by Cliff Bruner, which was recorded in 1939 and sold 100,000 copies. The main theme of the song, which is a true blues song, is about low pay, hardship, long hours etc. The same problems that beset the truck driving fraternity to this day. No change there then.

The King of the truckin' song was Red Sovine who died in 1980. He left some truly great songs behind him. His most famous recording was written by a songsmith named Faille and was *Phantom 309,* which is about a hitch hiker who is picked up by a truck driver called Joe, who, as it turns out, gave his life to save a bus load of kids and he and his rig, Phantom 309, are just that, Phantoms. He also co-wrote and recorded the somewhat twee and over sentimental *Teddy Bear* about a crippled orphan whose truck driver pappy was killed in a smash and whose CB handle is Teddy Bear. Other songs that Red sang include, *Woman Behind the Man Behind the Wheel, 18 Wheels hummin', Home Sweet Home* and *Long Night.* A lot of Red's songs were performed as monologues but were none the worse for that and he didn't solely rely on truckin' songs as his *Class of 49* shows.

Dave Dudley, born in 1928, died December 2003, born David Pedruska in Spencer, Wisconsin, was a contender for Red Sovine's crown as King of the Truckin' song. He is best known for the truckers anthem *6 Days on the Road (and I'm gonna make it home tonight*), released in 1963 and written by Earle Green and Carl 'Peanut' Montgomery. It tells the story of the trucker trying to make it home after 6 days away. The song includes the occasional gear crunching and air horns, it tells of dodging weight scales, way behind log sheets and popping little white pills to stay awake.

Other truckin' songs of Dudley's were *There Ain't No Easy Ride, Trucker's Prayer, Rollin' Rig* and that other great truckin' anthem *Truck Drivin' Son of Gun.*

Dudley's fame was such that a town was named after him in his home state, Wisconsin, namely Dudleyville, and he was made an honorary member of the Teamsters.

Give Me *40 Acres (and I'll Turn This Rig Around)* is another comedic truckin' song written by a songwriter called Green, who is probably the same Earle Green famous for *6 Days on the Road. 40 Acres* was turned into a hit by Red Simpson who made a number of other truck songs including *Diesel Smoke (Dangerous Curves), Beaver on my Lap (Bear on my Tail), I'm a Truck, Happy Go Lucky Truck Driver, Runaway Truck, Highway Man, and a version of Truck Drivers Blues* amongst numerous others.

Box car Willie, born Lecil Travis Martin in 1931 in Sterret, Texas, best known for his attire of floppy hat and dungarees to be evocative of the train hopping, American hobo, actually never worked on the railroad. He covered numerous truckin' songs including most of those already mentioned and also the Gray/Anderson composition *How Fast them trucks Will Go,* and *Freightliner Fever* from the pens of Lankford and Truman and many more. Willie, incidentally, was spotted by a British agent, Drew Taylor, playing in a club in Nashville. Taylor realised the commercial potential and singed him up, the rest, as they say, is history.

Commander Cody and his Lost Planet Airmen is probably the best 6 piece band portraying the truckers' lifestyle in song. Their 1972 classic album, *Hot Licks, Cold Steel* and *Trucker's Favourites* include what I believe to be, their best song, *Looking at the World Through a Windshield.*

Gear Bustin' Sort of Feller was written and recorded by Bobby Braddock and released in 1967. It failed to dent the charts at the time but has since become a truckin' favourite with its tongue twisting chorus lines: *I'm a double-clutching, scale-jumping, mile-making, tail-gating, cop-dodging, line-crossing, coffee-drinking, pin-balling, jack-knifing, part-timing, wind-jamming, late-running, gear-busting sort of feller.*

Bobby is a prolific song writer and penned D-I-V-O-R-C-E for Tammy Wynette and songs for Dave Dudley and others.

A Tombstone Every Mile written by Dan Fulkerson and recorded by Dick Curless is about a stretch of road in the state of Maine, on the East coast of America, which claimed a number of truck drivers' lives, and probably the lives of a few ordinary drivers. The accident rate was due to the old black ribbon becoming the white ribbon, covered in ice, throughout the long winter, causing skids, jack knives and countless other accidents. The song based on the truth about the number of casualties on the Haynesville Woods Road prompted the Government of the day to replace the said road with the 4 lane interstate 95, thus making the road safer and reducing the death toll. Dick Curless also recorded other classic truckin' songs such as *Big Wheel Cannanball* and *Long Lonesome Road.*

Terry Fell wrote and recorded *Truck Drivin' Man* in 1954. It was an immediate hit and it is said that the song was written in less than an hour. The song has been covered by Red Simpson and other C&W singers. Terry Fell died in 1998 aged 77.

The only lady C&W singer that I have come across singing about trucks is Kay Adams who sang a little ditty called *Little Mack*. Quite a nice song, but really, this is one for the ladies.

There are plenty more truckin' songs and artistes that sing them and as long as there are truckers driving the interstates hauling goods along the American highways there will always be truckin' songs thumbing a lift. As long as the Gypsy on 18 wheels is around, stories will be told of him plucking school buses from the paths of speeding trains or saving towns from runaway tankers loaded with nitro-glycerine and other heroic deeds. Long may he appear on television and on film and via the written word and also, long may he persevere as the coffee-swilling, hard working, pill-popping, burger-eating, jukebox-playing, waitress-flirting, womanising, truck-driving son of a gun. Long Live The Trucker.

CHAPTER 11
EXEL

FROM BRS TO EXEL AND BACK TO BRS

PRIOR to getting a full time post with EXEL I worked on most of the EXEL contracts, through BRS, delivering a multiplicity of goods to a multiplicity of places and customers.

It was whilst working for BRS in 1998 that my case for damage against BT and BICC came to court. After 10 years from the date of the accident and after numerous condemnations and denials from both sides the day of judgement was upon us. There were various and many approaches from the Defence to settle before going into the Court. These offers were dismissed as derisory by my Barrister and so to face the Judge we went. The case lasted the most of 2 days with yours truly emerging victorious with an award that if invested carefully would be quite capable of seeing me through my years of retirement. Finally after all the years of chasing 'The Big Money' I was in a state of relative wealth, although I would still have to work until I reached 60 years of age.

After a small celebration of my victory I returned to work for BRS and was given a job on one of the EXEL contracts. This contract was Crazy George's. Crazy George's was a chain of retail furniture shops that later became known as Brighthouse Furnishings.

The job I was given was a run to one of their distribution centres at Erdington in Birmingham. It was as I was making my way down the M6 that things took a turn for the worse. On this particular run I usually came off the M6 at junction 12, the A5 at Cannock and run through to the A38, down to Tyburn roundabout and into Erdington in a SE direction. On the day in question I decided to follow the M6 down to Spaghetti Junction and come off at junction 6 and up the A38 in a NW direction. After passing Hilton Park Services, driving in the middle lane, I came upon stationary traffic. The traffic between junctions 11 and 8 was nose to tail, stop, and start. I slowed down and was waiting for the traffic to start moving again when I felt a terrific bump from the rear, which almost pushed me into the vehicle in front of me. I looked in my rear view mirror and saw a Scania attempting to make its way to the hard shoulder. The front of the Scanny was well and truly smashed in, but obviously still manoeuvrable and the driver made it to the shoulder. The traffic started to move again and I indicated to pull over to get to the hard shoulder so that I could exchange insurance details and such with the driver of the Scania. I didn't know at the time that the impact had smashed my rear lights and rendered my indicators useless. I carried on indicating whilst moving forward but, obviously no-one knew my intentions and so no-one would let me in. Then there was the junction with the M54, very busy at this time of the day, with traffic joining the M6, and it was not until a mile or so further down that I managed to get onto the hard shoulder. I then ran down the hard shoulder to the nearest emergency telephone where I reported the incident to the police and was given an incident number. I waited for half an hour on the shoulder in faint hope that the Scania and its driver managed to get that far, and to check the damage that my vehicle had sustained. The damage to my vehicle was not that bad, due to the underslung tail lift which took the brunt of the collision. I then changed the lenses and bulbs in my indicators and tail lights, notified my home depot and telephoned the police again. They advised me that I had done all I could and to carry on with my job.

I finally reached Erdington, did my delivery and collection and headed back for the M6. The A38 was chocker block both ways so I went straight across Tyburn roundabout towards the Spitfire roundabout in an attempt to reach the M6 at junction 5 and dodge the traffic. I reached the Spitfire roundabout and as I was about to negotiate it, to head for the Motorway, I felt a bump from the rear. I looked though my rear view mirror again, to see a black guy get out of his gleaming, black Mercedes Benz, 320CLK, which like the earlier Scania was somewhat crumpled after he had used it as a battering ram to push me forward. My immediate reaction was to utter to myself 'Fucking Hell! What the fuck's going on today?'

I pulled across the roundabout, to clear the junction, and waited for the Merc and its driver to join me and swap details. He pulled up by the side of me, lowered his passenger window and leant across to speak. I couldn't help but notice he had a massive gold chain around his neck, another on one wrist and a Rolex watch on the other. He shouted 'Tain't yo' fau't, man, Ah fought yo'd pulled away, man, Ah'm goin' to the garage, man' and with that he sped away, but not before I got his number. I pulled on to Hilton Park to report this second, unbelievable rear end collision of the day, only to find that the police station on the services was no longer manned. I tried again and again and again and again at Stafford, Keele, Sandbach and Knutsford, only to be faced with the same scenario. I finally had to report the incident at my local police station at Harpurhey in Manchester which led to another lengthy conversation with the police and the making out of two statements, one for each incident. I was given two notices to produce my documents, which I duly did. Not a single accident for 20 years and then two in one day. Though neither of them were my fault I was made to feel like a criminal with the notices to produce and the making out of statements and accident report.

I phoned the Birmingham police a week later to be told that neither of the other drivers had reported anything to the police. A month later I received a letter saying that due to the lack of reports and evidence the case would be discontinued.

DRIVER'S HOURS, A RECIPE FOR DISASTER

Accidents have become an occupational hazard to drivers, due mainly to the sheer volume of traffic, time sensitive deliveries, pure bad driving and, of course, the stupid hours expected of drivers. A driver may, say, start at 03.00hrs and work a total of 15 hours in a day and then have only 9 hours off before his next shift when he again may work up to 15 hours. He or she may work up to 15 hours 3 times a week and have a reduced break, from 11 consecutive hours to 9 hours up to 3 times a week, although these reductions have to be compensated for by the end of the following week. The remaining 2 days, he or she may work up to 13 hours. Driving time is limited to 9 hours daily but this can be increased to 10 hours not more than twice a week. This mode of working when in charge of a 44 ton vehicle, capable of close to 60mph, is a recipe for disaster and unscrupulous bosses will take advantage of young or inexperienced drivers for their own ends, stressing that drivers must work the 15 hours and must take the reduced breaks, when these decisions should be at the drivers discretion taking into consideration tiredness, road conditions and weather conditions.

I was, again, working on the Crazy George contract and on one occasion, in early 1999, I was asked to do the run to the distribution warehouse at Uddington near Bellshill in Scotland. The job required that I start at 04.00hrs. I arrived at the depot at 04.00hrs and got my notes, vehicle keys etc. I did my vehicle checks, coupled up, checked all the trailer lights and running gear and set off at 04.30hrs.

I was a nice quiet morning and I had a pleasant run along the M62, onto the M61, along the M6 and joined the A74 at Carlisle. By the time I reached the A74M, the darkness was starting to leave the sky, and when I reached the M74 proper, it was almost daylight. As I was approaching the A723, the Hamilton and Motherwell exit at junction 6 of the M74, the skies went black with thunderheads. The heavens opened and the rain began to fall. It didn't start slowly. It came down in torrents immediately, accompanied by flashes of lightning and claps of thunder.

As I approached the entry slip road for those joining the motorway northwards, in what was now the rush hour, a car came up the slip road doing an estimated 50-60 mph. The driver, who was probably late for work, was driving like a maniac. He must have been aqua-planing and he lost control as he was about to join the flow of traffic. The car slid into the raised tarmac kerb of the hard shoulder, bounced off, spun sideways and shot, like a bullet between 2 cars on the inside lane. I saw what was happening and put on my hazard lights and slowed to a crawl.

After shooting between the 2 cars in the inside lane, the out of control vehicle careered in front of me. I was frantically waving my arm out of the off-side window in an attempt to slow down the vehicles in the outside lane. The car rocketed across the fast lane, ploughed into the central crash barrier sideways on, bursting a tyre in the process. It ricocheted off the barrier spun around, flashed in front of me, across the inside lane, hit, once again, the tarmac kerb and came to rest on the hard shoulder.

A youth of about 18 years clambered out of the wreck, put his hands on the crumpled wing and slowly sank to his knees on the hard shoulder. He appeared to be crying. Other vehicles pulled up behind him, whether to chastise him or comfort him I know not. There was little I could do. I was coming off at the next junction and as I made my way, carefully, over to the inside lane I saw, through my mirrors, the blue lights of the police arriving at the scene.

After a couple of years on the agency in late 1999, I was taken on full time on the North West Water Contract, which had now become the United Utilities Contract, employed directly by EXEL. EXEL, like a lot of other large companies and unlike the big companies of yesteryear, doesn't actually own any vehicles but has them on lease. This, of course, gets rid of all the responsibility of ownership such as servicing, breakdown, breakdown recovery, and a whole host of other things such as taxation etc. Fleets no longer carry spare tyres for the trailer or unit but take out contracts with commercial tyre companies, which save them the problem of changing their own with the plus point of extra payload.

The job entailed delivery and collection of components to all the NWW depots and also NWEB depots as well as to contractors on site and to their depots. When I started the depot had 2 artics and about half a dozen 4 wheelers and an 8 wheeler and a 4 wheeler fitted with HIAB lorry loaders. There was also a bit of low loader work involved. All in all, the job had quite a bit of variety. Most of the work was on tautliners except for the HIAB and low loader work.

I was asked if I would like to take my CITB, HIAB test so that I could drive the 8 wheeler if the regular driver, Stevie Dore, was off for any reason. The 8 wheeler and a flat bed, 4 wheeler worked out of the NWEB depot at Ashton under Lyne, where they were loaded with sub-stations, and transformers weighing up to 5 tons, for delivery to sites around the North west area. I, of course, said yes, and went out with Stevie on various jobs to learn the skills and techniques needed, another string to my bow, another feather in my cap, another apple in my barrel so to speak.

When I went out on my own, after passing the HIAB test, I was confronted with some jobs that were almost impossible for the HIAB vehicle. I once had to deliver a sub-station to a site in the Lake District, whereby I had to lift this massive piece of electrical engineering over the roof of a privately owned bungalow and lower it onto a concrete plinth that I could not see, on the other side of the dwelling. All I had to rely on were the distant voices of the fitters shouting 'Up a little, right a bit, down a little, right a little, left a bit, whoa!' and so on, until the station was sited. There was pole mounted equipment that had to be manoeuvred onto metal cross members set between a pair of telegraph poles, whilst the gangs were up the poles waiting to secure the equipment in place. It was a tricky task, working in the close proximity of men held on to poles with safety harnesses, with a 5 to 10cwt lump of metal swinging in the air on chains.

Sometimes the HIAB could not get close enough to site the equipment and a mobile crane, with longer reach and heavier lifting capability would need to be hired to complete the job.

I once again found that contempt for and a lack of understanding of the complexities of drivers and their jobs still existed. On one job I was discussing the merits and pitfalls of the job and the driver's duties in general when the guy I was talking to said 'drivers are ten a penny, I'm an engineer and I have to work to within thousands of an inch.' I replied 'that's fuck all, mate, I have to site this equipment up telegraph poles and I have to be fuckin' spot on.' He seemed somewhat lost for words.

Most of the time I was on artic work, tautliner or low

loader. The deliveries were to all the NWW and NWEB and the combined United Utilities depots throughout the North West for stock replenishment. Deliveries were also made to contractor's yards and even to the sites that the contractors were working on. Sometimes the sites would be in the middle of a farmer's field, where one could become easily bogged down, but usually a temporary stone roadway was laid. Other times one would have to drop the delivery at the roadside where the contractors were working.

The low loader work was very much similar to the work I had done for British Telecom plc, carrying large reels of cable battened down and secured with straps or chains. The chains, unlike the old days when we used tensioners that had to be tightened by using a length of scaffolding tube to obtain the leverage to close them now had ratchet tensioners that are much easier to use and much more reliable.

When I joined EXEL the NWW depot had no union representation, so I set in motion the mechanics of setting up a branch of the TGWU, of which I became the convener and as such, one of my first chores was to be instrumental in getting the overtime rate raised from time and a quarter to time and a half. Besides the drivers all the warehouse staff joined, though I believe when I left the company, nobody was willing to accept the convener's job and the branch ceased to exist.

ONE MAN AND HIS DOG

In the spring of 2000 when one of the regular Class 1 drivers on the NWW contract went on long term sick an agency driver named Rick Shaw was brought in to cover his job. Rick had worked on the contract numerous times before and knew all the depots. Because of this the transport manager asked for him personally. Rick brought with him every day, as a travelling companion, his pet Jack Russell terrier. One day he was given the Cumbria run, taking in Kendal, Penrith, Carlisle, Workington and Whitehaven. As usual he took his pooch with him. On his way up the M6 he called into Tebay Service Area to give his cab mutt a little exercise. Whilst walking around the grassy area of the services the travelling canine saw a number of rabbits frolicking and gambolling merrily in the newly mown grass and decided to join them in their frisky, playtime activities. The rabbits saw the little bow-wow bounding towards them and fled into their labyrinthine, subterranean warren with Jack Russell in hot pursuit. They all disappeared into the undergrowth and below ground. Rick searched high and low for the best part of an hour but his hound and the burrowing rodents were nowhere to be seen. He phoned the EXEL depot and was told that the animal should not have been travelling with him, and to get on with the job or face disciplinary action. Close to tears he had one more cursory look with no avail. He then carried on with the job. On his way back, later in the day, he took a detour and called back at the service area where he had another look for his beloved pet. He enquired in the shop and left a card with a contact number and a description of the missing Canis Minor.

A fortnight later Rick arrived in the yard for work and with him was a Jack Russell. Questions were asked, 'Was it the same dog?' 'Was it a replacement?' 'Was it all right?' etc. The story was that Rick was at home one night watching the tele, when he heard a scratching noise at the front door. He got up, his hopes soaring, and went to investigate. He opened the door to be greeted by a rather emaciated, scruffy, worn out, foot sore dog. Rick picked up the sorry looking bundle of hones, which was in danger of shaking its tail from its body in its apparent joy at being reunited with its master. The little beast was fed and watered and it's somewhat worse for wear foot-pads were bathed. An appointment was booked with the vet and Rick by his own admission cried buckets. The dog was prescribed plenty of tender loving care, which it duly received.

It's a strange phenomenon that animals lost or deserted miles away from home can, without the use of maps and compasses, and having to find their own provender, can find their way home to their masters and loved ones. If only humans had a fraction of that devotion and dedication the world would be a better place.

THE MYSTERIOUS CONES

Around about this time, and up to the present time, there seemed to be traffic cones appearing on any stretch of motorway or major trunk route that one used, usually segregating the outside lane from the others. Nothing ever seemed to be happening on the other side of these proliferations of cones and no workmen were to be seen.

It seems that The Highways Agency or the motorway repair people had ordered too many cones from the manufacturer, and having nowhere to store them, decided to fool the general public, and with a master stoke of British ingenuity, chose to use selected outside lanes of certain motorways or A roads as temporary storage space, thus reducing motorways to 2 lanes and trunk routes to 1 and in doing so causing more congestion on our already overcrowded road system. If this is not the case and work is indeed to be carried out behind these cones, the workforce must be taking invisibility pills. Of course, and joking apart, there are great stretches of our motorway system under reconstruction where men and machines can actually be seen to be working in their efforts to improve our motorways, but in the meantime causing massive tail backs, congestion and frayed tempers.

These reconstruction and new build sites are generally due to a lack of foresight by the powers that be, irrespective of their political persuasion, such as the development at Thelwell Viaduct on the M6 and Barton flyover on the M60, or the widening of Windy Hill on the M62, or instances whereby 3 lanes have been stretched to 4 by narrowing the existing lanes, thus rendering it impossible for LGV's to pass one another safely. Not to mention the ongoing problems at Spaghetti Junction or those nearby Lancaster on the M6. There are some sections where the hard shoulder has been sacrificed to make an extra lane. All this, in my opinion, is because the people who are paid millions to get it right in the first place, get it wrong in their initial projections.

A BIT OF BAD LUCK

In mid 2000, while I was still employed by EXEL, a second unfortunate occurrence happened to befall me. I awoke one morning at 04.30hrs to the sound of my alarm clock. I switched the alarm off immediately, to avoid waking my wife, and got out of bed. I had just put my socks on and as I straightened up I became dizzy and disorientated. I then lost consciousness and collapsed in a heap on the bedroom floor banging into the bed and the bedside cabinet as I fell. This gave my wife a rude and somewhat earlier than expected wakeup call. By the time she had extricated herself from the duvet I had started to come round and by the time she was by my side I was fully conscious although still a little muddled and confused. The partly spilled glass of water that was residing on the bedside cabinet was pressed to my lips and she asked me what had happened. Unfortunately I was at a loss what to tell her.

My wife phoned EXEL to let them know I was not feeling too good, which was a slight understatement, and that I would not be in that day, she then phoned the emergency doctor who told her that as I had fully regained consciousness and all my faculties, that I should make an appointment with my G.P. I did so and was told to come in immediately for some tests, which I also did. I was then given a referral to North Manchester General Hospital who, after further tests referred me to the cardiac unit at Manchester Royal Infirmary where I was fitted with a heart monitor that I had to wear for 6 months in case there were any further instances of temporary loss of consciousness, other than drunkenness.

The DVLC was notified and my LGV license was revoked. Luckily they allowed me to keep my car license and EXEL kept me on for almost 6 months as a yardman/shunter. I was sent on a forklift truck refresher course and a first aid course and I was trained up as the Health & Safety Representative for the depot as well as being one of the warehouse first aiders. It was my job to deliver manual handling training, make out risk assessments and deliver talks on health and safety to the workforce and any temporary agency staff that were employed. The loads to be delivered had never been safer. I strapped all components to their pallets with steel banding and shrink wrapped awkward loads so as to ensure stability in transit. After a while, though, I was seen as a liability to the company as I was considered to be none productive, even though the yard had never been ran more efficiently and safely and the loads for delivery were more stable. The incidence of accidents within the workplace, notifiable or otherwise fell noticeably, but I was still deemed surplus to requirements and a drain on the contract budget, the depot management sent me to see the EXEL Occupational Health people who decided that I was unit to carry out the duties for which I was originally employed, (ie. Driving duties) and so finished me on health grounds. So, once again, I was forced to accept sickness benefits and a small lump sum and pension.

CHAPTER 12
FOREIGN TRUCKS ON BRITISH ROADS

SINCE the instigation of the Common Market or the EEC or European Union there has been an influx of foreign trucks and drivers, delivering and collecting a variety of goods in Great Britain.

Foreign vehicles are not exactly a new thing in this country. Just as the British have been sending vehicles and drivers to the Continent and further afield for years, so the French, Germans. Spanish, Italians and Portuguese have been coming over here for decades. The Hungarian company Hungarocamion, which I think is or was the Hungarian state run haulage company, has been coming to these shores since I was a lad, has have a handful of Turkish and Greek companies.

The influx of which I speak stems from the opening up of the European borders including The Czech Republic, Slovakia, Slovenia, Lithuania, Estonia, Poland, Hungary, Bulgaria and Romania, some of which were once part of the Communist Bloc. All the newly joined countries welcomed into the European Union are making in-roads into this country and more will follow. This may not necessarily be a bad thing in time, but at this moment in time, there is, an element of unfair competition involved.

When Mustapha Fuq was made redundant at Brain Haulage, he bought a Scania 110, and ran a few trips to Saudi Arabia. He told tales of corruption on the borders of the Eastern Bloc Countries where he had to bribe police officers and custom officials, even though his paperwork was in order. He also told of how he could not enter Germany unless his fuel tanks were virtually empty, so that he would have to buy German derv, thus contributing to the German economy.

Foreign trucks come into this country with full tanks and belly tanks and cat-walk tanks abrim after fuelling up on the continent with cheaper fuel. They carry enough diesel on board to do all their deliveries and collections and then return to the Continent where they re-fuel, once again with cheap derv, contributing nothing to our economy. When British truckers driver abroad they have to pay all the relevant road tolls but when Johnny Foreigner comes over here he makes no contribution to the upkeep of our transport infrastructure thus introducing another element of unfair competition.

Foreign trucks including those from Southern Ireland don't appear to be fitted with top speed limiters, allowing them to get from A to B faster than their British counterparts. Willi Betz, the German haulier, who bought up SOMAT the Bulgarian state run transport company and its 2000 trucks, I hear, uses Eastern Bloc drivers including Russians and Kazakhstanis as well as Romanians and Bulgarians. His trucks are always double manned to obtain optimum usage whilst, I am told, his drivers are paid something that equates to our minimum wage, albeit this is a fortune to his drivers. Willie Betz operates over 4000 units and 7000 trailers and employs 8000 people Europe wide, and because of his bulk buying power buys his Mercedes trucks at preferential rates ensuring a modern fleet.

It seems, nowadays, that 1 in every 10 trucks ploughing the British motorway system is foreign. How are we supposed to compete in such biased conditions? It is no wonder our haulage industry is in a state close to collapse.

Van Bentum's of the Nederlands and all the Nederlander flower growers are running over here. Norbert Dentressangle, who was at one point the biggest independent haulier in Europe, has numerous trucks operating over here. Norbert is either staunchly patriotic or has some French government backing as all his trucks are Renault's. Giraud of France also has a number of vehicles ploughing our highways.

At one time most of the foreign vehicles that came to these shores were from directly across 'La Manche' or the North Sea or the Bay of Biscay. These being The French, Germans, Spanish, Portuguese and a smattering of Scandinavians and Italians. Now there is an equal amount from the Eastern Bloc countries working on low wages, low overheads and low practises. These Eastern Bloc drivers are in Britain for weeks on end and, so it is said, are paid very little or nothing at all whilst waiting for a back load. They are paid on mileage only.

These drivers like the Willi Betz and Greek and Turkish drivers, bring with them, in the trailer storage boxes, all the sustenance they may need for their stay here. Quite often one may see these drivers, who part up in 2's, 3's and 4's open up their storage boxes and take out folding chairs and a table, a primus stove, cutlery and crockery, their victuals and a carafe of wine and glasses and have a regular picnic. This practise can be seen on service areas, in lay-by's and outside the companies where they await a back load. If the weather is not conducive to dining alfresco, the table and chairs will be hoisted into the rear of an empty trailer and the dinner party will continue in relative comfort.

They park up overnight on service areas, without paying. They flout the law of the land by purposely and persistently speeding past speed cameras in the knowledge that the police and owners of the service areas will not pursue them, at great expense for little or no return, to the eastern Bloc countries from whence they came.

Eddie Stobart, after the fuel strike of the year 2000, realised the advantage of registering a number of his vehicles on the Continent to reap the benefits of low fuel costs, road tax etc., and so he registered some of his fleet in Belgium. Norbert Dentressangle appears to have gone the other way and has depots in Britain with British registered vehicles and British drivers.

Giraud also employs British drivers for his vehicles, though I believe all the units are registered in France.

There is, supposedly, a shortage, in this country, of 50,000+ LGV drivers. With professional drivers either not working, working in other industries, working part time or for agencies. Drivers have the bargaining power that they have never had before, but because we are individuals and not seen as team players we will probably let our best opportunity pass us by and we will, once again, be master of our own demise.

Between them, the British Government, who show very little interest in transport policy, the agencies, who at the very best, are a necessary evil and the foreign drivers, through no fault of their own are doing a pretty good job of screwing up the British haulage industry. If the stated shortage is truly the case, drivers should be being paid at a premium equal to any other tradesman's remuneration because that is, surely, what we are and what we are worth.

There is now a Young Drivers Training Scheme whereby a class 2 LGV can be gained at 18 or 19 years of age and when enough experience and age has been gained the young trainee may sit his class 1. I, personally, would not advise any youngster to take up employment in this overworked, underpaid, unfair, taken for granted, pushed from pillar to post, anti social, friendless industry. I've seen the good days and I wish they were back.

There are schemes being hatched, to train immigrants from Eastern Bloc countries, to drive vehicles in this country to alleviate the shortage of drivers. Of course, there will be stringent vetting processes, language tests and training programmes. One agency in the South is helping migrant workers to integrate by offering language lessons, accommodation and skills assessment. Such good intentions!

The Government and various other bodies cannot see the wood for the trees. It is patently obvious that the shortage of drivers is due to discontentment about pay, conditions and hours, besides the woeful state of the transport infrastructure. British drivers are totally disillusioned and any new drivers, be they British or foreign, will soon fall into this state of disillusionment. The powers that be and the various transport bodies, including the different, or should that be indifferent, transport unions, should be looking to alleviate the symptoms that affect our ailing transport system which is now in the Intensive Care Unit and close to death. Instead they ignore the problems, bury their heads in the sand and hope the problems will go away.

CHAPTER 13
EPILOGUE

BACK TO WORK

AFTER the surrender of my LGV license to the DVLA in Swansea, I was regularly monitored by the cardiac unit at The Manchester Royal Infirmary, and I was supposed to phone in and transmit anything untoward that had been recorded on the monitor that I had to wear. Because I never suffered any more losses of consciousness or any bouts of arrhythmia or a heart attack, stoke, vertigo, giddiness or dizziness or even high blood pressure there was no reason to phone in and nothing to report. Finally, the medical experts held their hands up in resignation and came to the conclusion that I had suffered a simple faint, which they said could happen to anyone and they pronounced me 'fit as a butcher's dog.' This, of course, satisfied me only partly. I had lost the job with EXEL Logistics which was going to see me though to retirement and had my vocational license revoked, albeit only temporarily, though I did not know that at the time. I was informed by the DVLA that I could re-apply for my vocational license, which I did, even though I should never have lost it in the first place, the license would not be returned without a formal application and medical proof of my fitness to drive, which, in my mind, was never in doubt.

My license was finally returned on the 18 months anniversary of its loss, during which time I had spent all my rainy day savings in order to exist and keep my family. Sickness benefit and my small BT pension does not allow one to live in the lap of luxury, and my investments are for the future. I had to find work fast and start earning more shekels to improve my liquidity and put me back on a firm footing.

Upon receiving my re-instated license, the only work I could get was through an agency. Full time employers view ones medical past with suspicion and make excuses not to employ anyone with a hint of frailty, despite medical evidence to the contrary. The fact that I was now in my mid fifties was also a contributory factor.

In 2002 I registered, once again, with BRS Taskforce where I was well known. BRS was, at the time, still the in-house agency for all EXEL Logistics contracts and I found myself working alongside people I had known and worked with for years. They main difference being that I was back working on a temporary basis with no guarantees of regular work and maybe working on a different contract every working day. The upside was that the agency driver, generally, was paid a slightly higher rate than the company man.

ONE GOOD TURN DESERVES ANOTHER

Shortly after regaining my license in 2002 and whilst working for BRS on the Rover/BMW contract for EXEL Logistics, I was to make a delivery and collection in Hartlepool and then a further collection on the Newcastle side of the Tyne. Having completed my first delivery and collection I pulled onto the A19 and headed for the Tyne tunnel. As I was passing by Peterlee I saw, in front of me, an elderly gentleman walking alongside the A19, thumbing a lift. He was walking with some difficulty and with the aid of a walking cane and even though it was against company policy to pick up hitch hikers, I thought to myself, 'look at that poor old sod, I'll give him a lift.' I was approaching a lay by and as I passed the old man, who as I have said was having great difficulty in perambulating, I pulled in and waited. Upon reaching the vehicle the old chap opened the passenger door and asked 'Have ya pulled up t'offer us a lift, son?'

'Yes' I replied 'where are you going?'

'Ne'castle' he responded 'and ah'd be grateful fer a ride nay matter how short.'

'Well I can drop you on the other side of the tunnel.' I said 'as I have a collection on the industrial estate there.'

This now, obviously, very ancient fellow started to climb up into the cab with extreme difficulty, so much so that I had to get out and help him up.

When I again resumed my journey, I said to this wizened but neatly attired gentleman 'you don't see many people as advanced in years as yourself hitching a ride. What's caused you to do so?'

'Ah'm 94 yerrs ahld' he said 'and a dain't have much in the way o' funds. Mah son's in the Hospital in Ne'castle daying o' cancer and a need to be wi' him.'

'I'm very sorry to hear that' I responded, and then said questioningly 'I don't want to appear nosey' I said 'but what age is your son?'

'He's 73 yerrs ahld' was the reply.

I thought to myself 'Now here's a unique situation, a 94 year old father, thumbing a lift to go see his dying 73 year old son in hospital, so I said to this old geezer, 'if you don't mind waiting while I load up at Freudenberg's, which is just round the corner on the industrial estate, through the tunnel, I'll drop you as close to the hospital as I can.'

'Whey aye mon!' he exclaimed. 'ye're a gent ta be true, but ah dain't maind waitin' 'cos in the long run it'll prob'ly save us time and most certainly 'll preserve mah ahld legs, which ain't too guid, but.'

Upon reaching Freudenberg's I related this tale to the fork lift truck driver, who said 'A've ainy got 2 pallets fo' ya, pull 'cross the gates 'n' open ya cu'tains and a'll put 'em on ya, an' ya c'n be gan.'

I did as I was requested and was loaded and ready to roll in less than 10 minutes, thus enabling me to get the old codger to the hospital with hardly a hitch, although I did have to help him in descending from the cab. Once down he shook my hand then hugged me and praised me for a saint before making his way, once again, with great suffering and obvious pain, through the hospital gates. I then got back in my cab and made my way back across the Tyne Bridge onto the A1 and back down to Manchester.

SOME BAD DRIVING PRACTISES

One sees some strange occurrences whilst truckin' on down. As I have been travelling the roads of Britain in the pursuance of a living wage I have seen drivers with polystyrene coffee cups balanced precariously on the dash board whilst eating a sandwich and steering with one hand, and letting go of the wheel to reach across and change gear with their right hand. I have also seen the coffee cup held between the knees of drivers doing 80+ mph.

I have seen young women applying make up whilst travelling above the national speed limit and other drivers with open road atlases spread across the steering wheel, probably so they can track their progress whilst saving time. In the same vein I have seen open newspapers spread across the steering wheels of cars in motion. How on earth can people read the newspapers whilst tailgating the vehicle in front? Then, of course, there is the ubiquitous mobile phone, of which the use of, whilst driving, attracts a £1,000 fine, but still one sees drivers that seem to have them glued to the side of their heads. Unfortunately it is not only the private motorist that acts in this totally dangerous and inconsiderate way. I have on occasions, sad to say, seen truck drivers acting in these indefensible fashions.

There is a tale of the driver that ran up the arse of the vehicle in front and when being interviewed by the police told the law enforcement officer that while applying her lipstick in the rear view mirror, the car in front swerved, causing her to take evasive action. This in turn caused her to drop the lippy which fell into the coffee cup on the dashboard, causing it to spill onto the map book on the steering wheel and pour onto her thighs, causing her to drop the sandwich she held in the other hand, as she attempted to retrieve the sandwich the mobile phone which was tucked between her neck and shoulder, as she conversed with someone else, fell to the floor, and as she bent to pick it up she ran into the vehicle in front which had unexpectedly stopped.

Apocryphal, I know, but having witnessed the examples of dangerous and inconsiderate driving given above, not completely outside the bounds of probability or possibility.

A LITTLE MORE ABOUT AGENCY WORK

Agencies, as I have stated earlier are not an ideal working solution and are more suited to the semi-retired who may only want 2 or 3 days work to supplement their pension, but at the time it was all I could get and with BRS servicing all the EXEL sites I considered it one of the better agencies.

Early in 2003 BRS was bought out by another agency, Blue Arrow Driving, and although the drivers that transferred over, including myself, went over on the TUPE (transfer of undertakings), agreement, my opinion was that things had changed drastically, and for the worst. If there was no class 1 work and one ended up piloting a class 2 vehicle or a 7.5 tonner, Blue Arrow would only pay class 2 or 7.5 tonne rate, whereas BRS paid a driver by the license he or she held and thus a class 1 driver received class 1 pay for any class of vehicle driven. My 40 years experience, like the TUPE agreement, counts for nothing in these days of the transient trucker.

Unlike the agencies permanent staff, only tiny contributions are made by the company to my Stakeholder Pension. I get fewer holidays than permanent employees and Bank holidays are part of my 20 days annual leave, although I believe that legislation is to be introduced, sometime in the near future, to ensure that all employees receive 28 days annual leave, thereby giving the agency driver the same rights as any other employee where Bank holidays are concerned. The agency even deny any responsibility for the provision of Personal Protective Equipment (PPE) although they do provide Hi Viz Vests, and even though, under new legislation, the onus is with the agency for this provision they expect us temporary workers to provide our own safety boots etc., whilst permanent employees have all PPE provided free of charge. When I requested safety footwear from Blue Arrow I was informed that I would have to buy my own. I immediately contacted the Health & Safety Executive, who in turn contacted Blue Arrow, who in turn provided me with safety boots free of charge. The agencies seem to work on the principle of keeping drivers in the dark and hoping their responsibility will not be challenged.

I don't receive the benefits of working for a large company such as healthcare, welfare, promotion opportunities and a whole host of other things. This is solely because I am classed as a temporary worker. This does not apply only to the agency that I work for but to most agencies that are steadfast in their attempts to discriminate against temporary workers and treat us as second class citizens unworthy of any social benefits, whilst they reap the profits from the extortionate rates charged for our labour. All within the current legislation, I hasten to add. Legislation that agencies can drive an Australian road train through.

ANOTHER INDUSTRIAL MISHAP

Through Blue Arrow, on 5th July 2004, I was sent to EXEL Logistics to work on the Rover/BMW contract once again. The job entailed a couple of deliveries and pick ups. One at Freudenbergs at Newcastle and another at Stadium Plastics at Hartlepool. I completed the Newcastle delivery and collection and headed through the Tyne tunnel onto the A19 and down to Stadium at Hartlepool. The delivery was taken off but one package had fallen from the rear most pallet. I had to climb onto the trailer to retrieve the package. As I descended from the trailer, using the under run bars as a ladder, my right foot landed on a piece of a broken pallet in the yard twisting my ankle violently. I also received a puncture wound to my left shin, as I stumbled from the pallet block I had stepped upon. The puncture wound was caused by another piece of debris on the yard floor. But for the rubbish on the floor, I believe I would have escaped unscathed.

When I went to sign for the load I reported what had happened, but only verbally. I thought I had sprained my ankle and even though I was suffering some pain I felt that I could drive back to Manchester. Upon entering the Manchester office of EXEL, the night foreman, a lad named Gary, saw that I was limping and asked me what had happened. I explained the earlier occurrence and was advised to enter the accident in the EXEL accident book before I left the depot.

The next morning my ankle was badly bruised and swollen and I could not put any weight on it. I went to the local hospital and after various prods, pokes and examinations and X-rays I was told that the ankle was broken. I was sent to the plaster room where I was put into plaster up to my knee. I was in plaster for 2 months and away from work for 3 months, living on sick pay plus my wife's wages, reluctant to break into my savings.

BUSINESS EXPRESS

When I returned to work I was given a placement, by Blue Arrow, with Business Express, the mail order arm of Littlewoods', on a long term, temporary basis, based at Shaw near Oldham. This was the kind of job I had been looking for. The working day was rarely more than 10 hours and the starting times were to my liking, nothing earlier than 0700hrs and reasonable finishing times. The vehicles were no older than 2 years. They were Volvo FM12, Globetrotters on lease from BRS. The work was clean and fairly easy and the earnings were at the higher end of the pay scale, made up of basic pay and various bonuses based on the number of trailers dropped and picked up, plus mileage and various other factors.

Because of the numerous trailer changes that may have to be done and because of the haste to boost bonus payments, it was inevitable that mistakes would be made. Drivers, even the older, more experienced men, were guilty of numerous blunders. Trailers were pulled off loading bays whilst the trailer legs were in the parking position. Drivers pulled away from trailers, forgetting, in their rush, to disconnect the air and electrical connections. Trailers were to be seen on the road without rear number plates. Some drivers, in their impetuosity, backed under trailers that had been dropped too high, resulting in the rear of the tractor smashing into the front of the trailer and the rear lights being smashed against the trailer landing legs. Numerous drivers were disciplined for this behaviour and lectures on safe working practises were given. Common sense seems to have prevailed lately and the bad practices have all but disappeared before someone was badly injured or even killed. The bonus payments are to be scrapped in favour of a higher basic wage plus overtime.

During my time in Business Express the injuries I had sustained over the years began to plague me more and more resulting in more and more days when I had to absent myself from the workplace. Not least of my problems was the most recent of my injuries, the broken ankle that I suffered in 2004. I had developed an unnatural gait due to the continual and incessant pain I was suffering. This pain caused me to turn my foot inwards and to walk on the outer edge of my foot. This in turn caused an increase of the back pain I constantly suffer from. The pain I suffer is worst in the mornings when I rise. I find I cannot put my foot on the floor and need assistance dressing myself. As the day moves on my mobility improves but I'm afraid it's never going to be perfect.

I was awarded, by the Industrial Injuries Board, a payment for the injury sustained and was told by my GP that I should consider my career as a large goods vehicle driver to be over and I was put on long term sickness benefit to await various prodding's and probing and X-rays and scans from experts and specialists. There has been talk of wearing a calliper and talk of re-breaking and re-setting the ankle. The payment that I was awarded was for 25% disability. Bone injuries such as my back injury are classed as degenerative conditions and so I cannot see that there will be much improvement in the future.

As I draw to the conclusion of this volume and to the end of my career in transport and also to my sixtieth birthday I reiterate that to those of us who have been bitten by the haulage bug, truck driving is not a job, it is a way of life. Not always a well paid way of life but like most other ways of earning a living that can be considered vocational, the basic pay, at times, comes as a secondary consideration and there were always the extra hidden bonuses that drivers managed to find, fiddle or filch to enhance, supplement, augment and generally pad out and swell their pay packets.

When I started driving in the 60's at age 18, drivers were generally treated like so much dirt on the sole of your shoe. Sadly little has changed and 40+ years later we are still treated as second class citizens, the poor relations in the manual worker sector. I consider after 40+ years, in this industry, I have paid my dues. I yearn for a permanent job, working normal hours for the last couple of years of my working life. I no longer have the desire to get up in the middle of the night and work 12 to 15 hours a day. I also consider myself unable to do some of the jobs that I once found easy, due to the after effects of the back injury I sustained whilst working at British Telecom plc, plus the other injuries I have, unfortunately, suffered over the years. So I plod on, doing just enough to justify my wages, waiting and yearning for the day I retire. Wishing my life away, I suppose, but that is how disillusioned I have become. I have, after all these years, started to loathe the job I once loved. Not because of the driving aspect, for that and the trucks are something I will always love, but because of the expectations of management and traffic clerks who work out routes on 'Autoroute' software on the computer. These people tell me, with my years of experience, that I can do London to Glasgow and back in a day, loaded out to 44 tons, through all types of weather and traffic. The 'Autoroute' you see, does not tell of motorway pile ups, traffic density, or snow or fog or rain or road works or any other delays one may encounter, and the traffic clerk does not have the sense to experience to make allowances for such delays. The said traffic clerk, who is usually some office junior who knows diddly squat about the intricacies of transport, takes it as read that 4½ hours, and no more, is what it will take to reach Central London, and if it takes that long to get there, then the return journey will be just the same. Not so, I'm afraid.

Each journey has become a white knuckle ride. The vehicles have been restricted to 56mph, down from 60, and the road system evermore congested but the same journey times are still expected from the driver. The traffic clerks seem to think that 56mph is the minimum speed, not the maximum.

Being a bit long in the tooth and not one to be badgered or bullied, I'll take the night out on London jobs or others of equally distant destinations, and claim driver fatigue, or drive at a more sedate pace to ensure safety. The company, you see, will not want to be seen as being instrumental in some major catastrophe, or indifferent to the drivers well being, especially if there is any chance that they may be liable to prosecution, and a charge, perhaps, of corporate manslaughter.

There is also the impact of the Working Time Directive and all its ramifications. The WTD has cut down the drivers' hours so that he may only work a maximum of 60 hours. A lot of drivers see this as wrong and believe that they should still be able to work longer extortionate hours to make more money. I believe, in these more enlightened days, that these drivers are wrong and should be looking for compensation for the reduction in hours. The driving fraternity should be striving for more money for less hours, not the same money for longer hours.

The digital tachograph is another responsibility we have to contend with. It, takes the form of a credit card sized swipe card with a memory chip capable of storing all the drivers' hours and activities of the past 3 months. These are impositions that I, at my age, can well do without. These and all the other changes in hours and conditions that we have had to accept over the years, without the advantage of a monetary increment, are for the benefit of the major supermarkets and multinationals who demand delivery and collection 24/7. They are certainly not for the benefit of the driver. These are the same major supermarkets that refuse to allow drivers to use their canteen facilities at their RDC's (Regional Distribution Centres), even after the driver has been there for a number of hours. So I carry on looking forward to the day I can hang up my truck driving boots and say goodbye to this once wonderful industry.

Over the years the job has declined. The pay, relatively speaking, is at the lower end of the pay scale. What other type of employer would put a man in charge of £120,000 worth of equipment with a cargo worth, maybe up to a million pounds and send him on his way with all the responsibility involved, at a rate as low as £7.00per hour? Granted the trucks have got much bigger, longer, heavier, and more powerful and a damn sight better. The new automatic gearboxes of Volvos and Mercs etc., have made the actual driving part of the job so much easier. So much so that it has become a case of engage the gearbox, point the truck in the right direction and go. This, of course, means that the driver can concentrate more on his driving and his surroundings and thus anticipate, more readily, any impending incidents.

To my mind it has taken away a great deal of the skill that we older drivers pride ourselves on. Gone are the days of roping and sheeting and constant mesh manual gearboxes. Gone along with these is the camaraderie that was so much in evidence when we used to share digs and cafes on the old 'A' roads and trunk routes and park up on council lorry parks to swap tales, mostly of the tall type.

The few drivers that are still employed in the general haulage, rope and sheet game, can rest assured that when it comes to folding their sheets in a high wind or on a rainy or snowy day they will have to do it on their own, unless there is another old driver nearby, as the new breed of drivers will just sit in their nice warm cabs and watch the older guys struggle. These same younger drivers will probably not offer any assistance even on a bright summer's day. I don't think the younger drivers see trucking as a long term career anymore, and I can now, honestly say, hand on heart, that I don't blame them. I would not recommend haulage, as a career to any young man or lady; rather, I would do all in my power to dissuade them.

Printed in Great Britain
by Amazon

54485447R00161